The Five Laws of Library Science

By

S.R. Ranganathan, M.A., LT., F.L.A.

Librarian, Madras University Llibrary
Secretary, Madras Library Association
Member, International Library Committee
of the World Association for Adult Education

WITH A FOREWORD
BY

Sir P.S. Sivaswami Aiyer, K.C.S.I., C.I.E.

AND AN INTRODUCTION
BY

W.C. Berwick Sayers, F.L.A.
Chief Librarian, Croydon Public Libraries
Lecturer in the University of London School of Librarianship

Published By
Ess Ess Publications
4837/24, Ansari Road
Darya Ganj
New Delhi-110 002
for

Sarada Ranganathan Endowment for Library Science
Bangalore

Five Laws of Library Science

Reprinted 2021

ISBN : 81-7000-498-1

Price: ₹ 1250

Published by
Ess Ess Publications
4837/24, Ansari Road, Darya Ganj,
New Delhi-110 002
Tel: 011-23260807, 41563444 Fax: 011-41563334
E-mail: info@essessreference.com
www.essessreference.com

For

Sarada Ranganathan Endowment for Library Science
702, 'Upstairs', 42nd Cross, III Block, Rajajinagar,
Bangalore-560 010
Tel: 080-23305109
E-mail: srels@vsnl.com

Printed in India at: Printline, New Delhi

CONTENTS

PREFACE

BY

THE MADRAS LIBRARY ASSOCIATION

WITH the object of spreading the essential ideas of the Library Movement and of directing thought towards the creation of a library service suited to our country, the Madras Library Association published in 1929 a collection of articles on the Library Movement contributed by persons interested in the subject and this collection has enjoyed a wide circulation throughout the country.

With the present volume on tbe "Five Laws of Library Science"—the manuscript of which Mr. S. R. Ranganathan has been good enough to place at the disposal of the Association—the Madras Library Association commences the publication of a series of books on the technical and practical aspects of library work.

The Association hopes that the publication will serve its purpose and further the cause of the Library Movement in India and elsewhere.

ACKNOWLEDGMENTS

The thanks of the author are due to the following persons and institutions:—

To the University of Madras, which gave the author generous facilities to make a special study of Library Science and Library Organisation in Great Britain, for permission to publish this work which is based on a course of lectures delivered under its auspices at Chidambaram in 1928;

To Professor E. B. Ross, to whom the author owes so much more, for a casual remark of his which convinced the author of the need for a book of this sort which seeks to reduce and relate all the principles and practice of library work to a few fundamental laws;

To Sir P. S. Sivaswami Aiyer, K.C.S.I., C.I.E., for his kind Foreword;

To Mr. W. C. Berwick Sayers, F.L.A., whose inspiring lectures on classification are still ringing in the author's ears, for his learned Introduction;

To Professor K. Swaminathan, who read the entire manuscript, for many valuable suggestions towards its improvement;

To the Madras Library Association, for having taken up the publication of the book;

To Mr. C. Sundaram, B.A., for reading the proofs for the author; and

To the Proprietor of the Madras Law Journal Press, for the efficient, expeditious and obliging way in which the printing has been carried out.

the pioneer of the library movement in the Madras Presidency and has been carrying on an energetic propaganda to spread it. He knows how to rouse and sustain the interest of the reader and has produced a very attractive and readable book. I have no doubt it will meet with wide appreciation and soon come to be recognised as a standard text-book of Library Science.

The Madras University is fortunate in possessing the author as its librarian. Its library has developed in his hands into a live human institution, which aims at a helpful personal touch between the staff and the readers who use the library. The enormous increase in the issue of volumes since the author took charge of the library is a striking testimony to the soundness of the principles on which it has been run and to the efficiency of his management in spite of the very defective housing conditions under which the library has been working.

The publication of this book by the Madras Library Association is not the least of its claims to the gratitude of the public.

P. S. Sivaswamy Aiyer.

FOREWORD

THE library movement is of comparatively recent origin in western countries and is the result of democratic influences which obtained an ascendancy towards the end of the last century. The desire to extend the benefits of learning to the people at large suggested the foundation of numerous public libraries. The possibilities of libraries as instruments of popular education have ever since occupied the attention of those interested in this movement. Much thought has been given in recent years to the best methods of popularising the use of libraries.

The vast increase in the number of books published year after year and in the additions made to libraries has given rise to a large crop of questions regarding the organisation, administration and management of libraries. Men's outlook in regard to these matters has undergone a radical change. Libraries are now regarded not as precious possessions to be jealously preserved from the intrusion of the vulgar, but as democratic institutions for the profit and enjoyment of all. How to attract readers to libraries, how to extend to all classes, the facilities for using them, how to render the maximum amount of help to those who desire to use libraries and how to save the time of the readers and the library staff alike are questions which, simple as they may seem, demand no little thought, imagination, skill and experience from the librarian.

A large mass of literature has grown up about this subject. Library Associations have been started in many countries, chairs have been founded in several Universities for the teaching of library management; and numbers of library journals have come into existence. Attempts have been made to systematize the knowledge on this subject and it is now claimed that it has attained the status of a science. "Whether the organisation and management of libraries is to be regarded as a science or as an art, it is needless to consider. There can be no doubt, however, that there are certain essential principles underlying the management of libraries according to present day needs and conceptions.

The author of this book has sought to expound these principles in a systematic form. He has been able to reduce them to five cardinal principles and has developed all the rules of library organisation and management as the necessary implications and inevitable corollaries of his five laws. ' Once the laws have been stated, they appear so obvious that one wonders that they were not clearly realised and worked out before.

Mr. Ranganathan's treatment of the subject is clear, logical and lucid. He has brought to his task extensive knowledge of the literature on the subject of libraries, personal acquaintance with the methods of management of libraries in Britain, a trained analytical intellect and a fervid but enlightened enthusiasm for the library movement. He has been

INTRODUCTION

I

THIS is one of the most interesting books that I have read in recent years upon our profession. It is unique, I believe, in that it attempts for the first time a comprehensive survey by a librarian who has a peculiarly Indian mind, and reflects his own racial culture on the basic theories of the art of book distribution as it is understood in the modern library world. To those who are new to our work it may be a wonder that so much can be made out of what superficially appears to be so simple a craft, but a perusal of Mr. Ranganathan's pages will take the beginner a long way along the path of enlightenment.

Mr. Ranganathan is unusually equipped for his undertaking. It is now several years since he placed himself for a while under the direction of the lecturers and teachers of the University of London School of Librarianship, and he became particularly associated with me. I found that he was a man of considerable culture, very original in his outlook, persistent and undeviating in his investigations, and wisely given to considering any suggestions that might be made to him. Not only did he attend the lectures in librarianship at the University of London, he made an intensive study of library work of all types by visits to libraries in various parts of the country. For some time he studied every day in the Croydon Public Libraries, where I watched his work with interest. He examined the processes of every department, and spent much time considering and criticizing the various processes. All the way through he was seeking the reasoning that lies at the back of all our doings.

Not only was he interested in books and libraries, he spent some of his leisure in examining the educational methods in the schools of the towns, and their relationship to libraries. His critical outlook went so far that he even started on a new classification of books. This, as he tells us in a later part of this volume, is employed in the University Library at Madras, and in a few other Indian libraries which are beginning to classify their books.

Such a course of study and such an attitude of mind could not fail to produce a type of librarian whose work would be of importance. The work before us is proof of this.

II

The practice of librarianship long preceded the formulation of any laws whatsoever. In all crafts this is so, of course. It is only slowly and from the continuous experience of workers that a theory can be deduced and given a statement. Ours may claim to be, however, one of the oldest crafts in the world, and some of the quite ordinary processes which have now been brought to such perfection that Mr. Ranganathan is able to formulate their results as "laws", existed in embryo form in the Assyrian libraries and probably in earlier ones. The clay tablet catalogues in the British Museum prove to us that there were then not only libraries, but a systematic library science. In later but still early years the work of such librarians as Callimachus in the libraries of the Pharaohs shows methods of management, especially in the classification of books, that are the wonder of modern librarians who have considered them.

Every great nation in the past has had its public libraries, even if their use was sometimes limited to special classes of the community, and in the general anarchy of European civilisation which followed the fall of the Western Roman Empire the monasteries still preserved and added to their libraries.

Library history was largely influenced by this monastic preservation of books, because for centuries libraries were limited to colleges and to other protected buildings, and their use restricted to the inhabitants of these institutions. To preserve the book was of as much and even of more consequence than to get it used. That spirit has been passing away since the middle of the nineteenth century. The great libraries of the world, with varying degrees of generosity, have been thrown open to external readers, and the attitude of the *conservateur* has given place to what I have ventured to call elsewhere the exploiter of books as the right description of the librarian.

The principal factor in the modern attitude towards libraries and books has been what are known in England and America as "public libraries". This term to-day has quite a different meaning from what it had before 1850, Then, public libraries were public in much the sense in which the public schools of England are public; that is to say, they were limited in their use very largely to the governing classes. The modern public library is a municipal institution supported by towns for the free use of the citizens without discrimination. They were Anglo-Saxon in their origin, and came into being at about the same time in Great Britain and in the United States. These libraries have now been built up with a special technique of their own, with, in many cases, very large stocks of books, and, literally, millions of readers.

One of the most significant social factors of the last half of the nineteenth and the first quarter of the twentieth centuries has been the widespread development of the reading habit amongst western peoples. Even the more conservative nations of Europe have now developed systems of libraries more or less on the Anglo-Saxon model.

III

The modern view, then, of libraries is that which regards all the population as its clientele. Even in university and research libraries facilities are now given to serious students without difficulty almost everywhere. This is the attitude which the librarian in India will, I hope and believe, make his own. It must be quite clear, however, that universal rules or notions must always be given a local and individual application. I do not think the library methods of America, much as I admire them, are root and branch suitable for Europe or even for England. The psychology of the people varies, and variants in library practice must be made to meet this fact. Even more amongst the peoples of India, with their immense history, powerful traditions, and distinctive racial qualities, the application of merely Anglo-Saxon ideas to a thing so intimate, personal and spiritual as literature, without modification, may not be wise. I have had many foreign students in the libraries under my care, and I have always tried to impress upon them that what they learn from us should always be considered carefully in the light of the needs of their own home countries. I feel that this is immensely important in India.

This, to my mind, gives its special value to Mr. Ranganathan's work. He deals with all the questions which exercise the minds of European librarians. Book selection, with a catholic mind which has determined that all sides shall be heard, and that no personal preference shall have undue influence; the best methods of library furnishing and equipment; a considered statement of what can be done by the catalogue and by the classification : these will be obvious to the reader. He writes, too, as an educationist—as all good librarians should— and I hope he has made quite clear that the development of a literate nation, with a full love for its great literature and a right understanding of the value of books, must begin with considered and generons provision for children.

In the West every child is a potential reader; it must be so in the East, even in places where the children have not yet had opportunities to do much reading or to get access to books.

IV

A wise American librarian once remarked to me that a log of wood with a book at one end and a librarian at another would make a perfect library. That was a picturesque exaggeration, of course, but it is the personal element that the librarian brings into the library which gives it its vitality. Many libraries, alas, lack vitality; they have staffs, but no librarians. The spirit of the real librarian has never been more beautifully or wisely shown than in Austin Dobson's epitaph on Richard Garnett, one of the greatest librarians of the last century:—

"Of him we may say justly,—Here was one
Who knew of most things more than any other;
Who loved all learning underneath the sun,
And looked on every learner as a brother."

The implications of this are profound enough to humble the most accomplished. librarian. It implies that the librarian must be a man of acquisitive mind who closes his mind to no subject of human interest. He is always a learner; he must always be awake to and welcome every development of human thought and every adventure of the human spirit. He must, however, be a man educated not only in the general sense but in every operation and process of libraries. He must be a lover of other men. When young people come to me as aspirants for library work I ask them, "Do you love books'?" They invariably reply that they do, but I ask them next, "Do you like people and serving people?" I rejoice that in India there are men who now have taken in hand the choosing and training of librarians. What the country holds in the way of libraries I do not know fully, but with its great literatures, in so many forms, there are no doubt many fields of research and many library possibilities as yet undreamed of even by the Indian himself.

Here, then, is a book that may be an inspiration to all those who, in higher or humbler office, will serve India in her libraries. Conceived in a broad, ungrudging spirit, it must enthuse those who enter upon our profession in that country with the immense, if sometimes undramatic, possibilities of a library. It will show it to be not merely a collection of books which accumulates age and dust, but a living and growing organism prolonging the life of the past and renewing it for this generation, but giving also to this generation the best that its own workers, thinkers and dreamers have to offer.

W. C. BERWICK SAYERS,

Chief Librarian, Croydon

Lecturer in the University of London School of Librarianship

Examiner in Library Organization to the Library Association.

CHAPTER I

THE FIRST LAW

THE first law of Library Science, like the first law of any other science, embodies an elemental truth. In fact, it is so self-evident that one may be Inclined to say that it is trivial. But, that is an invariable characteristic of all first laws. Take, for example, the first Upanishadic law of conduct (*Satyam Vada*—speak the truth), or the first law of motion.

The first law of Library Science is: BOOKS ARE FOR USE. No one will question the correctness of this law. But, in actual practice, the story is different. The law is seldom borne in mind by library authorities. "We may examine the history of any aspect of library practice and we shall find ample evidence of a deplorable neglect of this law.

Let us take, in the first place, the way in which books were kept in the fifteenth and sixteenth centuries. It was not uncommon in those days to have books actually chained to the shelves. The books were fitted with brass frames and rings, which were tied to iron chains, whose other ends were safely fastened to the shelves. Such chained books could not migrate from the shelves beyond the length of the chain. Their freedom was confined to the sphere determined by their chains. Certainly, such chaining was more conducive to the preservation than to the use of the books.. In fact, libraries were then regarded, not as organisations for furthering the USE of books, "but as institutions for preserving them.

It may be of interest to reflect for a while on this elaborate process of preservation. What must have been the purpose of such preservation? It is difficult to think of any purpose except that of preserving for the use of posterity. No doubt, it is a healthy, or at any rate, an unavoidable trait of human nature, that we think of our children—of our posterity—and that we are even prepared to deny ourselves many things, in order to hand them over unimpaired to posterity. But an inevitable deduction emanates from this practice. Even as we are anxious to hand over our books to posterity, every succeeding generation may be actuated by an exactly similar altruistic motive and in consequence books may have to be for ever in chains and may never be released for use. This aspect of the question seems to have escaped notice for a long time and 'BOOKS ARE FOR PRESERVATION' had usurped the place of 'BOOKS ARE FOR USE'.

This tendency to hoard books must have originated at a time when books were rare and difficult to produce. Before the invention of printing, it took years to copy a book. It is said that the copying of the *Mahabharata* was work for a whole life-time. Under such conditions, there was justification for forgetting that BOOKS ARE FOR USE and for overdoing the act of preserving them. But this tendency appears to have unfortunately developed into a regular instinct, as a result of long practice. Although the situation was thoroughly altered by the invention of printing, it took centuries to overcome this long-inherited habit. The first step was to declare an amnesty for the books and set them free from their chains. But, even after they were unchained and were permitted to be taken out for use and handled by readers, there was not, for a long time, a generous recognition, on the part of those that maintained and managed libraries, of the right of readers to an unhampered use of books. The, restrictions that were placed in the way of books being freely used were many and it is only in recent years that a vigorous movement seems to have set in to eliminate all such handicaps. Such a movement has by no means become universal as yet. There are several countries—and our land seems to have a fair claim to be classed with them—which are still hardly affected by this new movement.

I have heard of a Professor in a College, who ruled over his department for nearly a quarter of a century. The pursuit of his subject slowly narrowed the range of his vision and he became mecha-nieally minded. Trivial details began to loom large for him. Hence he came to attend personally to the meticulous discharge of every item of routine, from the opening of the doors and windows to the periodical emptying of waste-paper baskets. He was given to getting into a rage if everything was not in its place. Unfortunately, under the force of this inherited tendency, he came to regard the shelves rather than the hands of readers as the proper place for books. The assistants, whose advance in their cadre depended on the good will of the Professor, would rather forego the use of books than run the risk of exciting Ms rage by drawing the books from the shelves. The students of the first year course, who alone were strangers to his idiosyncrasies, would occasionally ask for the books of the departmental library. He used to dispose of them with this dilemma: "Have you followed the class lectures? If so, you do not want these books." "Were you unable to follow the class lectures? If so, you cannot profit by reading these books." The senior students would not approach him at all, since they had had painful experiences of the futility of such attempts. The result was that, when he retired at long last, his successor had to cut open the pages of several of the books bequeathed to him. In some cases, it was even found that it was not "worth while to waste time in cutting them open, since they had gone entirely out of date and had to be discarded. Would such a professorial career have been possible if the College had acted on the law—'BOOKS ARE FOR USE'?

The extraordinary strength and inexorability of this inherited tendency which stands between the books and their users, is brought out by the case of another Professor—this time a Professor of Philosophy. The Professor was a philosopher not only by profession but also by practice and temperament. He was also one of those that felt an urge for social service. One form of social service that our Professor of Philosophy decided to render was to give a chance for his neighbours to become learned. To this end, he used to invest most of his savings in books. When he had made up a good collection, he built a nice little reading hut to house the books. He used to spend most of his spare time in this reading hut, so that he may serve out the books personally. He was, however, very disappointed at the ultimate indifference of his neighbours. So, one day he took an enthusiastic librarian-friend of his to his reading hut to take his advice. On his way he was waxing eloquent over the excellent books he had bought for the library, the depressing indifference of the people of his locality to the use of books and so on. The conversation that ensued as soon as they entered the charming but desolate reading hut threw a flood of light on the persistence of the long-inherited preserving instinct which could smother even the sincere resolve and the good intentions of an honest philosopher.

"Where are your books, my friend?"

"All these ten almirahs are full of them. I spent a hundred rupees on each of these almirahs. I had them specially made, etc., etc., etc,"

"But, my dear Professor, "why have you lined their lovely transparent glass doors with these ugly sheets of brown paper?"

"You don't know how these visitors bother me. If I don't stick up this brown paper, they look at the books through the glass door. They ask for this book and that and I have to pull out all the books."

Poor vanquished philosopher! Comment is needless.

While such things are common with us in the twentieth century, we have only to go a century back to find the iron sway of this hoarding instinct over American Libraries. T. W. Koch of the Northwestern University records a significant but typical story[1] of a librarian of Harvard. The Harvard University Librarian "once completed an inventory of the library and was seen crossing the yard with a particularly happy smile". "When he was asked the reason for his exceptionally pleasant mood, he exclaimed with pride "All the books are in excepting two. Agassiz has those and I am going after them".

On the other hand a modern librarian, who has faith in the law that 'BOOKS ARE FOR USE,' is happy only when his readers make his shelves constantly empty. It is not the books that go out that worry him. It is the stay-at-home volumes that perplex and depress him. He too will constantly cross the yard to meet his Agassizes. But he will go to

(1) KOCH (Theodore Wesley): *On University Libraries*, page 27.

them, not to snatch away the books they are using, but to distribute the new arrivals that need to be introduced to them as rapidly as possible.

The different stages by which the force of the law, "BOOKS ARE FOR USE," worked out the gradual removal of the restrictions induced by the aforesaid inherited instinct may be summarised as follows:—The chains were first removed and sold as old iron; but access was limited to the chosen few. Then those that could pay were allowed the use of the books. Then came the further step of making them free to all, but only for use in the premises of the library. Then, lending to the favoured few; then, to all who paid the fee; and at last, lending free to all. Perhaps we are just reaching this stage in our land. But this was by no means the end elsewhere, where the first law had been familiar sufficiently long to lay bare all the implications embedded deep in its bosom. In such places, aggressive methods, which have made other enterprises successful, came to be employed to push forward the use of books. Then branch libraries were opened in the larger cities in order to provide a fair collection of books and an inviting reading room within a few minutes' walk from each home. Then books were sent out for a nominal fee to those who could not conveniently come after them. The latest is that boxes of books are sent free to the homes of those that would offer to get them introduced in their neighbourhood. What further triumph is in store for the first law, it is difficult to guess. But as stated by J. P. Quincy, one is tempted to adapt a well-known Celtic paradox by saying that a public library is as good as a private one and, for the effective study of books, has decided advantages over it.[1]

LIBRARY LOCATION

The location of a library may, in general, be taken as an index of the degree of faith that the authorities of the library have in the law, BOOKS ARE FOR USE. When I happened to visit a municipal town in the south, the city fathers of the place invited me for a discussion about building a library for the town. The question of site turned up at a very early stage. Practically all of them suggested a place on the outskirts of the town. One of their reasons for suggesting such a remote site was that there was too much dust in the centre and that the books would be spoiled. Another reason adduced was that, otherwise, "all sorts of fellows" would get into the library. It never struck them that the function of the library was to make "all sorts of fellows" use its books and that the dust problem should not be allowed to drive away the library beyond the zone of accessibility and usefulness. On the other hand, they were shocked to hear me suggest a site on the bazaar street running

(1) JANZOW (Laura M.): *The Library Without the Walls*, page 19.

RURAL LIBRARY SERVICE.

through the heart of the town. I had to cite the example of several of the cities of the West and expound elaborately the gospel of library organisation before they would concede that there was at least something to be said in favour of my suggestion.

In a Kellett Hall lecture of not long ago—before the bus service came into being—a talented speaker humorously fixed the co-ordinates of one of our big libraries as follows:—"Find a place in the city which is at least a mile from any tram-line or any railway station, which has not even a rickshaw-stand within a radius of half a mile, which has the nearest college or students' hostel at a distance of three miles. There is perhaps only one place in the city answering such a description and that is the place chosen for our library." And yet nobody grumbled; because a library was regarded more as an ornament to the city than as an institution whose primary function was to spread the use of books.

On the other hand, in all western cities which have a living faith in the First Law of Library Science, and which vote for and maintain libraries, because they are anxious that books should be used, the main library is usually housed in the centre of the city—at a place to which most of the citizens will be obliged to go daily on some business or other. It also works through several branches and delivery stations in different parts of the city, so that distance may not stand in the way of the free and full use of books. Dublin, for example, has five such district libraries for her population of 3,24,000. Even thrifty Edinburgh, with its population of 4,20,000, has already established seven branch libraries. Manchester has found the need for thirty branches to get her books fully used by her people, who number 7,44,000. Birmingham, with her population of 9,19,000, does not find her twenty-four branch libraries adequate to spread the use of her books. Toronto, which has only a population of 5,50,000, has already established fifteen branches and intends to build more of them. Cleveland, which is the home of about eight hundred thousand people, distributes her book collection through 25 branches and 108 delivery stations, while 46 branches and 275 delivery stations are found too inadequate for the 3,000,000 people of Chicago.

Once the idea that 'BOOKS ARE FOR USE' is firmly established, once the libraries realise that their existence is justified only by the extent to which their books are used by readers, there will be no difference of opinion about their location. A location, such as the one described by our Kellett Hall lecturer, would never be thought of. A shrewd shopkeeper, who wants his wares to sell, puts up his shop in the *Sannidhi* of a popular temple. A coffee-house owner, who wants his business to thrive, establishes his *cafe* near a big students' hostel like the Victoria Hostel. A betel-vendor, keen on his daily turn-over, pitches his tent opposite to a big and popular hotel. So also a library which is keen about its books being fully used will plant itself in the midst of its *clientele*. Conversely, the *Sannidhi* of no popular temple is without a shop and the vicinity of all Victoria hostels invariably gets studded with coffee-hotels and betel-shops. The same is the case with libraries. Wherever people habitually congregate, that is a potential site for a library. An extreme but a happy illustration of this deduction from the First Law of Library Science is afforded by the "Garden Library" of Lisbon.[1]

Lisbon, the capital of Portugal, built on Seven Hills like our Tiruppati and comparable to our Madura in size and population, has gained a unique place in the library world. A Portuguese proverb claims "Who has not seen Lisbon has not seen a thing of beauty".[2] Whether such a claim is valid or not, Lisbon has certainly excelled all other cities in her unique Garden Library which is certainly a thing of beauty.

On the flank of one of its Seven Hills, overlooking the blue surface of the Tagus, there is a sunny little public garden with a marble basin in the centre round which flowers riot in rain-bow tints and children shout and run in joyous ecstasy.

At the far end, there is a giant Cedar-Tree spreading like an umbrella defying sun and rain. Inside its intense shadow deep silence prevails; and you find a line of chairs encircling an enchanting collection of volumes in a lovely bookcase. Students

(1) *Wilson Bulletin*, Volume 4, page 65.

(2) RECLUS (Elisee): *Universal Geography*, edited by E. G. Ravenstein, V. I, p. 484.

in their flowing cloaks, workmen white with lime-dust, raw rustics with timid and listless eyes, office and shop employees munching their lunch, soldiers, printers, electricians, sailors and dock-hands, all share the contents of this unique Library, unhampered by any formality but aided by the nimble, sweetfaced Librarian who flutters from end to end with her beaming smiles.

Who conceived this idea? It was a private Educational Society known as the "Free University". Hoping to foster a love of reading among all classes, the Free University founded this Garden Library, supplying the books and the furniture. The Lisbon city-fathers, who were themselves believers in the First Law of Library Science, warmly approved of this venture and lent the services of a Librarian.

There are only less than a 1,000 volumes but they are changed from time to time. They have a little of everything—Classics, Living Authors, Travels, History, Electricity, Chemistry, Shorthand, Book-keeping, Building, Smithy, Navigation and so on. And these are eagerly sought by all the visitors to the Garden. The Library is open daily from 10 to 6. Statistics show that during the first year there were no less than 25,000 readers using this Library. May the shadow of the ancient cedar in the public garden of the city of the Seven Hills never grow less! May it long provide shelter for this patriotic enterprise, in the service of the gospel, 'BOOKS ARE FOR USE'!

In schools and colleges also, the location of their libraries may be taken as a reliable index of the degree of faith which the authorities have in the law, 'BOOKS ARE FOR USE'. The evolution of ideas regarding the location and the size of school and college libraries has been closely parallel to the gradual growth of the belief in that law. In a school, which I knew intimately, the library consisted of a few hundred books made up mostly of specimen copies of text-books given away by the teachers of the school as not worth private appropriation. These few hundreds of books were carefully locked up in a wooden book-case, which was itself locked in a room, ten feet square, and ventilated by a single small window. But the tragic feature of it was that the headmaster invariably held his classes—including his innumerable special classes—in the hall leading to that room, almost blocking the entrance to it. Those that know the mortal dread in which headmasters were held in such schools, twenty-five or thirty years ago, will realise what this meant for the books of the library. For those who do not know, it may be said that the appearance of the headmaster's figure at the street-corner was enough to make a group of school-boys, playing at marbles in the evening sun, fly for their life and take shelter in the darkest corners of the kitchens of the nearest houses, where their timid tell-tale eyes and ways would make the mothers exclaim 'Is the headmaster going to the temple?' Hardly any of the boys would dare to come out of his hole, until the greatest dare-devil among them made bold to peep out stealthily and announce, in a cheering tone, that the line was clear. With this information, it may be easy to realise how effective such a location for the school library should have been in preventing the library books from being used. Certainly, that school did not believe, in those days, that 'BOOKS WERE FOR USE' and that school was by no means an exception.

Not long ago, the Principal of a big college invited a librarian to pay a visit to his college library and to suggest some improvements. He gladly went. He was received with great kindness and taken through a maze of narrow, dark, ill-ventilated rooms or corridors, which had almirahs along the walls. When the other end was nearing, he asked the Principal where his library was and when he would take him to it. To his surprise he was told that they had all along been passing only through the library. Wondering at this queer provision, in a college, of a place for the boys to play hide and seek during their lunch-interval, the librarian asked the Principal why such an unhappy situation was selected for the College library. The prompt and innocent reply of the Principal was, "These rooms are unfit for anything else and they have to be put to some sort of use." Would such a naive reply have come forward, if the First Law of Library Science had any hold on the authorities of that college?

What now prevails in our schools and colleges obtained some sixty or seventy years ago in the schools and colleges of the West. Speaking at the dedication of the Library of the Colorado College, in March 1894, Mr. Harper, the first President of the Chicago University, said 'A quarter of a century ago, the library in most of our institutions, even the oldest, was scarcely large enough . . . to deserve the name of library...I know of a college, having an enrolment of one hundred and fifty students...and yet in a room ten by twelve having the name of library has not two hundred and fifty volumes . . . So far as it had location, it was the place to which the Professor was accustomed to make his way occasionally, the student never... The place, seldom frequented, was some out of the way room which could serve no other purpose"[1]. Almost the very words of the Principal mentioned in the last paragraph!

But all this changed, the moment the First Law of Library Science came to establish itself in the minds of people. At present, several of the colleges in the West, which believe that 'BOOKS ARE FOR USE' and feel that one of their primary duties is to develop the book-habit in their undergraduates, assign their very best room for library purposes. Not only do they give their best room, they allot quite a number of such rooms for the library. At least in one college of the West, whose "books were

(1) HARPER (William Rainy): *The Trend of Higher Education*, pp. 120-121.

placed in corridors, cellars and attics" till this law weighed with it, the floor area of the libraries of the college is now nearly half the floor area of the whole college. To quote Harper again, "To-day the chief building of a college, the building in which is taken greatest pride, is the library. With the stack for storage purposes, the reading-room for reference books, the offices of delivery, the rooms for seminar purposes, it is the center of the institutional activity...A greater change from the old can hardly be conceived...The time is near when the student will do little of his work in the study; he must be in the midst of books. As the scholar, though having thousands of volumes in his own library, must find his way to the great libraries of the Old World when he wishes to do the work of highest character, so the University student, though having hundreds of volumes in his own room, must do his work in the library of the institution...His table must be where, without a moment's delay, without the mediation of a zealous librarian, who perhaps thinks more of the book than of its use, he may place his hand upon that one of ten or twenty thousand books which he desires to use...That factor of our college and University work, the library, fifty years ago almost unknown, to-day already the center of the institution's intellectual activity, half a century hence will, by absorbing all else, have become the institution itself."[1]

---

(1) HARPER (William Rainy): *The Trend of Higher Education*, pp. 121-125.

LIBRARY HOURS

The influence of the law 'BOOKS ARE FOR USE' has been no less profound on the Library Hours. So long as the inherited notion about preservation had the upper hand and the concept 'BOOKS ARE FOR USE' had not fully asserted itself, the library was more often closed than kept open. Perhaps it was more frequently opened for the book-worms to be chased out and the books to be dusted than for the readers to enter or for the books to be issued for use. The registers of books borrowed for the decade 1730-40 from the Bodleian library of Oxford are said to show that only rarely were more than one or two books issued in a day. Sometimes a whole week is said to have passed over without a single entry being made. An interesting memento said to be preserved by that library dates from 1806. Finding the library closed, a scholar, angry with disappointment, affixed to the door of the library a scrap of paper containing words which the Muse of Greece supplied him with for the relief of his feelings:—"Woe unto you who have taken the key of knowledge! Ye enter not yourself and hinder those who come". In his *Story of the University of Edinburgh*, Sir Alexander Grant deplores how, in the early nineteenth century, the hours of the University Library restricted the facilities afforded to the students for making use of the library. Books might be taken out only during two hours on two days of the week. According to Koch, the library of the Amherst College was open, in 1850, only once a week from one to three in the after-noon. The students of the Princeton University could use its library only for one hour twice a week, while their contemporaries at Missouri were allowed only one hour for two weeks. In the Columbia college, which was started in 1859, for many years, "freshmen and sophomores were allowed to visit the library only once a month to gaze at the backs of books, the juniors were taken there once a week by a tutor who gave verbal information about the contents of the books, but only seniors...could draw from the library during one hour on Wednesday afternoons".

If the library hours were, till late in the last century, of such small magnitude in the land of libraries, one can easily imagine the conditions that obtain at present in our school and college libraries, of course, wherever they exist! The practice of one big college may serve as an illustration. Theoretically, it has 'two issue-days' per week. But, let not the occurrence of the word 'day' by any means mislead one to multiply the 'two' by twenty-four or even by twelve to arrive at the number of library hours per week. In practice, the professor-in-charge, whose displeasure no discreet boy would dare incur, had conveniently interpreted the "two issue-days" as two quarter-hours. One might wonder what takes place in the library during the remaining hours of the week. Well, the books enjoy their eternal undisturbed repose behind locked doors, in a dark, closed room. Another of our libraries experimented for a long time with its hours. Those people in its locality, who were literate enough to use its books, had their office-hours between 11 A.M. and 5 P.M. on week-days. Saturdays and Sundays were usually holidays with them. During such days, they were accustomed to devote the morning hours to social visits, household-purchases and such other week-end business. After the luxury of a late meal, and a midday nap, they would find themselves fit for study or for a serious visit to the library only in the after-noon. The hours finally arrived at by the library, after its endless experiments and investigations, fitted in with this habit of its *clientele* in an ideally wrong way. It actually decided to keep itself open between 10 A.M. and 5 P.M. on week-days and from 7 A.M. to 2 P.M. on Saturdays and Sundays. Can a more effective decision be imagined for a place where the First Law of Library Science was almost a heresy? In another place, when the authorities of a library were solemnly discussing ways and means to meet a great increase in the issue of books, a veritable Daniel came "to judgment".

"When do you have the greatest rush in the day?" asked the Daniel.

"In the evening, between 4 and 6", somebody said.

"There you are," came forth the solution, "Close the library at four instead of at six. That will end the bother".

Some weak member meekly murmured, "They are the only hours when most of the students and teachers can use the Library".

"Too much reading is no good, you know", retorted the strong-willed Daniel.

Poor First Law! So summarily and unceremoniously thrown overboard! But you must not refuse your clemency to South India; for, all climes and times have an equal claim on you. South India is not alone in showing you disrespect at this late hour. Remember the recent lamentations of a Parisian librarian: "Generally speaking, a school library in France was a closed cupboard opened once a fortnight or once a month".

But the magic of the *Mantra* 'BOOKS ARE FOR USE' has made marvellous changes in the library hours in the other places of the West. Even the Bodleian, groaning under the undiscriminating weight of medieval tradition, has, we are told, recently broken the shackles of an old injunction about lights, which had till now made its hours keep pace with the erratic sun of the north. The long prohibited electric light is now making its hours not only uniform but also fairly long. Other libraries had surrendered to the dictates of the First Law even earlier. According to the recent American Library Association's survey of the libraries,[1] 'the hours, during which the libraries are open daily, vary from ten to fourteen'. The

(1) AMERICAN LIBRARY ASSOCIATION: *A Survey of the Libraries in the United States,* Volume 2, pp. 94-95 & 159-160.

Amherst college which, eighty years ago, was keeping its library open for bare three hours in a week, now keeps it open for nearly a hundred hours in a week. In fact its daily hours are said to be 8 A.M. to 10-30 P.M. The Cornell University does similarly. The Oregon University opens the library daily at 7-30 A.M. and closes it only at 10 P.M. Even the Madras University Library has fixed 7 A.M. and 6 P.M. as its hours of opening and closing, for every day in the year. God willing, it may soon emulate the Western Universities even in their nocturnal vigils. It is not only the college and University libraries that have responded to the call of the First Law of Library Science. The response of the Public Libraries has been no less eager. The majority of them, which keep BOOKS FOR USE, are open daily from 9 A.M. to 9 P.M., while some, as in San Francisco and Seattle, work even till 10 P.M.

There is no need to multiply statistics. It may be asserted boldly that the *a priori* reasoning about library hours leads only to results that are consistent with practice in the West. In no country, where the concept, 'BOOKS ARE FOR USE', has taken root in the Public Mind, will any library be allowed to close till the majority of humanity go to bed and so cannot use it. Nor can it be kept closed after they rise from bed. Nor will any library be allowed to close on any day of the year,— not even on Sundays, even in Christian Countries. The Public demand long hours and the library authorities appreciate the soundness of this demand. It is indeed considered criminal to close a library at any time when people can conveniently use it. One might ask, what about the cost of establishment, if it is to be kept open for long hours and on all days. Modern society maintains that any extra money spent on library establishment is legitimately spent and is well spent. After all, what is the proportion of the extra cost of establishment to the enormous benefit that will flow from a wider use of the library. What a large sum of money is locked up in the books of libraries! Is it not penny-wise and pound-foolish to grudge a few rupees more on the establishment and to restrict the full use of such a treasure? Sometimes, wisdom consists in throwing good money after better.

"*** *** ****; but if you please
To shoot another arrow that self way
Which you did shoot the first, I do not doubt,
As I will watch the aim...to find both."[1]

But in the matter of library hours, the palm goes to the University College, London. In the inaugural address to freshmen, which was delivered in my year, by a lucky coincidence, by Dr. E. A. Baker, the Director of the School of Librarianship, he mentioned in proud terms that the University College was a pioneer and a breaker of traditions and cited several facts in support of his claim. I don't remember, however, that he included the

(1) SHAKESPEARE (William): *Merchant of Venice*, Act I, Scene 1.

achievements of the college in the matter of library hours. To put it shortly, the library hours of the University College are not fixed by the college at all. They are left entirely in the hands of each individual student. The fact is, each student is given a latch-key for the library of his or her Department and he or she is at liberty to use the library, at any time he or she likes—day or night—the last word on library hours! This ideal is whole-heartedly endorsed, in its final report of May 1927, by the Public Libraries Committee, appointed in 1924 by the President of the Board of Education of Great Britain. It observes "Inasmuch as there is no hour of the night or day at which a citizen may not feel the need to peruse some book which is not in his possession, the ideal arrangement would be that libraries should always be open to the public."[1]

LIBRARY FURNITURE

Next let us see the effect of the dictum 'BOOKS ARE FOR USE' on library furniture. One may say with confidence 'Show me your library furniture and I shall tell you whether you believe in the First Law of Library Science or not'. To begin with, in the days when the rival dictum 'BOOKS ARE FOR PRESERVATION' ruled, the library racks were built only with a view to preservation. The problem was to accommodate the maximum number of books in the least space and at the lowest cost. The Rule of Least Space left the height of

(1) *Report on Public Libraries in England and Wales*, 1927, page 75.

the book-racks entirely to be determined by the height of the ceiling. Not even an inch of vertical space should be wasted. Hence each rack should begin at the very bottom and go right up to the ceiling. Similarly, another corollary of the Rule of Least Space was that not an inch of horizontal space, beyond the absolute minimum, should be wasted. This required that the gangway between book-racks should be as narrow as possible—just enough for an attendant to pass through—say a foot and a half or two at the most. Again, in the absence of chaining, each rack should be at least provided with doors, locks and keys. The Rule of Least Cost required that the furniture of the reading-room should be as simple and as cheap as practicable. The reader had no business to expect comfort. Other furnishings, the reading-room need not have. No hangings to make the room more attractive. No charming pictures or inspiring portraits on which the tired eyes of a reader may now and then rest and refresh themselves. But the advent of the First Law of Library Science threw on these, Rules of Least Space and of Least Cost a delightful spell which has completely transformed them.

A DIALOGUE

First Law: Your methods are intolerable. They *must* go.

Rule of Least Space: Can you kindly descend to the level of particulars?

First Law: Take your book-racks first. How do you expect the top of these sky-scrapers to be reached?

Rule of Least Space: Use a ladder!

First Law: That is more easily said. It is all-right with the trained nimble library attendants. Perhaps you do not know, that I am going to allow every reader to pick out any book he wants directly from the shelf.

Rule of Least Space: It is news to me. I have never heard of that.

First Law Oh! I see,....Is it so? Yes, any reader will go to the shelf. Now imagine a corpulent reader climbing a ladder, for the first time in his life, in his enthusiasm for a book. Imagine his fiddling at the top, falling down and breaking his neck. Who is to pay the damages? What will your sister, the Rule of Least Cost, say to that?

Rule of Least Cost: No doubt, it is a matter for serious thought.

Rule of Least Space: What do you suggest then?

First Law: No rack should be higher than what can be comfortably reached by a person of average height, while standing on the bare floor.

Rule of Least Space: A height of 6½ or 7 feet?

First Law: Admirable. That is the right height. You are very reasonable.

Rule of Least Space: Well, I have noted it. Anything else?

First Law: The regulation width of your gangways is too small.

Rule of Least Space: It was fixed for different conditions, you know. We only intended a library attendant to pass through.

First Law: Excuse me if I laugh. So long as it was only an attendant that had to use it, it was open to you to tell the library authorities that they should recruit only slim 'one-dimensional' beings as attendants, if they don't want their staff to get jammed between the racks.

Rule of Least Space: No offence at all. These points have to be made clear. Your admitting the readers to the shelves is quite a novel idea. That makes all the difference. But, dimensions are more my province. Without fear of being considered pedantic, I may say that you seem to contemplate a race of readers who have expanded into all my three dimensions with a vengeance and demand a gangway which should be capable of admitting the biggest of them!

First Law: You are nearly right. I should like however that the gangway should be broad enough to permit two of them to walk along abreast of each other.

Rule of Least Space: Ye-es. I quite see your point. $4\frac{1}{2}$ to 6 feet will be all right?

First Law: Thank you. One word more. Although it is not quite relevant to what we were talking about, I should like to thank you most heartily for the selfless manner in which you took a bold stand against the Library Authorities when they proposed to stop all further purchase temporarily, because the stack-room was choked with books and that there was no more space.

Rule of Least Space: Well, . . .

First Law: I see, from your exchange of smiles with your sister, that there is more behind it.

Rule of Least Cost: Really, it was so good of my sister to have accommodated me and sided with me in that matter.

Rule of Least Space: She just convinced me that if that proposal came to be adopted she would be nowhere, since the cost of old books—and particularly the scientific periodicals and other publications of Learned Societies which are indispensable for research—will increase tenfold in a short while.

First Law: Even then, I am indebted to you. Who, in these days, is prepared to be so very selfless and look to the comforts of a sister in distress?

Rule of Least Space: Thank you. I am so glad we part as friends although you will admit you were almost in a rage at the beginning.

First Law: I am sorry. I crave your pardon. The fault is due to my enthusiasm for my cause. I meant nothing personal. I shall make amends, by giving some cheering news to your sister.

Rule of Least Space and Rule of Least Cost: What is it! What is it!

First Law: I don't want doors, locks and keys for the book-racks. You may save the cost of all of them. . . .

Rule of Least Cost: I am, in a sense, pleased; but what about rats and squirrels? And again, you say all sorts of folk will come into the gangway. What will prevent their passing the books through the windows?

First Law: It is a very intelligent question. But, you need not trouble yourself about it. I am asking the architect to make the room itself vermin-proof and thief-proof.

Rule of Least Cost: And air-proof! Is it?

First Law: No, not necessarily. Will you be good enough, in return not to make the reading-room man-proof?

Rule of Least Cost: I don't quite understand you.

First Law: Just make the chairs cozy and comfortable and the table-space ample. Also, just sanction the necessary sum to make the floor sound-proof.

Rule of Least Cost: That is not much. That is easily done.

First Law: I should also implore you to furnish the reading-room as nicely as possible —like a first class drawing-room, say, like this lovely room of yours, with beautiful hangings, flowers, pictures, fans, lights, etc. Remember the lights particularly since it is my policy to allow the serious students to stay on after sunset, if they are so minded, to continue their study.

Rule of Least Cost: That is an idea.

First Law: One more request. I trust you don't think I am going too far.

Rule of Least Cost: Never mind. It is better to let us know at once all your requirements.

First Law: Just make provision for ample supply of reliable drinking water, for a few W. C.'s, for a bath-room and—I am almost afraid to say it—for the establishment and maintenance of a refectory.

Rule of Least Cost: Why afraid? We are only exchanging ideas. Be frank.

First Law: Then, I shall add, provide also a retiring room, with perhaps a couple of lounges where the scholars, who come to stay the whole day, may stretch themselves and close their eyelids now and then for a few minutes. Of course, I may assure you that due precautions will be taken to see that such a first-class privilege is not abused by any.

Rule of Least Cost: What novel ideas! Beautiful. . . though costly. But ... per—haps . . . eco—nomical al—so. . .

Rule of Least Space: Costie! . . . Costie! What are you pondering over, with eyes closed?

Rule of Least Cost: Ye—es, Dear Spacie, Meditating . . . Cogitating, if you like. I just got on the 'Time-Machine' to explore what this would mean in the long run. I have seen, Spacie, that, at that distance of time, all this little sum that we may have to spend extra on such things to get the books better used will lead ultimately to real healthy National Economy. Yes, the whole thing is clear to me now. Am I right, Mr. First Law?

First Law: Yes, you have put it correctly and in a businesslike manner.

Rule of Least Cost: To put it in a word you don't want the library to continue any longer as a dead storehouse of books. You want it fitted up as a first-class workshop.

Rule of Least Space: Costie! You remind me of the revolutionary words of Lord Lytton at the inauguration of the Public Library at Manchester in 1851. You remember his words,[1] "A Library is not only a school, it is an arsenal and an armoury. Books are weapons; either for war or for self-defence."

Rule of Least Cost: Yes, I do. But they are the words of a pre-League of Nations-man. Our friend wants us to conceive the library as a regular peaceful workshop, which will prove to be a panacea for the ills of humanity and—what I am more concerned with—eliminate all wastage both in local administration and in the State.

Rule of Least Space: I can never keep pace with you in your *Economic* flights into the Future. Mr. First Law, are you satisfied? That is all that we want.

Rule of Least Cost: I am sure he is.

---

(1) EDWARDS (Edward): *Free Town Libraries*, p. 73.

First Law: Workshop! Exactly. That is the word. You have caught it. I am sure hereafter we shall always see eye to eye and get on in a friendly way. I am glad of your sympathy and I may tell you at once that, in addition to doing all this, I want the constant help of your watchful eye to save every possible pie to buy the very books, for whose use, after all, I am giving you all this trouble.

Rule of Least Cost: You are a regular missionary, I see. But, now that we have understood each other, may I take the liberty of making one or two suggestions?

First Law: Most certainly. I want them.

Rule of Least Cost: I think, the retiring room, the refectory and the elaborate furnishings of the reading-room—like a first class drawing-room, as you put it—may wait. Perhaps you don't realise how it will re-act in certain quarters. You must remember that, for some time to come, library authorities will consist of persons who spent their earlier days before your advent. You can hardly expect them to develop a library habit at this late stage of their life. In these circumstances, how do you expect them to evaluate properly all such innovations, all so suddenly sprung on them.

First Law: I was not altogether unaware of this difficulty. In fact, in speaking to your sister, it is such considerations that made me reluctantly refrain from asking for space for a 'Lecture Room' and an 'Exhibition Room'. I thought I might rather leave it for my sister, the Third Law, since she is more directly interested in such things.

Rule of Least Space: I have been here for such a long time. I can tell you what will happen. The entire blame will be put on the head of the poor Librarian. All sorts of motives will be attributed to him, such as thirst for cheap popularity, and his life will be filled with worry.

Rule of Least Cost: My sister is quite right.

First Law: I didn't realise that. Perhaps my missionary zeal—as you put it—and my over-enthusiasm have blinded me to such worldly wisdom, which are so natural to you...the shrewd financier that you are...I want the good will of the Librarian and his staff more than anything else, if my mission is to succeed. In fact, he is the person that I am going to see next. I don't want that he should in any way...innocent man...in any way get into disrepute for no fault of his.

On the other hand, I not only want that *he* should co-operate with me but also that he should have the good-will and co-operation of the library authorities. Otherwise, he can't be of much use to me. I don't want to weaken his position for anything in the world . . . . Thank you for the advice. I thought, I came to teach; but I go back wiser.

Rule of Least Cost: So it is with us. Cheerio!

Rule of Least Space: Wish you good luck with the Librarian!

First Law: Thank you. Good-bye.

LIBRARY STAFF

Let us now pass on from the Library Furniture to the Library Staff. The advent of the First Law has had the most vital effect on the Library Staff. It has affected the question of staff in several ways and we should examine each one of them with the greatest possible care and thoroughness. Whatever be the Library Location, the Library Hours, the Library Furniture and the way in which books are kept, it is the Library Staff that ultimately make or mar a library. In fact, an enormous struggle has been going on for the past fifty years to adjust the Library Staff to the needs of this new concept, BOOKS ARE FOR USE. If the mere number of papers that have been written on librarianship can be taken as a measure of this struggle, one can get some idea of it from the admirable *Bibliography* of Cannons. Not less than 58 closely printed pages of this book is devoted to the subject of the staff and it must be remembered that the list has been brought up only to the end of 1920.[1]

So long as the preservation of books was the chief concern of a library, all that it wanted by way of staff was a competent care-taker who could fight against the four enemies of books: fire, water, vermin and men. And it was not unusual to make a post in the library the sinecure for persons unfit for other jobs. It was not unusual, for example, for libraries to be manned by the deaf and the maimed, by stammerers and hunch-backs, by the dull and the short-tempered—by never-do-well's of all sorts. The term "Keeper" by which the librarians of ancient libraries are still designated is indeed a significant survival of the pre-First Law days. The parody of a passage in Plato's *Republic* given by Dr. A. D. Lindsay, Master of Balliol College in his Presidential Address of 1928, fits in appropriately with this conception of a librarian.

"Then on which occasions concerned with books is the librarian a more useful partner than another?

In cases of depositing and keeping books safe.

Is not that as good as saying 'When there is no need to read books but only to keep them unread?'

Yes.

Then librarianship is useful in regard to books when books are useless?

(1) CANNONS (H. G. T.): *Bibliography of Library Economy* ...1876-1920, pp. 225-282.

It looks like it.

Librarianship, then, my friend, cannot be of any great moment if it is useful only for books when they are useless.'"[1]

In fact librarianship was not till recently considered to be of any great moment for any purpose.

Indeed, it took a long time even to realise the need for a professional librarian. If there was a librarian's post, it was not known whom to recruit for it and if there was a librarian, it was not known what to do with him. For nearly half a century, even the University College, London, which has now become a centre for training librarians, used to leave its library "to the care of an assistant, sometimes dignified with the title of librarian but never paid more than £80 a year or to that of a library beadle.'"[2] In his *Story of the University of Edinburgh,* Sir Alexander Grant records, "Between 1635 and 1667 there was a succession of no less than ten librarians; probably none of these persons had a peculiar vocation for the employment." When it finally got a librarian who would not leave it, not knowing what to do with him, it asked him to maintain "the Graduation Book where for a series of years he entered the laureations". Even that not filling all his spare time, he was made to act, in addition, "as Secretary to the College, an office which was henceforth combined with that of Libra-

(1) *Library Association Record (New Series),* Vol. VI, pp. 237-8.

(2) BELLOT (H. Hab.): *University College, London,* p. 418.

rian!" So long as BOOKS WERE ONLY FOR PRESERVATION and until it came to be realised that "BOOKS ARE FOR USE," how else could a librarian's time and energy have been utilised? Edinburgh was by no means unique in thus obtaining from the librarian some such miscellaneous work in return for the salary paid to him. Her neighbour Glasgow did similarly. We are told that, until 1858, "Matriculation and enrolment was carried through by the Librarian" in the University of Glasgow.[1]

The position in the New World too was not very different. It was only in comparatively recent times that at Harvard or Yale, a librarian was appointed who should give his entire time to the care of the library. When the Kenyon College, a residential institution, was established in 1826, the duties of the librarian fell upon the Principal's wife, Mrs. Chase. But librarian's work was not the only work that was assigned to her. "The chief care of the household affairs fell upon Mrs. Chase. She also kept the accounts of the institution and *looked after the library*"[2] (Italics mine).

According to Koch,[3] "It was not long ago that the library was generally thought of as a place for the semi-retirement of the aged professor or the incompetent instructor. Even now, it is a common occurrence for the librarian to be asked whether

(1) MURRAY (David): *Memoirs of the Old College of Glasgow*, p. 54.

(2) SMYTHE (George Franklin), *Kenyon College*, p. 39.

(3) *Ibid.*, pp. 40-41.

he has not something to which a broken down scholar can turn his hand. The necessity for training, energy, alertness and specific fitness for library work is still not seen by many who, even from their casual acquaintance with libraries, should know better what kind of help is required to run a library".

William Frederick Poole, who was librarian at Newberry in the closing years of the last century, is reported to have said before his death, "None of the Universities have as yet quite come up to the high standard of having a professor of bibliography, but they are moving in that direction". In 1894, President Harper[1] could only hope "some of us will see the day when in every grand division of the University there will be professors of bibliography and methodology whose function will be to teach men books, and how to use them". The same University President was however convinced[2] that "The equipment of the Library will never be finished until it have upon its staff men and women whose sole work shall be, not the care of books, not the cataloguing of books, but the giving of instruction concerning their use".

Turning to our own country we are yet to get a Harper as the head of any of our educational institutions. The conditions hardly seem to favour even the entertainment by us of such a hope. Most of our Colleges have no doubt begun to include in

(1) SMYTHE (George Franklin), *Kenyon College*, p. 123.
(2) *Ibid.*, p. 124.

their "Annual Staff Return" a post under the dignified title "Librarian". Although the salary shown against the entry may imply a deplorable lack of appreciation of the need for a real librarian, who can get the BOOKS USED, his true status can be realised only by those who have served on the staff of a college for some time.

In most of the degree colleges, the so-called librarian is usually a clerk, and nothing more, by training, temperament and status. He is not given much initiative, nor is he capable of any. His time is largely spent in maintaining the files and in carrying them, now and then, to a far-off room occupied by the dignitary—the Professor-in-charge-of-the-Library—to whom he is responsible and by dancing attendance on whom, he hopes to keep his place. His assistant is usually an attendant whose educational attainments are a little too good for a peon's place. His duty is to dole out books across the barrier at stated hours in the week and otherwise to keep dusting the shelves or trimming the books and the files. There is none on the Library Staff who could link it up with the instructional force of the college, not to speak of following up the course of studies pursued by the college; none who could look up material on request, not to speak of collecting the material in advance, in anticipation of future demand; none who could instruct the ordinary students in the use of the books of the library, not to speak of assisting the research students in the methods of using original sources. The

Professor-in-charge may do such things—there are exceptional professors-in-charge who actually do such things and all honour to them. But the Professor-in-charge is a Professor and not a Librarian and he is ordinarily made to understand his duties to begin with the passing of office-copies and end with the signing of fair-copies. On the other hand, one must be really thankful if the Professor does not succumb to the temptation to keep all good new arrivals in his exclusive private custody thus gaining a temporary advantage over the pupils whom he has to teach. If he does, as it not infrequently happens, the class of librarians to which he can be appropriately assigned has been carefully defined by the Master of Balliol in the parody of another passage of the *Republic*.

"And he is an excellent guard of an army who is clever in stealing the plans of the enemy and all their dispositions?

Certainly.

Then, whoever is a clever guarder of anything is also a clever thief of it?

Apparently.

Then, if the librarian is clever at guarding books, he is also clever at stealing them?

That is certainly the drift of the argument."

The plight of the Intermediate College libraries is still worse in the matter of Library Staff. More often than not, a raw youth, who has just scraped through the School Final Examination is installed in the librarian's *gadi*. The Intermediate Colleges usually have a populous school department. This department it is that often relieves the Principal from the awkward predicament of finding work for this youth, to keep him from mischief. The daily consolidation of the hourly attendance of the pupils, the monthly writing-up of the nominal rolls in the attendance registers, and the terminal posting of entries in the Secondary School Leaving Certificate books are, as a rule, made his monopoly. If they do not engage him fully, he must assist the Accountant in the collection of school-fees, or, the troublesome task of maintaining the stock of stationery and forms awaits his attention.

But the worst occurs in School Libraries. The School Libraries have not recognised the need even for a librarian-clerk. It is usually the drill master or the drawing master that is asked to look after the library—if there is one. In a school that I knew, the stoutest and cruellest of the staff, who was nicknamed Mohammad of Ghazni in honour of the number of his unsuccessful attempts at Matriculation, was marked out as the guardian angel of the library. And, he proved to be too zealous a guardian. When an inquisitive child of the school picked up courage to approach him and ask for a book for "extra-reading" it was late in the evening and he was dead tired after the day's task of teaching for six hours.

"What do you want?" thundered Mohammad of Ghazni, almost scorching the child with his reddish eyes.

"*Peeps Into Many Lands: Japan,* Sir," stammered the child.

"How many marks did you get in the last Quarterly?"

"Fo—Forty-two out of fifty, Sir."

"Go and get the remaining eight marks before you can think of "extra-reading",

came forth the emphatic injunction in company with the right-hand fist of the Mohammad of Ghazni, which settled on the forehead of the quivering child with such painful force, that the child ran away sobbing—never, never to return to the library.

If the school believed that BOOKS WERE FOR THE USE of children, would it have consigned them to the care of such a frightening monster? On the other hand, would it not have put them in charge of a charming Children's Librarian, whose specialised training and sympathetic outlook, would have attracted all the children of the school to what is now rightly called "the heart of the school". Then, how different would have been the reminiscences of the children of the school! Consider, for example, the pleasant recollections of a New World contemporary of our sobbing child. "I can almost say that I owe to the library the greatest mental stimulus of my life. The picture of that Librarian's intelligent grey-eyed face, the very odour of the library room itself are indelibly impressed in my memory. Personally my debt to the library as an institution and to librarians as a class is a greater one than I can ever hope to pay even with everlasting gratefulness".[1]

LIBRARY STAFF AND SCHOLARSHIP

Even after the First Law had succeeded in convincing people of the need for a full-timed and special staff for the library, it took a long time for library authorities to appreciate the qualities and qualifications that are essential in a Library Staff, if it is to carry out all the mandates of that Law. The struggle experienced by the First Law in establishing proper standards for librarianship was even more strenuous than that experienced in fixing the proper Library Hours. Its predecessor "BOOKS ARE FOR PRESERVATION" had left behind it many a hardened tradition. Tradition, as is well known, is obstinately indifferent to reasoning of any type. She would not easily listen to the arguments of the First Law. Analogy, however suggestive, could not carry conviction to her. A grain dealer, it is conceded, should know about grains of all sorts. A draper should know everything about apparel. An insurance agent cannot be a success if he does not know all about life-tables and their significance. No one would be admitted as a teacher unless he knows the subject he has to teach. But it took a long time to realise that a librarian,—who has to deal with learning, who has to find for each person his appropriate book, who has to persuade people to benefit by the

(1) *Adult Education and the Library*, Vol. III, p. 52.

knowledge treasured up in books, who has, in fact, to help the life-long education of all and not merely that of the beardless urchins,—must have learning, must know his books and must possess scholarship of a wide range.

In his humorous retrospect of the "Early Days," Mr. Frank Pacy, the late Secretary of the British Library Association, refers to certain interesting impressions produced by the scholarship of the early British librarians. "The man who showed us the library knew nothing about anything." "The Westminster Librarian not only looked like a chimney sweep, but was very deaf".[1] Fortunately, those days are gone. Nowadays, nobody in the West questions the place of Librarianship among the learned professions.

But, in our country, few people realise even to-day the need for a scholarly staff in a library. Not long ago, a librarian received, from a high-placed educational officer, a pathetic note of recommendation saying, "The bearer, you will find, is very aged. He appeared for the S.S.L.C. Examination more than a dozen times. There is no prospect of his passing it 'in this *Janma*'. How can he get even a clerk's post? But I am interested in him. Can you take him on your staff? That is the only chance for him". When a big metropolitan library came to be started, one of the first appointments in "the superior service" of the library went to a peon

(1) *Proceedings of the Fiftieth Conference of the Library Association*, p. 57.

of a neighbouring office, for the simple reason that he was an honest fellow and that there was no other way in which his emoluments could be increased. Perhaps, the precedent for this was that the Janitor of the Bodleian Library was made its sub-librarian in 1712.[1] Similarly, when a District Board permitted a Union Chairman to appoint a part-time librarian for his Union Library on a monthly allowance of Rs. 10, the Chairman is said to have promptly given that allowance to his personal attendant, since he was a serviceable fellow and would jealously guard the library. It is reported that not long ago, a learned professor laid down the dictum that the academic qualification of a library clerk need not be even as high as that of an attendant in a Chemist's shop.

But more amusing is the inference that a librarian cannot be a scholar. The embarrassment felt by a prominent official in an up-country town when he was asked to receive a librarian as his guest could only be relieved by one of his junior clerks offering to entertain that librarian in his own house. When, however, quite ignorant of this arrangement, the librarian went straight to the official's house and sent in his card, the appearance of the suffix "M.A.," to the name of the librarian instantly made his feeling of embarrassment give place to one of amazement, and by the time they reached the stage of post-prandial *pan supari*, the

---

(1) BIRRELL (Augustine): *Collected Essays and Addresses*, Vol. III, p. 206.

amazement had transformed itself into pity and soaked with sympathy the learned official condoled with the Master of Arts for the fate that had overtaken him and cursed the hard times that had driven a man of his ability and scholarship to the predicament of having to mind a library. But this sincere pity was overpowered by righteous indignation when he discovered that the librarian's salary was higher than his own and that the authorities had wasted over a librarian's post not only a Master of Arts of the country but also such a huge slice of its revenue. But, my concern is that this learned official appears to be the type rather than the exception.

The learned official's opinion comes naturally to those that seldom use a library and have never felt the influence of a well-conducted modern library. But every person that makes a frequent and serious USE of a library and "has worked up a subject" once in his life expects to find on the library staff at least one member who "speaks his language" and knows the bibliography and the method of his subject. The President of a Western University once remarked: "Every person in charge of a library must be capable of teaching. Executive ability is no doubt necessary in a librarian, but, unless it is coupled with wide scholarship, it is not at all sufficient."

What kind of a scholar should the library recruit for its staff? Certainly not the scholar pictured in the comic papers as one without common sense, nor one of the pedant variety who is unduly formal and subtle; nor one of the specialist type who learns "more and more about less and less". The Library requires on its Staff persons who have scholarship in Mark Pattison's sense, *i.e.*, judgment, discipline and scientific habit. Their speciality must be bibliography and their attitude must be that of a student. In the words of the "Public Libraries Committee" of Great Britain they must have a sufficient knowledge of and sympathy with all branches of knowledge to be able to do justice to them in the selection of books, to give the readers the guidance of which they stand in need and to divine in the quickest manner the place where the information sought by the readers can be found. They must be capable of using books as tools not only for the dissemination of knowledge but also for the extension of the boundaries of knowledge.

It is on account of this that a University degree is considered a normal entrance requirement by the library schools of the West and the highest University degrees are required from those who aspire to the highest places in library service. This also explains the recent practice, in go-ahead libraries, of attracting to the Library Staff persons with ripe professorial experience as part-time Reference-librarians. It is from this point of view that Arnold Bennett wrote that if libraries "spent less on books and more on an educated Staff, far better results would be obtained. It is not books that lack in the libraries; it is the key to their effective employment. That key is the individualities and attainments of Librarians and their staffs".

LIBRARY STAFF AND PROFESSIONAL TRAINING

But mere scholarship cannot make a librarian. Many people think that, because they can read books, they are qualified to be librarians. Such ignorance is well illustrated by the anecdote of MacAlister narrated by Augustine Birrell[1]:

"Only the day before yesterday, on the Calais boat, I was introduced to a world-famed military officer who, when he understood I had some connection with the Library Association, exclaimed: 'Why, you're just the man I want! I have been anxious of late about my man, old Atkins. You see the old boy, with a stoop, sheltering behind the funnel. Poor old beggar! quite past his work, but as faithful as a dog. It has just occurred to me that if you could shove him into some snug library in the country, I'd be awfully grateful to you. His one fault is a fondness for reading, and so a library would be just the thing."

"The usual titled lady also turned up at the Conference. This time she was recommending her late cook for the post of librarian, alleging on her behalf the same strange trait of character—her fondness for reading."

(1) BIRRELL (Augustine): *Collected Essays and Addresses*, Vol. III, pp. 227-228.

The pathos attendant on such ignorance is only comparable to what was felt when an innocent lad applied for a "Mathematics Reader's" post in one of our Universities, basing his claim on the ample qualification that he had just taken his B.A. (Pass) degree in Mathematics and that he was "fond of reading".

But the superior arrogance of those, who can more than read books, who feel competent to criticise literary style or have gained some acquaintance with a special department of knowledge, is more annoying. They imagine that anything in a library, beyond their scholarship, is manual, clerical and rather beneath their efforts, not knowing that they are yet only good material out of which librarians might be made. Not infrequently one comes across a bumptious upstart, who has the cheek to say, "What is there in *indexing?*" meaning by 'indexing', *Cataloguing.* One only wishes that he was allowed to try his hand at 'indexing' for a couple of months to discover for himself what a mess he is capable of making. Another, a venerable old man, may say "What is the training that is necessary to hand over books across the barrier? In my days, so and so did it so admirably and he had no ghost of a professional training". He has only to be asked "How many volumes did the library of his days have on its shelves? How many of them refused to leave the shelves even once in his long life-time? How many volumes were added to his library in a year? And how many of his learned contemporaries ever knew of a library or its purpose?" Another, a specialist quite jealous of the rights of his line of experts, may make a flippant remark, "That is not the way to classify. This is the way to catalogue. Reference-work is not in your province. It is the preserve of the Professors" and so on. One has to tell him "Mr. Specialist, I am a specialist in my line as much as you are, Sir, in yours. If *your* field is clouded in mystery and needs prolonged formal initiation, so is mine. Remember what you will think of any uninitiated Tom, Dick or Harry who attempts to poke his nose into your sphere."

The fact is that so long as the task of a library was to PRESERVE BOOKS, there was no need for giving any special training to the care-taker-librarian. The moment 'BOOKS ARE FOR USE' stepped into the place of 'BOOKS ARE FOR PRESERVATION', Librarianship was invested with several tasks, which required a well-thought-out professional training, with as much grind and as much technique as that required for any other learned profession, such as Medicine, Engineering, or Law. A Doctor, an Engineer, and a Lawyer will flare up into righteous wrath, if anybody ventures to question the need for their professional training. But the same Doctor, Engineer, and Lawyer would naively question the need for professional training for a librarian. That is due simply to the fact that Medicine, Engineering and Law are *old* professions which have cleanly forgotten the struggle they had in establishing their need for specialised training while Librarianship is a *new* profession. It is natural for people in a privileged position to fight every inch before admitting a stranger to the same privilege. This fight will not end unless and until the present-day Doctor, Engineer and Lawyer are replaced by those that have had, from their youth onwards, the pleasure and benefit of being served by a technically trained profession of librarians.

This may look like a vicious circle. But with the rousing chorus of the new song 'BOOKS ARE FOR USE' people have already broken this vicious circle elsewhere, and we may take advantage of it. Great Britain had long ago decided:

"(*i*) to educate public opinion to demand that trained librarians should be the rule and not the exception;

(*ii*) to enforce on library authorities their responsibility for giving due weight to training in their selection of candidates, and for giving facilities to their staff to continue their training, both technical and educational, while in their services;"[1]

America has gone ahead and established fourteen accredited institutions for the teaching of Library Science. The Ministries of Education of most of the countries of Continental Europe have taken upon themselves the task of providing the country with librarians of proper professional

(1) *Report on Public Libraries in England and Wales*, p. 83.

attainments. Japan had long ago established its own library school while China has the Boone's School for Librarians. What is more important, in some of the Western countries, the Library Profession has long ago passed the stage of infancy and reached the ripe age of throwing out several branches, which show a tendency to develop such independence and individuality, that, ere long, we shall have several semi-independent library professions, spreading round their primitive stem, even as the pillar roots shooting forth profusely from the branches of the giant banyan-tree appear to be outside the tree but are still of it, giving shelter to thousands of birds.

Our hope is that a small beginning is being made even in our land. A seedling of the species, Summer School of Library Science, was carefully tended for two years in the nursery of the Madras Library Association. When it was fit for transplantation, it has found its way into the fertile garden of the Madras University which can, not only tend it with greater ease, but can also find a market for its fruits. May that seedling grow from more to more and may its harvest of fruits enrich the land from the Himalayas to the Cape Comorin!

LIBRARY STAFF AND STATUS

The next effort of the First Law, on behalf of the Library Staff, had to be directed towards the removal of another incubus bequeathed by the concept 'BOOKS ARE FOR PRESERVATION'. Even after a learned technically trained staff came to be recruited, the library authorities blinded by tradition would not perceive the need for revising the scale of salary that was originally designed but to attract and retain the care-taker-librarian and the clerk-librarian. It may even be that that scale had become inferior to that of a head-peon, or a *maistry* or a wireman. Though such an anamoly would not prick the conscience of the authorities, it was a matter of serious concern for the First Law. Such a scale would by no means attract the right type of men. Even if it did, the person, that it was able to pull out from the army of the unemployed, would be merely marking time, with his mind and heart elsewhere. Even the little experience he might gather would soon be lost to the library as he would take the earliest opportunity to step out. For a generation or two, in the early days of the First Law, when the library authorities consisted mostly of persons who had never come under the influence of a library whose guiding motto was 'BOOKS ARE FOR USE', when the work of the Library Staff could be neither appreciated nor evaluated properly, it was indeed an uphill task for the First Law to convince the authorities of the need for fixing an equitable scale of salary.

The First Law knew that a discontented staff was a social danger. Even apart from such a general slogan, it realised that an underpaid staff could not work up the enthusiasm necessary for the successful carrying out of its mission. Even if they did, the enthusiasm, the zeal and the solicitude of a poorly paid staff would not produce the desired result. The words of the poor, however beneficial, are seldom heard.[1] They would be put down as interested officiousness although the contempt induced by their low salary in the reader's mind would recoil on the reader himself. One may say, let the reader hang himself. But to that extent, the use of the books of the library would suffer and *that* is a matter for serious thought, for those who believe in the First Law.

Rightly or wrongly, human society has evolved its Economics on a Money-basis. An unsophisticated scrutiny of the foundations of the Theory of Value may disclose to the embarrassment of many that the feet of Mammon are made of clay. But, what is the good? Are the majority of men guided by the ultimate value of things? "An emphatic no", is the answer supplied by that astute Professor of Worldly Wisdom, Bhartrihari.[2] "On the other hand," says he, "He who has wealth is believed to have the bluest blood running in his veins. He is taken for a scholar. He passes for the most well-informed. He is considered the most discriminate. His power of speech is praised as

---

1. हेतुप्रमाणयुक्तं वाक्यं न श्रूयते दरिद्रस्य The *Panchatantra*, p. 152, Harvard Oriental Series, Vol. III.

2. यस्यास्ति वित्तं स नरः कुलीनः स पण्डितः स श्रुतिमान् गुणज्ञः ।
स एव वक्ता स च दर्शनीयः सर्वे गुणाः काञ्चनमाश्रयन्ति ॥

BHARTRIHARI: *Nitisataka and Vairagya Sataka* (Bombay Sanskrit Series), p. 11 of the text or p. 99 of Gopinath's edition with Hindi and English translations.

unequalled. And his figure is described as the most handsome. It is the gold in his possession that settles the quality of every one of his attributes".

> With reason may ye wele se,
> That Peny wyll mayster be,
> Prove nowe man of mode;
> * * * *
> He makyth the fals to be soende
> And ryght puttys to the grounde.[1]

Thus, money rules the world. It determines the status of men as well as the value of the services rendered by them.) Unfortunately, people are prepared to benefit by a service only in proportion to the value set on it by money. Thus, a famished staff will render the efforts of the First Law as futile as paucity of books or paucity of readers. In the trinity of the library—books, staff and readers—the richness of the staff in worldly goods appears to be as necessary as the richness of the other two in number and variety, if the theory 'BOOKS ARE FOR USE' is to be translated into practice. It will have to be so, so long as men's status is left to the capricious and arbitrary rule of Mammon.

An important handicap that is attendant on library service, in getting what it deserves, is that

(1) *Syr Peny*, a 14th century poem, *cf.* COULTON (G. G.): *Social Life in Britain from the Conquest to the Reformation*, pp. 369-370.

the benefits of its service are latent. A doctor gets his fifteen rupees for crossing the threshold once, since people believe that the life or death of the patient at the next moment is dependent on his service. A lawyer gets his hundred rupees for standing on his legs for one hour since people believe that the ownership of property at the next minute is dependent on his service. But the benefit of the service of the library staff, like the benefit of the service of the teacher, is not discernible at the next moment—not even in the next year or decade. Its benefit, although more universal and lasting, will come to the surface only a generation or two later, when the people, that had to open their purse and pay for it, are dead and forgotten. This is a distressing attribute, with which God seems to have invested it, perhaps when in a mood of wilful mischief.

In spite of it, the First Law has already nearly succeeded in the Western countries in overcoming the effects of such a mischief. Western Society is now prepared to agree that a University Librarian must have the status and salary of a Dean of the University, that a College-Librarian must get a treatment similar to that of a Professor, that a School-Librarian is in no way inferior to a Teacher and that the Librarian of a city is entitled to the same pay, the same rights and the same privileges as those of the other officers of the city, such as the Engineer, the Health Officer, the Revenue Officer and the Educational Officer.[1] When will India fall into line with her Western sisters? Will

(1) A NOTE ON THE STATUS OF LIBRARIANS IN MEDIEVAL INDIA.—Some interesting light is thrown, on the place the Libraries occupied in the educational institutions of medieval India, by the '*Inscriptions of Nagai*' published as No. 8 of the Hyderabad Archæological Series.

Nagai is a village near Wadi and it is said to be the site of an old city, which has now disappeared leaving behind it several monuments and inscriptions of great historical value.

A Kannada inscription in the sixty-pillared temple called 'Aruvathu Kambada Gudi' of that village, said to be of the date corresponding to the 24th of December, 1058, A.D., gives an account of the public institutions founded by Madusudana, a famous general and minister of the Chalukya King, Raya-Narayana. One of the institutions founded by him was a residential college called Chati kasala for two hundred scholars studying the Vedas, and fifty-two studying the Sastras. The institute was manned by three Vedic teachers, three Sastra teachers . . . and six librarians (Sarasvati-bhandarikas)'.

If the appointment of as many as six librarians is significant at all, perhaps one may reasonably infer that the Library attached to the college should have been of considerable size and usefulness. One is further tempted to compare this medieval college library with our present-day college libraries which are so notoriously indifferent and grudging both in improving their book-resources and in providing them with the necessary human aids for helping the proper exploitation of their resources by their teachers and students.

A later verse in the same inscription shows that Madusudana was far ahead of us in fixing the status of college librarians. For, his allotment of land to the teachers and librarians in lieu of their salary was as follows:—

48 Units (Matter) of land to the Professor of Prabhakara darsana.

35 Units to the Professor of Bhatta darsana.

30 Units to the Professor of Nyaya.

20 Units to the Professor of Vedangas.

30 Units to each of the six librarians and so on.

This shows that Madusudana has treated the professors and librarians almost equally and it may further be inferred that their she benefit by the experiences of her sisters or will she close her eyes to them and proceed herself to tread every inch of that old weary path? If she does, her children can never, never, overtake their cousins, in their onward march. Let us hope and pray that she won't take that fatal course but straight-away plunge into the foremost crest of the wave of progress, triumphantly put her librarians on a par with those of other countries and thus add to the chance of the First Law of Library Science bringing the long-neglected children of India, to the same position of vantage as that Law has been able to secure for the other nations of the world. Amen!

LIBRARY STAFF AND THEIR RESPONSIBILITY

Thus the primary task of the First Law was to educate the library authorities, with regard to Library Staff. We have seen that it performed this task step by step in four stages. First it convinced them of the need for a special staff, then for a learned staff, next for a trained staff, and finally for a well-paid staff. Its second task, in this matter, has been to tune the staff itself to the proper pitch. It would, indeed, be a tragedy if the Library Staff themselves forget, Sugriva-

---

academic qualifications also should have been of the same order.

The present day educational institutions of the West, which make a correct evaluation of the place of libraries, give professorial status to their librarians and, in return, insist upon high academic qualifications in them. It is earnestly hoped that the standard set by our illustrious countryman Madusudana, which is in such close agreement with the present-day practice in other countries, will soon be reached by our Universities, Colleges and Schools.

like,[1] the very noble cause which secured them their scholarship, training, emoluments and status. The plums of office are like the apple of Eden. And those, that are in their enjoyment, stand in need of a periodic searching of heart, in the light of the indignant words of the sons of Kausalya and Sumitra.[2] Every moment the Library Staff should remember that "BOOKS ARE FOR USE". At no time should they lapse into the mood of their ancestor at the Bodleian, of whom it is said "He was a very good librarian in some ways; but he hated anyone getting at his books.[3] They should never forget that in libraries books are collected for USE, prepared for USE, kept for USE and served for USE. The endless technical processes and routine—getting suggestions from experts, acquiring by purchase or gift, accessioning, classifying, cataloguing, shelf-registering, shelving, charging, and discharging—all these are carried on only FOR USE. To fulfil this paramount mission of the First Law to the fullest extent the Library Staff should not only remind themselves of that mission constantly, not only acquire the scholarship and pro-

---

(1) பெறல் அரும் திருப்பெற்று உதவிப்பெரும்
திறன் நினைத்திலன்; சீர்மையின் தீர்ந்தனன்;
அறம் மறந்தனன்; அன்பு கிடக்க நம்
மறன் அறிந்திலன்; வாழ்வில் மயங்கினன்.

KAMBAN: *Ramayanam*, Kishkindhakandam, VIII, 2.

(2) VALMIKI: *Ramayanam*, Kishkindhakandam, Sargas 33 and 34.

(3) *Library Association Record*: (*New Series*), Vol. VI, p. 237.

fessional training necessary but also develop certain attitudes and interests which are equally indispensable.

LIBRARY STAFF AND READERS

First comes the attitude towards Readers. It may seem rather unnecessary to have to say that Readers form an essential part of a live library's business. But, unfortunately, there are some who cannot get out of the habit of looking upon Readers as a nuisance. Others there are, who would just allow some Readers to step in, provided they remember that they are there by sufferance and have no right to demand anything, least of all, any comfort conducive to study. There are still others who won't mind paying some attention to the needs of the Readers, provided it won't interfere with the meticulous discharge of their administrative routine. Their motto is 'Administration' first, everything else including 'Readers' next. About a century and a half ago, when the First Law was not widely known, a Library with such an outlook would have perhaps been tolerated. In fact it was unfortunately so.

For about half a century from 1763, the Bodleian Library of Oxford was in the hands of the Rev. John Price of Jesus College. Quite early in his library-career, captain Cook's *Voyages* was published in 1771 and there was quite a demand for the work. But our Librarian Price promptly loaned his library copy to a friend of his and asked him to keep it as long as possible, lest he should be 'perpetually plagued by enquiries after it'.

Librarian Price would fain have had a library without readers. In fact, it is said of him that 'he discouraged readers by neglect and incivility'. In spite of this, he was allowed to rule the Bodleian, without any let or hindrance, for full half a century and to instal in his *gadi* his own son-in-law, who was a chip of the old block and managed to keep it with equal thoroughness for another half a century.

But Librarian Price is an anachronism to-day. A modern library cannot exist without Readers. 'The neglect and incivility' have crossed the floor, so to speak. For it is no longer the Reader that has to put up meekly with the 'incivility' of the Library Staff, but, unfortunately, it is the Library Staff that has silently to put up with the incivility that emanates, occasionally, from inconsiderate bumptious Readers.

The library has now to develop the methods of a modern shop. It is true that, in a great many libraries, it may not be possible to have enough assistants just waiting around for someone to come in. They will have queries to look up, letters to answer, catalogue-cards to write and a thousand and one other things to do. But, even so, it must be a rule that the moment a Reader enters the library, whatever is in hand must be stopped instantly and the impression given to the Reader should be one of welcome and attention.

We know it is very annoying if, just as one is in the middle of adding up a column of figures, someone pops in, and it is more annoying if one finds that he simply wants to browse round and does not want anything in particular. But these are the little things that are sent to try us and we must keep a cheerful outlook and on no account show any discourtesy. It is an excellent thing to remember that the 'Customer loveth a cheerful assistant'.

The conduct of the library assistants should on no account give room for gossip of the following type: "We went into that palatial nice looking library not long ago. There was one human figure with the irritating odour of Eucalyptus oil about him, in charge of the library at the moment, doubled up over the counter table, apparently addressing envelopes. No notice was taken of us at all when we entered and it was quite a few minutes before that figure let us know that it was alive. When it did, its expression so obviously said, "I wish people would not come in when I am obliged to get this job done"; but it actually said "What can I do for you?" without getting up from the seat. By the time we had stated our wants and it was able to say "Sorry, that book is on loan", we were not at all sure that it *was* sorry or even that it knew the book we wanted and we wondered whether the book was not on the shelf all the time".

On the other hand, when the Readers go home, it must be possible for them to say "The young lad who received us at that library had such a bewitching smile that it brightened up the whole room, and we felt quite certain that we had come in to the right place. Everything is made so comfortable in that library. Any day, I shall prefer to spend my off-time there".

LIBRARY STAFF AND PSYCHOLOGY

Next to being welcomed, the readers must be 'sized up' and humoured. To be successful in this task, the librarian must be a psychologist. To go a step further, every person on the Library Staff must also be a psychologist, if the best results are to be obtained. Does this mean that every person on the Library Staff should take a formal course in the study of the theory of psychology? Far from it, though it may not do much harm. Even a child learns, by observation, the particular kind of tactics that is necessary to have its own way with parents and teachers. So also every person on the Library Staff, who gets innumerable opportunities to observe people, should acquire, by practice, a working knowledge of psychology and the ability to understand human nature. It is the librarian's job to handle every type of reader, not merely just those that are pliant. The really successful librarian must be able to handle difficult readers. Otherwise, his books will be left unused to that extent. How often the librarian attributes his failure to the reader being unreasonable! Knowledge of books is only half the battle. It is almost as fatal not to know the difference between Tom and Dick as not to know that between Newton and Einstein. To handle the difficult reader successfully, one has to understand him. Does he growl? If so, does he mean it or is it merely a pose? Is he really ill-natured or is only his manner unpleasant? One will be turning away many a potential reader from the counter, if one shirks the problem of the visitor who is unreasonable, unpleasant, fussy or super-critical. Success can be secured by our accuracy in quickly sizing up the easy ones and by the patience and intelligence we show in studying and working with difficult ones.

A few years ago a turbanned Indian happened to be on 'floor duty' in the Reference Department of an English library. A top-hatted Englishman came in with the usual familiarity but was dismayed to find the outlandish figure in the staff-enclosure.

The Indian librarian offered his help carefully suppressing the feeling induced by this look of dismay.

"No, thanks" came out the polite reply, and the Englishman went from shelf to shelf.

After a few minutes, the Indian approached him with another "Can I help you?"

"Thank you. Where are the books on 'Temperance'?" was the only reluctant response.

Then book after book of the 'temperance' region was opened and closed in quick succession. The watch was pulled out every minute from the pocket. He was evidently in a hurry. He had not got his reference and it was already 4-45. Poor man! "If you can tell me what exactly you want about temperance, perhaps I may be able to help you'', thus came another offer from the Indian on floor-duty.

This time, with his head turned the other way, the top-hatted gentleman said, ''I have to preside at a temperance-meeting. I want something for my introductory speech. Can you help me? My train is at quarter past five''.

Instantly, a volume of the encyclopædia which was in another part of the room, gave him the something he wanted, and he went away with a profusion of thanks scintillating from his smiling lips. ''What is this queer behaviour due to?'' was the problem raised by the new reference librarian, when the library was closing for the day. ''Shyness, my friend, shyness'', was the solution given by an experienced colleague, who added, ''If you want to be a reference librarian, you must learn to overcome not only *your shyness* but also the shyness of *others*!''

A common situation is that a visitor comes in; you have never seen him before; he states his wants; you show him the books you think will suit him. All the time you must study him to see if your first impression is correct or if you must revise it. Above all, you should not impose your ideas, your likes and dislikes, on him. If you offer him the new large-paper edition of Vanbrough and he says, 'I don't like Vanbrough. He is awful', it is better not to press the point unduly but to endeavour to pass on to the next shelf. Don't argue about it. Alas! we are all human and in try-

F—9

ing to prove that we are right, we lose sight of our main object which is to help the visitor in finding out what he can use with pleasure and profit. Work with the reader. Don't work on him. You can lead him. But you cannot drag him. Work with him on his own ground. If he is vain, play that quality. If he talks about himself, listen with respect but don't let him go too far from the point, *viz.*, the choice of books. If he is unreasonable and fussy, show him as early as possible that you can be assertive and that you know your rights and powers. But don't yield to the temptation of settling down in pleasant conversation, for its own sake, however agreeable it may be.

Visitors fall into two groups: those who want immediate attention so that they may be on their way as soon as possible and those that want to make unhurried selection without too much assistance. Errors in diagnosis at this point create an immediate and lasting unfavourable impression. The mistake lies in using a stereotyped greeting to all visitors. An answer should be sought to the question—"Into which group the visitor falls"—and he should be treated in accordance with the analysis.

"A regular Polonius come to advice!", one might jeer. But a slight reflection will show how much disservice would be done to the First Law of Library Science by overlooking some of these apparently commonplace precepts. Any librarian who has had to do with a large staff will recollect how often, in his career, he has had the necessity to preach them to his colleagues. If there is a doubt that the testimony of such a librarian may be an interested testimony, here are the weighty words which have been deliberately embodied in a Report 'Presented by the President of the Board of Education to Parliament by Command of His Majesty' in May 1927. "Willingness to give help, patience in the face of stupidity, control of temper under provocation must be inculcated in every assistant and attendant in a library; while the higher rank need to cultivate a study of human nature which may almost claim the dignity of a special branch of psychology. The human factor is of such supreme importance in library administration that schools of librarianship and courses of instruction may well be asked to devote a portion of their attention to giving advice on this topic".[1]

LIBRARY STAFF AND PERSONAL SERVICE

The pleasure of understanding human nature and handling difficult cases should not, however, be regarded as the beginning and end of librarianship. They are only means to an end. What is a library? A library is a collection of books kept for use. Librarianship, then, is connecting a user and a book. Hence the very life of a library is in the *personal service* given to the people. At any rate, that is what obtains in the libraries that wholeheartedly believe that 'BOOKS ARE FOR USE'.

(1) *Report on Public Libraries in England and Wales*, p. 88.

This First Law of Library Science is a hard task-master. Once you admit its dictum, you cannot escape the logical conclusion to which it will drag you. It will say, for example, "If the library KEEPS BOOKS FOR USE, the task of the librarian is not to dump down a mass of books and tell readers to help themselves. Nor is it to forcibly feed them on books of *your* choice. It is to help them; and, to help any one is to co-operate with him in carrying out his own plans and wishes—to help him to help himself." That is the kind of *personal service* that the First Law expects of the Library Staff, if they mean to help it in its mission. It is a noteworthy fact that individual requests for such *personal service* are increasing. Books selected to fit individual needs and accompanied by tactful guidance should be the response to such requests. Some may wish to broaden their outlook on life; some may wish to supplement their formal education at school; some may wish to extend it by entry into new fields of knowledge; some may wish to gather data of a particular type; others may wish to read for the pure joy of reading. To such varied individual needs, the Library Staff must attend with equal efficiency. To render such *personal service,* the knowledge and experience of the Library Staff should be such that they will be able to recommend, with due discrimination, suitable books on the same subject to men and women who differ widely in ability, education and purpose. For example, everybody wants to read about

Relativity and we have scores of books on Relativity. Will any and all of these books suit the requirements of any reader whatever? Can Lodge's *Relativity,* Durell's *Readable Relativity,* Haldane's *Reign of Relativity,* Einstein's *Meaning of Relativity,* Russell's *A. B. C. of Relativity,* Whitehead's *Principles of Relativity,* Eddington's *Mathematical Theory of Relativity* and Birkhoff's *Origin, Nature and Influence of Relativity* appeal similarly to all? One may be too trashy for a particular person, but that may be the only book that brings Relativity to the level of the comprehension of some. Another book may be too speculative but that may be the only aspect of Relativity that may appeal to some. A third may be too mystic but there are souls that revel in mysticism. The treatment in yet another book may throw a challenge to the ripest senior wrangler but that may be the very hard nut that the senior wrangler has been longing to catch to exercise his powers of cracking. It is this wilderness of print, confusing in its magnitude even to those who deal with it constantly, on the one hand, and the equally bewildering variety of the tastes and capacities of the readers on the other hand, that make the *personal service* of the Library Staff indispensable to effect contact between the right reader and the right book at the right time and in the right manner. As William S. Learned puts it 'The library of the future will be a community intelligence service. It would require a more highly specialised personnel which must command all the College teachers' familarity with the literature of a strictly limited field, *plus* the power which the college teacher may and often does lack completely, namely, the power speedily to read his applicant's mental equipment and point of view and to sense intuitively the character of his personal need'.[1] To fulfil the demands of the First Law in this matter of *personal service*, the Library Staff should even be prepared to run to specialists and experts whenever necessary, for advice regarding the books that can be recommended to readers who may be interested in the pursuit or enjoyment of abstruse branches of knowledge.

In addition, they must have personality, tact, enthusiasm and sympathy. In fact, the relationship between the librarian and the reader should be the easiest and the most agreeable, not of a superior telling an inferior what books he ought to read, not of a teacher instructing a child, but of two equals exchanging points of view and information on books. In a word, the librarian should be 'friend, philosopher and guide' to every one who comes to *use* the library. It is such sympathetic *personal service* and "such hospitality that makes a library big, not its size" as the Poet Rabindranath Tagore puts it.[2]

---

(1) *Adult Education and the Library*, Vol. IV, p. 16.

(2) *Library Movement: a Collection of Essays by Divers Hands*, published by the Madras Library Association, p. 2.

LIBRARY STAFF AND SOCIAL SERVICE

If the logical outcome of the concept 'BOOKS ARE FOR USE' is such a high order of ungrudging *personal service*, it can be easily seen that it is only persons, with an irrepressible inward urge for *social service*, that can prove to be librarians, reaching the high standard set by the First Law. It can be seen that neither scholarship, nor professional training, nor high salary can by themselves make a librarian, however necessary they may be. Scholarship may lead to phlegmatic exclusiveness, professional training may result in arrogant self-complacency, and high salary may engender stand-offishness. They can all be bent to serve the purpose of the First Law if and only if there is that 'mental set'—inborn or cultivated—that mental set which moved our Saint Tayumanavar to burst forth in rapturous strains pleading with Him who is the Greatest of the Great:

"If you but give me the fitness to serve my fellow-beings, the state of happiness will come to me of its own accord."[1]

While such a delight in *social service* is necessary for any librarian, it is absolutely indispensable in one who has to turn the first sod of the library

---

(1) அன்பர் பணி செய்ய எனை ஆளாக்கி விட்டு விட்டால்
இன்பநிலை தானே வந்து எய்தும் பராபரமே.

TAYUMANAVAR: *Paraparakkanni*, verse 155.

TAMBYAH (T. Isac): *Psaḷms of a Saiva Saint, being selections from the writings of Tayumanaswamy tr. into English*, p. 36 (Verse No. 76).

movement in any society or country. The following pithy words of Edward Edwards, one of the pioneers of the Library Movement of the 19th Century England, enumerating the difficulties and the rewards of a pioneer librarian will be a source of consolation and encouragement to many a Library Staff of to-day in this part of the world:

"He must find comfort amidst the discouragements of ill-appreciated work... The labour that has to be performed under the direction of men who can neither understand its difficulties, nor estimate its results, is but likely to be at length rendered grudgingly. It becomes increasingly hard to keep in mind that applause is no right aim of work; that the pursuit which is much affected by immediate rewards, or the want of them, must be either unworthy itself, or be unworthily carried on." "But there is ample ground for steady and cheerful perseverance. Every step that is taken to extend the usefulness of a library;—to diffuse far and wide the best thought of the best thinkers;—carries one mine the more beneath the social abuses which have so often placed a prevailing influence over public institutions within the grasp of cunning money-grubs or of noisy stump-orators."[1]

But there is no need to invoke the aid of that fiction of a mine or to hope for a reward, however, remote. The FIRST LAW would say, "Plant

---

(1) EDWARDS (Edward): *Memoirs of Libraries*, Vol. II, pp. 96-7.

your cheerfulness and perseverance in my words, BOOKS ARE FOR USE. Your duty is to serve with books. Service is your sphere. Not rewards. Falter not. Go forward uninfluenced by any reward, real or fictitious, remote or immediate". To the librarian, the celebrated words of the Lord Sri Krishna have a special appeal:

> "Work alone are thou entitled to, and not to its fruit
> So never work for fruit, nor yet desist from work."[1]
>
> कर्मण्येवाधिकारस्ते मा फलेषु कदाचन ।
> मा कर्मफलहेतुर्भूः मा ते संगोऽस्त्वकर्मणि ॥

(1) *Bhagavadgita*, Chapter II, Verse 47—p. 71 of the edition with the text and translation by D. S. SARMA.

CHAPTER II

THE SECOND LAW AND ITS STRUGGLE

In the last Chapter, we traced the slow emergence of the First Law and examined, in a brief manner, its effect on the method of keeping books, on library location, on library hours, on library furniture and on library staff. The changes brought about by the First Law in all these matters were of a fundamental character. If the final effect of the First Law should be described in one word, that word is *revolution*. Once the outlook was revolutionised, other things followed in course of time.

The Second Law of Library Science comes on the heels of the First Law to carry this revolution a step further. If the First Law replaced the concept 'BOOKS ARE FOR PRESERVATION', the Second Law widens the concept 'BOOKS FOR THE CHOSEN FEW'. If the revolutionary cry of the First Law was 'BOOKS ARE FOR USE', the revolutionary cry of the Second Law is 'BOOKS ARE FOR ALL'. If the approach of the First Law was from the side of books, the approach of the Second Law is from the side of users of books. If the First Law vitalised the library, the Second Law magnifies the library into a nation-wide problem. If the First Law threw open the existing libraries, the Second Law plants new libraries and brings about the culture of new species of libraries. If there was reluctance to act up to the First Law, there is, in the initial stages, positive opposition to the Second Law. Thus, the revolution brought about by the Second Law is of a more advanced nature and brings humanity nearer the goal.

EVERY PERSON HIS OR HER BOOK! What a volume of ideas rests in a potential state in these six words of but seven syllables! How exacting will be the task of carrying out these ideas! What a variety of vested interests is arrayed in opposition against any attempt to put these ideas into force! These are points that require careful examination in a study of the Second Law.

It may be convenient to start from the very beginning. What are libraries? Libraries are collections of books built for a special purpose. What is that purpose? 'USE' is the answer supplied by the First Law. What is the use of books? Books give information; they educate. They may also give solace and furnish a harmless means of recreation. Let us first concentrate on their educational value. If books are tools of education, the law 'EVERY PERSON HIS OR HER BOOK' presupposes the concept 'EDUCATION FOR EVERY PERSON'. This lays bare the fundamental issue. The history of the answer to the question, "Is every person entitled to education?" will show how the Second Law too has been in actual practice seldom borne in mind by library authorities.

THE CLASSES AND THE MASSES

It is customary to begin all academic history from Aristotle. What is Aristotle's answer to this fundamental question? "It is the intention of nature to make bodies of slaves and freemen different from each other. . . And since this is true with respect to the body, it is still more just to determine in the same manner, when we consider the soul."[1] These plausible premises led Aristotle to the characteristic conclusion that "a slave can have no deliberative faculty".[2] The result of this rigorous reasoning was that "while Athens and Sparta offered education to freemen, nine-tenths of the population were excluded from the privilege of learning".[3] In translating this in terms of books, we find that 'BOOKS FOR THE CHOSEN FEW' was the ruling concept and that the Second Law had no recognition. Even in Rome, which heralded the establishment of municipal and state schools, the privilege of learning rarely crossed the occupational and income lines. The narrowness of the Middle Ages is described by Margaret Hodgen in the following words, "The spirit of exclusion which the land-owning classes asserted towards ambitious villeins bound for the church; the church toward laymen

---

(1) ARISTOTLE: *Politics*, Book I, Chapter V, p. 13, of Edward Walford's translation.

(2) *Ibid.*, Book I, Chapter XIII, p. 30 of the translation.

(3) HODGEN (Margaret, T.): *Workers' Education*, p. 8.

seeking intellectual independence; the merchants towards outsiders looking to enjoy profits of commercial enterprises, was in turn asserted by all toward the educational aspirations of the poor.'"[1] We are even told that "vassal fathers were punished for allowing vassal sons to attend school.'"[2]

The spirit of exclusion persisted for centuries. Here is a specimen of eighteenth century opinion. "To make the Society happy and People easy under the meanest circumstances, it is requisite that great numbers of them should be Ignorant as well as Poor. . . . The Welfare and Felicity therefore of every State and Kingdom, require that the knowledge of the Working Poor should be confined within the Verge of their occupations and never extended (as to things visible) beyond what relates to their Calling. The more a Shepherd, a Plowman or any other Peasant knows of the World, and the things that are Foreign to his Labour or Employment, the less fit he'll be to go through the Fatigues and Hardships of it with Cheerfulness and Content. Reading, Writing and Arithmetic . . . are very pernicious to the Poor, who are forced to get their Daily Bread by their Daily Labour.'"[3] What a benevolent dispensation! What a show of inevitableness in this eighteenth century reasoning! With such ideas running rampant, one can easily imagine how effectively the concept 'BOOKS FOR THE

(1) HODGAN (Margaret, T.): *Workers' Education*, p. 13.
(2) JACKSON (G. L.): *The Privilege of Education*, p. 39.
(3) MANDEVILLE (Bernard): *The Fable of the Bees*, F. B. Kaye's edition, Vol. I, p. 288.

CHOSEN FEW' would have thwarted the emergence of the rival concept 'BOOKS FOR ONE AND ALL'.

Even the nineteenth century was for long under the spell of this concept of a bipartite division of persons into a small governing class consisting of those who, almost as it were by divine right, occupied the privileged position and the large class of the others who, as it was supposed, by the essential constitution of things belonged to the lower orders, had no right to education and hence had no right to the instruments of education, *viz.*, books. The well-to-do and influential classes—the *freemen* of the nineteenth century—resisted outright on grounds of sheer self-interest even the bare suggestion that the poor should be given the rudiments of education. The story is told of the Marquis of Westminster refusing to give even a farthing for the London Mechanics' Institute because of his apprehension that the education of the workmen would make them rebel. "True," he said, "but *we* must take care of ourselves".[1] The struggle that books had in reaching *every person* is amply illustrated by the experience recorded by Francis Place, a Charing Cross tailor of the early years of the last century. He "had to be more and more careful that none of his ordinary customers should be allowed to go into the library at the back of the shop". "Had these persons been told that I had never read a book, that I was

(1) WALLAS (Graham): *Life of Francis Place*, p. 112.

ignorant of everything but my own business, that I sotted in a public house, they would not have made the least objection to me. I should have been a 'fellow' beneath them, and they would have patronised me; but . . . to accumulate books, and to be supposed to know something of their contents, was putting myself on an equality with themselves, if not indeed assuming superiority; it was an abominable offence in a tailor, if not a crime, which deserved punishment. Had it been known to all my customers that in the few years from 1810-1817, I had accumulated a considerable library, in which I spent all the leisure time I could spare, . . . half of them at least would have left me''.[1] We find Green complaining even late in the nineteenth century that "It is one of the inconveniences attaching to the present state of Society in England, that all questions of education are complicated by distinctions of classes''.[2] Even so late as 1918, the *Hansard* discloses that the Education Bill of Mr. H. A. L. Fisher was opposed on the ground that, if the workmen are to be given such a long and elaborate course of education, "How are the horses to be kept at work, the cows to be milked, the sheep to be tended and the folds to be pitched? How is education going to help a man who has to spread manure on a field''.[3] A veritable incarnation of Barnard de Mandeville!

(1) WALLAS (Graham): *Life of Francis Place*, p. 37.

(2) GREEN (Thomas Hill): *Works*, Ed. by R. L. Nettleship, Vol. III, p. 387.

(3) *Hansard*, Vol. CIV, p. 344.

That the political instinct of those in privileged positions was vehemently opposing the advent of the Second Law of Library Science is pointed out in unmistakable words by all students of Politics. Viscount Bryce says, for example, "That all the despotic governments of sixty years ago, and some of them down to our own day, were either indifferent or hostile to the spread of education among their subjects, because they feared that knowledge and intelligence would create a wish for freedom".[1]

The arguments of those that opposed the Ewart Bill—the first Public Library Bill of England—were "that too much knowledge was a dangerous thing and that libraries might become centres of political education".[2] In his Presidential Address to the Leeds Conference, Dr. Guppy remarked, "It is somewhat perplexing to find that in the middle decades of the last century, many of the most eminent men were debating, with all seriousness, not what was best in literature to put before the people, but whether it would be safe, and wise, and politic to admit the general public to libraries at all. So far from readers being considered competent to handle and examine books, it was a question whether the rough uncultured democracy should be permitted, even with most stringent precautions and regulations to invade

(1) BRYCE (James): *Modern Democracies*, Vol. I, p. 79.

(2) *Library Association Record* (*New Series*), Vol. IV, p. 199.

the sacred precincts of the Library''. When a library school was inaugurated at Moscow in 1913, the following question was asked in the National Duma by the leader of the extreme right: ''How can the government tolerate library courses, which would pave the way for a revolution''.[2]

Thus the Second Law had to face not merely an inherited instinct as was the case with the First Law but it had to face a very strong opposition based on political and economic instincts. However misleading these instincts might have been, there is hardly any ground to doubt their *bona fide* nature. In fact, as it may be easily seen, they were mere derivatives of a more fundamental instinct, *viz.*, the instinct of self-preservation. But, society had not been lacking in far-seeing souls that could perceive the mistaken nature of such opposition. There were indeed men who would draw just the opposite inference from that very instinct of self-preservation.

The location of factories near sources of power caused a redistribution of population and the towns were inundated with a flood of people unaccustomed to civic responsibilities. The crowding together of tens of thousands of the illiterate poor was creating a host of unspeakable nuisance. For a time the black-coated gentry were able to maintain a safe distance from centres of dirt, disease and petty

(1) *Library Association Record (New Series)*, Vol. IV, p. 194.

(2) *Bulletin of the American Library Association*, Vol. XX, pp. 261-2.

criminality. But they could not remain aloof for ever. Poverty rudely encroached in course of time. It brought disease and unsavoury sights to the doors of the vicarage and the manor. In their eagerness to defend themselves the gentle folk hurried to their most trusted advisers. The first of these, the economists, recommended a judicious dose of education. Adam Smith, for example, recommended that "The public can impose upon almost the whole body of the people the necessity of acquiring the most essential parts of education, by obliging every man to undergo an examination or probation in them, before he can obtain the freedom in any corporation, or be allowed to set up any trade either in a village or town Corporate".[1] He took advantage of this predicament of the well-to-do and even pleaded as follows: "The education of the Common people requires, perhaps, in a civilised and commercial society, the attention of the public, more than that of people of some rank and fortune . . . The public can facilitate this acquisition by establishing in every parish or district a little school, where children may be taught . . . Though the state was to derive no advantage from the instruction of the inferior ranks of people, it would still deserve its attention that they should not be altogether uninstructed. The state, however, derives no inconsiderable advantage from their instruction. The more they are instructed, the

(1) SMITH (Adam): *An Enquiry into the Nature and Causes of the Wealth of Nations*, ed. by Joseph Shield Nicholson, pp. 328-329.

less liable they are to the delusions of enthusiasm and superstition, which, among ignorant nations, frequently occasion the most dreadful disorders. An instructed and intelligent people, besides, are always more decent and orderly than an ignorant and stupid one. They feel themselves each individually, more respectable and more likely to obtain the respect of their superiors, and they are, therefore, more disposed to respect their superiors. They are more disposed to examine and more capable of seeing through, the interested complaints of faction and sedition; and they are, on that account, less apt to be misled into any wanton or unnecessary opposition to the measures of Government''.[1]

Although, generally speaking, the words of Adam Smith fell upon deaf ears, there were some who could appreciate the soundness of his reasoning. In fact, it induced Mr. Whitbread to introduce a Bill in Parliament in 1807 for universal education, though, it goes without saying, it was rejected by an overwhelming majority. In spite of the ridicule of die-hards, the *''Society for the Diffusion of Useful Knowledge''* did much to spread education among the masses, under the inspiring leadership of Lord Brougham. The *Penny Cyclopædia,* the *Penny Magazine,* the *Gallery of Portraits* and the *Pictorial Bible* are the surviving monuments of the missionary zeal which championed the cause of 'BOOKS FOR ALL', in the thirties of the last

(1) *Ibid.,* pp. 328-330.

century. While the majority of the magnates and officials of the early Victorian era desired that the young peasant should till the same fields, with the same tools in the same seasons as his father before him, enlightened souls like Matthew Arnold were impatient with the tardy recognition shown to the newly emerging concept 'EDUCATION FOR ALL'. As Her Majesty's Inspector of Schools, he lamented, in 1853, that "The children of the lowest, poorest classes of the country, of what are called the masses, are not, to speak generally, educated; the children who are educated belong to a different class from these, and consequently of the education of the masses, I, in the course of my official duty, see, strictly speaking, little or nothing".[1] The first twenty pages of Graham Balfour's *Educational Systems of Great Britain and Ireland* give a brief but vivid picture of the ingenuity and tenacity with which a handful of far-seeing patriotic statesmen secured the educational enactments of 1870, 1880 and 1891, which successively made 'EDUCATION FOR ALL' first permissive, then compulsory and finally free.[2] Once 'EDUCATION FOR ALL' had been established, it required but a decade or two for our Second Law 'BOOKS FOR ALL', to enter the field and quietly bring about the realisation of

---

(1) SHARPLESS (Isac): *English Education*, p. 10.

(2) *Law Reports, Statutes*: 33 and 34 Victoria, Chapter 75, Section 74; 43 and 44 Victoria, Chapter 23, Section 2; and 54 and 55 Victoria, Chapter 56, Section 2.

Huxley's dream,[1] of 'a ladder of learning' from the gutter to the Universities.

How literally the Second Law has realised this dream of Huxley may be seen from the account given in *Adult Education and the Library*,[2] about the progress of a fisher-boy along the paths of learning. He was born in Norway. In his fourteenth year, he was withdrawn from the school. His father said, "You are not worth educating" and the lad was sent to the eternal task of fishing in the desolate coast of the North of Norway. But the Norwegian Government maintained at this outpost of the world a good library, though small, and had its books periodically changed and replenished. By burying his head and heart in its books, this lad, pronounced to be *not worth educating*, educated himself more than he himself realised. He, then, went to the New World, began his Preparatory School in his twenty-third year, took his degree in his twenty-eighth year and settled down as a professor in his own college. This career of Professor Rolvaag of St. Olaf's College is by no means unique. We, in Madras, remember the story of the marvellous achievement of books, read in the light of street lamps, in raising a boy born in obscurity to the bench of the High Court. This sway of the Second Law has resulted in reclaiming for the benefit of the world many such promising

(1) *Life and Letters of Thomas Henry Huxley*, Vol. III, p. 7.
(2) *Adult Education and the Library*, Vol. III, pp. 12-13.

men from the very depths of society. A generation or two ago, her rival, 'BOOKS FOR THE CHOSEN FEW' would have sworn by their prenatal social status and forced them to drag on and die, without ever reaching their full stature.

"Here is a woman who earns her own living as a chef in a hotel . . . She noticed one day that her eldest daughter frowned impatiently when the mother made a mistake in grammar. The mother decided that she would not lose one bit of her daughter's respect on that account. She asked the readers' adviser to recommend books which would help her to avoid the most common errors of grammar and pronunciation. She wanted a progressive course on good English suited to her special needs. Later she asked for books which would keep her informed on present-day happenings and so on and so on".[1]

There is again the case of a policeman who asked for books which would help him to discover why crimes are committed. "What's the use of arresting people if you can't help them?" he asked.[2] He devoured books in Sociology and Psychology. If he had lived before the advent of the Law 'EVERY PERSON HIS OR HER BOOK', what chance would he have had either to study books in Sociology and Psychology or to discharge his official duties in a manner, not only satisfactory

---

(1) *Adult Education and the Library*, Vol. III, p. 20.
(2) *Adult Education and the Library*, Vol. III, p. 22.

to his conscience but also beneficial to society. How useful and popular *our* police will become if they are made to read like their New World contemporary books in Sociology and Psychology in addition to the sections of the Police Manual!

The prophetic nature of the words of Adam Smith has been demonstrated to the very letter by the services rendered by the Second Law of Library Science to the public of the city of Grand Rapids in the State of Michigan. The water-supply of the city could not keep up with the growth of the city, . . . As a result a large part of the citizens depended on wells for much of their drinking water, because they would not drink the unfiltered river water. The typhoid-fever rate was very high—several hundred cases a year—with a correspondingly high death rate . . . The city Government and the business interests of the city finally secured the appointment of a Special Commission of high-grade business and professional men to study the whole situation and to report a plan to be submitted to a vote of the citizens. After long and careful study they recommended the adoption of the plan to take the water from the river and to filter it by the rapid sand or mechanical filtration process . . . Eight or ten days before the election, full or half-page newspaper broadsides were distributed to every house in the city claiming that filtration was a failure, by publishing facsimile reproductions from newspapers and technical magazines, etc., of items with reference to typhoid fever in certain cities, and then followed by the statement that the said cities had filtered water. In short, the whole purpose of these broadsides was to discredit the report of the Special Commission in order to have it defeated. New broadsides appeared about every other day and were always distributed to every house in the city. They came out over the name of "a young unemployed Engineer". The library immediately checked up a number of the reference to other cities in the annual reports and municipal documents in its collection . . . on the trail of the young engineer's published broadsides and made the knowledge it found available to the newspapers, with the librarian signing the published statements of the facts the library found. Here is a sample of what we found. Reading, Pennsylvania and Albany, New York, both had filtered water supplies serving other parts. The typhoid epidemics were in the sections of those cities served by the unfiltered supplies. The broadside advertisements were correct in stating that Reading and Albany both had typhoid epidemics and both had filtered water, but, nevertheless, these statements were both damnable lies in the impressions they conveyed. Thus, "the library was the first . . . to rally the forces to save the day for pure water. Pure water won at the polls and Grand Rapids, except for sporadic cases brought in from outside, has as a result eliminated typhoid fever from the city . . . I have always believed that the library would have been derelict in its duty had it failed to give to the public the knowledge it had on such a vital matter''.[1]

Instances of this nature can be multiplied *ad nauseam*. But as it is not our purpose to record here the achievements of 'BOOKS FOR ALL' suffice it to say that, to-day, the Second Law of Library Science has triumphantly planted its democratic flag in many a land having blown to pieces the black-coated barrier of exclusiveness and snobbery. During the last century, Europe and America, Japan and Russia, were as impervious to its appeals and as impregnable to its attacks as India was. But, to-day, Europe and America, Japan and Russia have capitulated to it, while India is still defiantly holding her own. Who is responsible for this strange phenomenon? Who has been helping India to stick to her guns in this battle against 'BOOKS FOR ALL', while she has been establishing a world record in losing battles in other spheres?

Whatever might be the complex of contributory causes, her ''English-educated'' sons cannot escape their share of the blame. Macaulay and Wood imported English education into India with the best of motives. They evolved their famous 'filtration theory' with the highest of hopes. They could not have reasonably foreseen that the filter would develop human jealousy and selfish exclusiveness. Certainly, they never, for a moment,

(1) *Essays Offered to Herbert Putnam, on his Thirtieth Anniversary as Librarian of Congress*, pp. 374-376.

dreamt that the filter will work in the contrary way and get itself coated with another super-filter that will grant a place in the sun only to those English-educated Indians, who could get their English-education on English soil. Yes. This tragic triumph of India in her fight against the intrusion of the Second Law of Library Science, nay, even of its precursor 'EDUCATION FOR ALL', is not a little due to the almost criminal apathy and neglect of duty on the part of her better placed "English-educated" sons. They have developed an abnormal short-sight which disables them from seeing beyond their nose, at any rate beyond their privileged circle. They glibly speak of India, and her millions, when they mean only the two per cent. of her millions who can lisp in English. Remind them how you will that Macaulay intended that they should, actively and ungrudgingly, spread their knowledge among the masses. No, they will rather prefer to take their lesson from Bernard de Mandeville. Honourable exceptions there are and all honour to them. But the majority act as an impervious clog in the filter.

Our only hope lies in the supreme resourcefulness of the Second Law. History has shown that it is an adept in the art of strategy. If Macaulay's filter has proved a snare, ere long it will divert its course and keep clear of this clog in the 'filter'. The Second Law will not take a defeat. It must win ultimately. With the world opinion backing it, it may win even at no distant date. If they are shrewd business men, the 'English-educated' Indians should greet it with an olive branch and volunteer their services in its holy war on lingering ignorance. Then only, they will gain any respect in the eyes of the world and then only can they survive amidst the forces that will be set free on the day the Second Law plants its flag on Indian soil and puts the BOOKS in the hands of ALL, even as it has done on their soils.

THE MEN AND THE WOMEN

The antithesis has not been merely between the classes and the masses. As we trace the prejudices of ages in the light of the Second Law of Library Science, we come across several others. It is not merely the income line that has, for long, divided humanity into those that are entitled to the use of books and those that are not. Sex, for example, was another factor that restricted the enforcement of the Law, 'BOOKS FOR ALL'. In our own country, the Second Law has not yet fully succeeded in overcoming such sex disabilities.

No doubt, the conditions have begun to change. Signs of the onslaught of the Second Law are not wanting. The surging wave of 'BOOKS FOR ALL' may, ere long, wash away even the hardened bank of the feminine conservatism of the Indian Home. But that should not close one's eyes to the tenacious fight that is being fought to-day, in several homes against the encroachment of the 'pernicious habit' of reading among ladies. Nor should one delude oneself with the fond, but blinding boast that our country had, in days past, kept the road wide open for her women to emulate the stronger sex in the pursuit of learning. It does not help us now to be told that women could and did read as well as men from the Vedic days onwards down to the day when an alien tongue drove a cultural wedge into the till-then homogeneous home. It is only half the truth to say that the use of a foreign medium for current thought has sequestered Indian women from the world current that has enabled her sisters in many a clime to keep abreast of their brethren. The glorious record of women like Maitreyi, Panchali, Lilavati and Auvaiar and the still-surviving memory of the learned ladies that formed the fitting life-companions of the intellectual giants of places like Tiruvisalur, should not blind us to our present plight, when for every Maitreyi we have thousands of Katyayinis, when the bulk of our sisters are straggling a century behind, unlettered, untutored, and unprovided with books. But, if it can be a source of consolation and encouragement, it may be mentioned that the concepts 'EDUCATION FOR ALL' and 'BOOKS FOR ALL' definitely crossed the sex-barrier only within the last half-century or so in most of the countries.

From the days of the primitive man, the majority of women have generally occupied a sheltered place and have not had, therefore, a higher cultural or professional training such as would enable them to deal with large affairs. In earliest as well as recent civilisations, the limits to which feminine accomplishments might extend have generally been definitely fixed by custom and those who dared to exceed them have run the risk of being thought 'unwomanly'. In Athens, it seems, it was an accepted dogma that no respectable girl should be educated. The Athenian wife for example, "lived a virtual prisoner within four walls . . . They could not in their own persons inherit property, but were regarded as an appanage of the estate . . . Their education was trivial".[1] The social ostracism practised to prevent ladies from getting their share of education and books is indicated by the following statement about the education of women in Greece: "Literary education and intellectual pursuits belonged to those who were without the home circle, the hetaerae".[2] In the writings of St. Paul there appeared similar restrictions which seemed to set women off as an inferior, dependent class. After referring to the sixteenth verse of the third chapter of Genesis regarding the status of women, he wrote, "And if they will learn anything, let them ask their husbands at home".[3]

For a long time it was even commonly believed that women were not capable of education. Here

---

(1) WRIGHT (F. A.): *Greek Social Life*, pp. 6-13.

(2) MONROE (Paul): *Source Book of the History of Education*, p. 34.

(3) I Corinthians, 35.

is Chesterfield writing to his son "Women, then, are only children of a larger growth; they have an entertaining tattle, and sometimes wit; but for solid reasoning, good sense, I never in my life knew one that had it, . . . A man of sense . . . neither consults them about, nor trusts them with, serious matters".[1] Again Rousseau says of women that she is 'an imperfect man', that in many respects she is only 'a grown-up child'.[2] He adds, "The search for abstract and speculative truths, principles, and scientific axioms, whatever tends to generalise ideas, does not fall within the compass of women; . . . as to works of genius, they are out of their reach, nor have they sufficient accuracy and attention to succeed in the exact sciences".[3] Rousseau would willingly repeat Moliere's words:—

> It is not seemly, and for many reasons,
> That a woman should study and know so
> many things.

Rousseau's conception of the capacity of women is only what was too common in France and other countries in the eighteenth century.

The nineteenth century tried to excel the eighteenth by inventing anatomical explanations for the woman's incapacity to benefit by books and

---

(1) CHESTERFIELD (Lord): *Letters,* letter LXXVI, pp. 141-142 of Vol. I of John Bradshaw's edition.

(2) COMPAYRE (Gabriel): *Jean Jacques Rousseau,* p. 85.

(3) ROUSSEAU (Jean Jacques): *Emile,* Tr. by Payne, p. 281.

learning. Here is a piece of serious scientific demonstration which dates from 1866.—"A man has will and understanding, and a cerebellum and a cerebrum by which they act; and so has a woman. In this they are alike. But in man the understanding predominates, and in woman the will; and here they are different. If this be so, we may, of course, expect to find a larger development of the cerebrum, or upper brain, in man, and a larger development of the cerebellum, or lower brain, in woman; and this is so. A man's head is higher, and fuller in front, than a woman's; while a woman's head is broader and larger behind than a man's."[1] Another contemporary of this anatomical psychologist cannot see any virtue in wasting such elaborate reasoning to establish such an obvious thing. "The great argument", he would say, "against the existence of this equality of intellect in women is, that it does not exist. If that proof does not satisfy a female philosopher, we have no better to give".[2]

If girls' schools existed, "they aimed at 'breeding', deportment and the accomplishments, not at learning".[3] In his *Essay on Projects,* Daniel Defoe gives a pathetic description of the customary education of girls in the following words: "One would wonder indeed how it should happen that women are conversible at all, since they are only

(1) ARTHUR (T. S.): *Advice to Young Ladies,* pp. 152-153.

(2) *Saturday Review,* 1860, quoted by Thomas Woody.

(3) MONROE (Paul): *A Cyclopaedia of Education,* Vol. V, p. 801.

beholding to natural parts for all their knowledge. Their youth is spent to teach them to stitch and sew or make bawbles; they are taught to read indeed and perhaps to write their names or so; and that is the height of a woman's education".[1] If any lady acquired learning, the attitude towards such learned ladies was one of contempt and ridicule. We have it recorded that Dr. Johnson once laid down the dictum that "man is, in general, better pleased when he has a good dinner on his table, than when his wife talks Greek". His contemptuous parallelism between a woman preaching and a dog walking on his hind legs is also well known. We have the story of an American bachelor who explained his single state saying,

> "One did command to me a wife both fair and young
> That had French, Spanish and Italian tongue.
> I thanked him kindly and told him I loved none such,
> For I thought one tongue for a wife too much,
> What! love ye not the learned? Yes, as my life,
> A learned scholar, but not a learned wife."[2]

---

(1) *The Cambridge History of English Literature*, Vol. IX, p. 404.

(2) WHARTON (Anne): *Colonial Days and Dames*, pp. 195-196.

The effects of such disparagement of women's powers, the lack of incentives to learning and the ridicule, that was offered to the few who would learn, had a disastrous effect in shaping the opinion of the women themselves with regard to their right to education and books. They would fain continue for ever on the established folkways of traditional ideas. Many an Indian of to-day may hear within the walls of his home an unmistakable echo of the emphatic words ''Book larnin' don't do no good to a woman'' uttered by an American lady about a couple of generations ago.[1] Indeed the obstinate feminine conservatism which keeps the Second Law at bay and wallows with self-complacency in a book-less, education-less state reminds one of the victims of Comus, who are

> ". . . . . changed
> Into some brutish form of wolf, or bear,
> Or ounce or tiger, hog, or bearded goat,
> . . . .
> And they, so perfect in their misery,
> Not once perceive their foul disfigurement,
> But boast themselves more comely than before."[2]

However dogged custom has been, during the slow passage of many centuries, to keep 'EDUCATION' and its companion the Second Law of Library Science on one side of the sex-line, it is

(1) WOODY (Thomas): *A History of Women's Education in the United States*, Vol. I, p. 132.

(2) MILTON (John): *Comus*, 69-75.

F—13

certain that in this age of social unrest, when practically every custom and institution of every society is exposed to the unsparing scrutiny of critical minds, women and women's right to education and books have been thrust into the forefront of discussion. The whole vexed question of the woman's 'sphere' and of her education viewed in the light of that 'sphere' has engaged the minds of men for more than a generation and is, at present, nearly settled in the only right manner admissible. It is now admitted that even University education is desirable for at least a great number of women. That education will unfit woman to be wife and mother, that the physical strain will be too great, or that she is intellectually incapable of mastering higher branches of learning, were serious arguments a generation or two ago and unquestionably acted as impediments, but are now only slumbering memories in the social mind of a busy world and come to the centre of consciousness only in some sequestered nooks, still undisturbed by the effects of the Great War. The antediluvian view, which would utterly restrict the woman, making her at best a tolerably intelligent and obedient slave, is already vanishing. The worst view that may now be tolerated is that which would give her a measure of freedom by taking a half-step forward towards her education, arguing that, by this cultivated-mother influence, the life of society may be improved at the very fountain-head. But the most radical view, that is fast gaining ground, would propose absolute equality of opportunity in education and in political, social and economic life, maintaining that a woman need not, unless she herself so desires, pay her obligation to society, biologically, any more than man, but should be equipped so as to be equally free to choose a literary, scientific or industrial career.

So far we have seen only the first phase of the war on the sex barrier. The Second Law of Library Science had no part in this phase of the war. It was all left to its precursor 'EDUCATION FOR ALL'. But the campaign against sex-distinctions involved more battles than that against class distinctions. Even after the sex-barrier was broken through by its companion, the Second Law was not able to march in freely. For, until the latest radical view began to appear on the scene, people argued "Yes. Education is necessary for a woman and she is capable of it. But woman's education to prepare her for her allotted sphere—the home—can be obtained through apprenticeship to her mother, in the home. There is no need for any formal schooling or book-learning, which would lead her away from the hearth".

The little learning I have gained
Is all from simple nature drained,[1]

was a correct description of the state of affairs in the latter half of the last century, a state which

(1) WOODY (Thomas): *A History of Women's Education in the United States*, Vol. I, p. 129.

was not favourable for the success of 'BOOKS FOR WOMEN'.

Fortunately, however, even before the radical view asserted itself and blew up the sex-barrier, it came to be realised that such a natural process of education is not practicable in the crowded life of to-day, that formal education and book-learning are necessary even for cooking, nursing, and the care of children. The increasing incapacity of the home to hold the monopoly of the education of its daughters and the changing conception of education did much to prepare the public mind to receive the gospel 'EVERY WOMAN TOO HER BOOK'. Even assuming that the sphere of the woman was the home, it came to be realised that *home-making* is at once an art and a science. It is a progressive art and a developing science. It has a serious organic contact with the Fine Arts on the one side and the severest sciences on the other. It would include, for example, care of children, nursing, first aid, foods and nutrition, of course, cooking, marketing, laundering, millinery, sewing, budget-making and thrift, kitchen-gardening and horticulture, home hygiene, home sanitation, home decoration, the making of simple repairs, home courtesies and obligations of family and family life.[1] While such is the complex of elements involved in the profession of *home-making*, women

(1) *School and Society*, Vol. XXXII, p. 279. '*Home Economics in the Curriculum.*'

ought to be constantly trained for these duties as men are trained for their trades and professions.

There is much in the plea, "When the other sex are to be instructed in law, medicine or divinity, they are favoured with numerous institutions richly endowed, with teachers of the highest talents and acquirements and with expensive libraries. . . . Woman's profession embraces the care and nursing of the body in the critical periods of infancy and sickness, the training of the human mind in the most impressible period, childhood, the instruction and control of servants, and most of the government and economics of the family estate. These duties of women are as sacred and important as any ordained to man; and yet no such advantages for preparation have been accorded to her".[1] While such a reproach was justifiable till about three or four decades ago, every effort is now being made in all forward countries to have that reproach removed by a proper orientation of the initial education at school and by a profuse supply of books for that education to be continued to the end of one's life. 'EVERY WOMAN HER BOOK' is the guiding motto of the libraries of to-day. They now take care to see that their books reach behind the *purdah*. They endeavour, for example, "to get all mothers, whose names appear in the official records of birth when a new baby

---

(1) BEECHER (Catherine) and STOWE (Harriet): *Principles of Domestic Science*, pp. 13-14; quoted in Woody's *History of Women's Education in the United States*.

comes into the home, into contact with the Library's book-service on the care of children"[1] Such a discriminating distribution of books in restricted fields of knowledge marks the second stage.

It is however in the third phase of the war that the sex-barrier was completely overthrown in the march of the concept 'BOOKS FOR ALL'. This phase is taking shape only in the present century. It began with a critical investigation into the inherited tradition about the 'woman's sphere' and about the 'woman's inferiority' in matters intellectual. The first to lay the axe to the root of the pseudo-scientific opinion of the nineteenth century was Karl Pearson. In his paper of 1897 entitled "*Variation in man and woman*",[2] he clearly demonstrated that there was, in fact, no indication of greater male variability, when actual anatomical measurements of actual human beings are treated with mathematical insight. After a rigorous statistical examination of varied anatomical data, he concluded his long paper in his characteristic carping manner with the words "I . . . assert that the present results show that the greater variability often claimed for men remains as yet a quite unproven principle . . . The "sequacity" exhibited by the multitude of semi-scientific writers on evolution is possibly a sign of the very small capacity for intellectual

(1) *Essays Offered to Herbert Putnam . . . on His Thirtieth Anniversary as Librarian of Congress*, p. 368.

(2) PEARSON (Karl): *The Chances of Death and Other Studies in Evolution*, Vol. 1, pp. 256-377.

variation possessed by the literary male".[1] The evidence collected by Karl Pearson was extended and corroborated by the further statistical data published by Montague and Hollingworth in the *American Journal of Sociology* in October, 1914.

This anatomical investigation was followed by the psychological demonstration of the absolute absence of sex difference in mental variability by the elaborate mental tests carried out by Trabue, Courtis, Terman and Pyle. Again, there was the time-honoured traditional opinion that the functional periodicity has an unfavourable effect on woman's mental capacity. Havelock Ellis, for example, makes the sweeping remark that the monthly physiological cycle "influences throughout the month the whole of a woman's physical and psychic organism".[2] Dr. Hollingworth's experimental investigation of 1914 into this allegation disclosed, on the contrary, that the data, gathered by her, undermined rather than supported such opinions.[3]

After experimental psychology thus established that the division of labour between the sexes, which had existed throughout historic times, was not the result of psychological differences at all, and that women are as competent intellectually as

(1) PEARSON (Karl): *The Chances of Death and Other Studies in Evolution*, Vol. I, pp. 376-377.

(2) ELLIS (Havelock): *Men and Women*, p. 284.

(3) HOLLINGWORTH (Leta Statter): *Functional Periodicity*, being No. 60 of *Teachers' College Studies* of the Columbia University.

men to undertake any and all human vocations, it came to be realised that "the education of women, especially in the higher stages, will make available to the country a wealth of capacity that is, now, largely wasted through lack of opportunity"[1] and it even came to be argued that an educated woman, a woman when given 'HER BOOKS' "is a far better and surer guarantee of the education of the coming generation than a literate man".[2] Then came the opportunity for the Second Law to break through the sex-barrier and triumphantly proclaim, "Education should develop women's tastes and aptitudes precisely as men's. The rights of women to choose their books should be precisely the same as those of men. The books that I distribute should be different, not on the ground that the one is a man and the other a woman; but, they should be different only on the ground that each is an individual".

Thus, the Second Law of Library Science is now no longer satisfied with offering to women books on *Home-making* or with books of orthodox devotion; on the other hand it insists that all books have a perfect right to enter any home for the benefit of all the members of the home irrespective of sex.

---

(1) INDIAN STATUTORY COMMISSION: *Interim Report*. Review of the growth of Education in British India by the auxiliary committee (*known as the Hartog Committee*) appointed by the Commission, p. 151.

(2) *Ibid.*, p. 151.

LADIES' LIBRARY, BARODA.

STORY HOUR, CHILDREN'S LIBRARY, BARODA.

THE CITY-FOLK AND THE COUNTRY-FOLK

A third antithesis that had to be overcome by the concept 'BOOKS FOR ALL' was that between the city-folk and the country-folk. The municipal toll-gate seems to have held up the Second Law even longer than the income-line or the sex-barrier. We have seen that the income-line was nearly crossed in most countries about half-a-century ago. We have also noticed that the scaling of the sex-barrier was begun at least a generation back. But the cry 'BOOKS FOR ALL' was able to get beyond the city-walls only in our days. To be more precise, the right of the country-folk to books came to be respected in most of the countries only after the Great War. Although the first systematic travelling library service was inaugurated by Maryland and Ohio as early as 1905 it is only in the last decade or so that serious effort is made by most of the nations to supply the inhabitants of the scattered country-side with the books they want.

That the country-folk lack the opportunity for learning and culture is clear from the contempt that is suppressed in the English word 'Rustic' and the Tamil word '*Nattuppurattan*'.[1] It is also indicated by the common connotation of the Sanskrit epithet '*Grāmya*'.[2] In his *Hellenica*, Xenophon naively suggests by implication that

(1) Literally means a villager.

(2) *Grama* means a village while *Gramya* means vulgar.

habitual residence in villages would be enough to deprive one of some of the commonest rights and privileges. He says, "They did not, however, dispossess them of the presidency of the shrine of Olympian Zeus, even though it did not belong to the Eleanos in ancient times, for they thought that *the rival claimants were country people*"[1] (italics mine). Such a differential view has been persisting all through the centuries. Hannah More, for example, "would not 'banish ignorance' from the villages; vice she would have ousted if she could, but knowledge, except of their duties and their 'place' she would have advised her . . . villagers to leave to their betters"[2] in the urban areas.

The fact is that, even at a very early stage, the increasing complexities and the grave menaces attendant on the civic problems of a crowded city made out a strong plea for 'EDUCATION FOR ALL' and 'BOOKS FOR ALL' in the case of the city-folk. That inexorable mistress, Necessity, however, did not, for long, put a similar pressure in regard to the country-folk. While the consequences of ignorance and lack of books are immediate in an urban area, they are latent and become visible only very late in rural areas.

Nevertheless, the farmers of the village form a most important class in a country. Tilling the land is one of man's fundamental and original occupations. Adam was a gardener and Abraham,

---

(1) XENOPHON: *Hellenica*, Book III, Section II, Sub-section (30); page 215 of Vol. I of the *Loeb Classical Library*.

(2) ASHBY (M. K.): *The Country School*, p. 29.

a shepherd. Agriculture feeds the world. It calls for progressive skill and the national need of an alert, adaptable peasantry can be met only by extending the use of books to the country-side. Even in an industrial country like England, where only 20 per cent live in villages and the cities form the chief centres of production, it is felt that the future of the nation would be jeopardised if the handful of people who live in the country-side are not given THEIR BOOKS. How much more serious and vital should be the rural library problem in our land, where, even confining ourselves to British India, only 12.9 per cent of the population of 247 millions live in towns . . . there are only 29 cities with a population of 100,000 or over . . . and 2,100 towns with a population between 5,000 and 100,000, while the number of villages is not far short of half a million?[1] Further, the Indian towns and cities are not comparable in their function to the industrial towns and cities of England. As Mr. V. Ramaswamy Ayyar, the learned president of the Indian Mathematical Society, humorously remarked in a recent Retreat of the International Fellowship, the function of most of the Indian towns is like that of the receiver of an air pump. Very little of their stir and bustle is due to productive activities. They are largely engaged in sucking the wealth that is

(1) INDIAN STATUTORY COMMISSION: *Interim Report*, Review of the growth of Education in British India by the auxiliary Committee appointed by the Commission (commonly known as the Hartog Report), p. 37.

produced in the villages and discharging it beyond the seas. It is in view of this, that the Linlithgow Commission recorded, "It is upon the homes and fields of her cultivators that the strength of the country and the foundations of her prosperity must ultimately rest".[1]

But, in the present state of international competition and struggle, the agricultural and other rural industries are proving to be more and more futile and less and less worthwhile, if carried on in the old time-honoured methods of production and marketing. The chief needs of these rural industries are the daily stimulus of new ideas and the constant provision of instruction in such ideas. New methods in farming are being invented from year to year, and new markets have to be found from time to time. Inter-communications that are being established in ways hitherto undreamt of have to be understood and machinery and labour-saving devices are in urgent need of adoption.

Till recently families lived on the land and produced by hand nearly all that they ate or wore. The oxen and the wooden plough were about all the labour-saving devices at hand. People made their own butter, candles and clothing, evaporated their own salt, and ground their corn in primitive hand-operated mills. Business was carried on chiefly by barter. But, in the short period of one generation, epoch-making inventions in agricul-

(1) ROYAL COMMISSION ON AGRICULTURE IN INDIA: *Report*, p. 67.

tural machinery and methods have been perfected and are being introduced elsewhere. At such a flux, the 'SCHOOL OF BOOKS' must constantly supplement the school of practical experience.

Improvements in marketing have also contributed much to the need for a progressive peasantry and to the need for the frequent feeding of the peasantry on books and magazines. No longer have small loads of produce to be taken over a muddy road to be sold or exchanged. Good metalled road and the motor-truck and a net-work of railroad and the parcel express have greatly changed the methods of transport. The steamship and the motor-boat gather up the products and quickly deliver them in the world's great markets. The betels of Kumbakonam have now to find a market in Madras and far-off Benares. The plantains of Erode have to be marketed throughout the province, and so too the fruits of the orchards and vineyards of Coorg. The cotton of Tinnevelly and the paddy of Tanjore have to search for markets overseas. Farm-products can no longer be bartered in the village. They have to be judiciously sold in exchange for *hundies.* These conditions will not be temporary or transient. They have come to stay and, year by year, they will become more and more pronounced. From now on, we may look upon farming as being a capitalised industry, calling for knowledge and executive ability and attracting men of capital and brains. The man of small energy or capacity and the man lacking in growing scientific knowledge will find it increasingly difficult to avoid being pushed to the wall. We can no longer depend upon a peasantry perpetually steeped in ignorance and confined to traditional ways. If the country is to keep abreast of the world, the peasantry must be constantly lifted from their ruts and be enlightened with the most up-to-date scientific and economic facts and ideas. How will this be possible except through books and periodicals? *Can* we any longer afford to delay giving the COUNTRY FOLK THEIR BOOKS?

Nor is it left to the city-folk to deny their rural brethren the pleasures of books and the other amenities of life. For, in the words of the recent Royal Commission on agriculture, "Upon the ancient structure of village life, certain influences are at work which must sooner or later profoundly modify its characteristic self-sufficiency and which, in some parts of the country, have already begun to produce their effects". "The development of communications and the consequent quickening and cheapening of travelling facilities are bringing the villages into closer touch with urban areas . . . contact with towns introduces new ideas and desire for better conditions of living". The farmer's life is, in fact, mentally changing. The old isolation and the narrow provincialism are rapidly ending. He and his wife will, no longer, be markedly "of the country". They, and particularly their children, dress much better than formerly. The movements of the family are no longer limited by the locomotive power of its bullock. The inter-urban bus will take them to town almost any hour and a trip to town, which lately consumed the better part of a day, is now only a matter of an hour or so. It is easy to go in the evening after the day's work is done. The cinema and the theatre, once unknown, now offer their attractions. City connections—financial, social and political—are established. The children attend the High School in the neighbouring town or city, copy town ways and form new friendships there. The social horizon is thus greatly enlarged. Marriages are accordingly made at much greater distances than formerly and with new social classes.

This rapid and intensive intermingling of the city-folk and the country-folk would lead the latter to demand for themselves all the facilities that the former enjoy. Farm-workers and farmers would begin to argue "We pay *our* toll to the exchequer as much as the city. Then, why this differential treatment? Why should the city-folk alone have their City-Libraries and all the amenities that centre round them? Why should not the State provide us with similar library and other facilities? We too have brains. We too want to improve our knowledge of the world. We too want to be up-to-date in our methods of work. We too want 'OUR BOOKS' ". Modern democracy has invested such awakened peasants with the power to

'DEMAND THEIR BOOKS', if they are not voluntarily forthcoming, and to make their demand heard. Such, in fact, was the genesis of the first systematic travelling library.

"In Washington County, Maryland, there lived many people who had few books to read, for whom buying books was too costly a procedure, but who were hungry for good literature. Some of these people come to Miss Mary L. Titcomb of the Hagerstown free library and *asked that books be sent to them* (italics mine) . . . This gave Miss Titcomb the idea that a wagon fitted with book-shelves and laden with a wide assortment of books, going over the mountain roads to the homes, would be a splendid way of giving the people a chance to read . . . This was in 1905. In 1910 the horse and wagon gave way to the automobile. Now nearly 300 counties have followed the example of Hagerstown, Maryland."[1] Nay, the counties of several other parts of the world are also beginning to follow that example. It is the initial *demand* of the country-folk of Maryland that started the idea.

The wise administrators of the Carnegie United Kingdom Trust have shown how to create in villagers a demand for books, in case they are oblivious either of the benefit of the use of books or of their right to demand them. We have it on

---

(1) FELTON (Ralph, A.) and MARJORIE (Beal): *The Library of the Open Road*, being Bulletin No. 188 of *Cornell Extension Bulletin*, pp. 14-15.

the authority of no less a person than Sir William Robertson, the first Vice-President of the Trust. In describing the genesis of the Rural Libraries of Great Britain, he said: "We baited our hook very generously. We said 'We will not only undertake to provide the Capital outlay, but also undertake to provide maintenance for five years', so that the local authority—always in terror of rates—need have no fears on the ground of having to increase the rates. We had to lure them on; as we were convinced that by the time the five years had expired a real, abiding appetite for reading would have been—not created, because it was latent, it was there,—but discovered; so that if the local authorities at the expiry of that period were reactionary and wanted to go back on the scheme, they would not be allowed to do so by the people. We went from county to county . . . We did not wait to be approached by them, we were the initiators of the scheme, and we took the initial step of inviting them to consider such an offer".[1] Such a deliberate, calculated campaign for less than a decade[2] was enough to carry 'BOOKS FOR ALL' beyond the city-walls and to spread it triumphantly into all but three of the counties of England. As a result, the demand of the English country-folk for 'THEIR BOOKS' became so insistent that Parliament had to provide by the Amending Act

(1) *The Proceedings of the Carnegie Rural Library Conference held on November 2nd and 3rd*, 1920, p. 12.

(2) The first County-library Scheme of England was inaugurated in Staffordshire in 1916.

of 1919[1] for a Rural Library Scheme on a county basis and to appoint a Public Libraries Committee in 1924 "to enquire into the adequacy of the library provision" and to explore, among other things, "the means of extending and completing such provision, throughout England and Wales".[2]

The recent reforms have invested the Indian ryots also with a similar power to demand THEIR BOOKS and to ask for a nation-wide Rural Library Scheme, with all the latest amenities that go with it. It may not be long before they realise the possession of this power and exercise it. That day can be hastened by inducements such as their contemporaries in Britain received from the Carnegie United Kingdom Trust. Even if there is no such prospect for the ryots of India, systematic and continued propaganda by bodies like the Madras Library Association can do much to carry the message of the Second Law to the countryside and to open the eyes of the villagers to the use of books and to their right to have them.

But, even from a narrower and strictly selfish point of view, the city-folk would be well advised to concede to the demands of the Second Law to give the COUNTRY-FOLK TOO THEIR BOOKS. It is to their interest to help in the reduction of the ever-increasing drift of the popu-

(1) *Law Reports, 'Statutes,'* 9 and 10 George V, Chapter 93, Section 1.

(2) PUBLIC LIBRARIES COMMITTEE: *Report on Public Libraries in England and Wales*, p. 8.

lation from the village to the city. Various causes excite such a drift; but there are some whose effects can be minimised by a judicious capitulation to the Second Law of Library Science.

Take, for example, one such cause, clearly set forth by the Linlithgow Commission. The village fellows of an educated boy "regarded him as possessing a qualification in virtue of which, he could, almost for the asking, obtain employment of a kind which was beyond their reach . . . This has contributed to the drift of educated boys from the village to the town, which still continues though the conditions which gave rise to it are rapidly changing. The supply of educated men for ordinary routine work under Government and in business-houses nearly exceeds the demand . . . In so far as it is accentuated by the drift of educated boys from the villages to the towns, there to swell the ranks of the educated unemployed, it can, in our view, only be remedied by the spread of education in rural areas *in combination with an improvement in the amenities of village life.* It is hopeless to endeavour to put the clock back by restricting education to a minimum"[1] (italics mine).

This tendency to drift spreads easily from the boy to the parent. A large majority of farmers have at least two to four months of leisure during summer. These summer months induce a vacation

(1) *Royal Commission on Agriculture in India*: *Report*, p. 539.

habit. Accordingly, the farmer spends a few summers with his son or daughter "in town" or in some distant city, leaving his lands in the care of a hired agent. The attractions of the city entice him and his family, to such an extent, that he rents his lands to tenants, often closing down his village-house entirely, and the whole family moves to town to enjoy its social and educational advantages. The next step—he goes home, sells out and comes back to settle permanently in the city with no more thought about the village and farm. One of the most important social questions, now facing those interested in rural welfare, is how to prevent this purposeless drift.

Even if an educated boy has got the strength of mind to go back to the village, the dreary conditions prevailing there, the absolute lack of means of intellectual recreation and of guidance in his daily pursuits leads to one of two results. Either he comes in time to neglect and finally lose sight of his serious interests, fall into a morbid state of mind and becomes a lifelong victim to cards or he runs back to town dreading the dullness of village life.

Apart from disastrous economic consequences, such a drift to the city unnecessarily adds to the congestion in the cities, increases the cost of living of the city-folk and renders the maintenance of Public Health more difficult and more costly. The fact is, the country needs a new rural class and new conditions in the rural parts to keep them to their rural duties and functions. This necessitates inevitably books in the villages—books of all kinds—so that the long engagementless summer may be endurable and so that the inquiring mind may find food ready to hand without wandering to the towns to seek for it. Once the Rural Library Scheme is started, it can be—in other countries it has been—made to extend its sphere far beyond books. It will send to villages cinema-reels and lantern slides, both for recreation and for information. It will help in the organisation of musical concerts, lectures, dramas and exhibitions of all kinds. It will endeavour to function up to every new opportunity for service reasonably within its field. Further, as a centre for the community life, the Rural Library has certain advantages over other rural institutions. It is common property for all and has a democracy about it which the temple and the *mutt* do not, as a rule, have.

In fact, if the Law 'BOOKS FOR ALL' be allowed to cross the city-walls, it will attempt to invest the village with all the possible amenities and intellectual opportunities that have been, till now, found only in urban areas. In this way a progressive Rural Library Scheme will become a powerful agency in minimising the undesirable drift from the village to the city.

Although it is our intention to reserve all technical details to a later volume of this series, the supreme importance of the Rural Library Scheme for India will justify a short digression into the problem of the organisation of village libraries. While a Taluk may ultimately prove to be the most convenient unit area for the scheme of rural libraries, at present it may be more expedient to start on a District basis. Although the area of a district may prove to be too large, the resources of a District Board as well as its capacity for sustained work and direction are much greater than those of a Taluk Board.

The inauguration and the initial shaping of a District Library Service will depend largely on the resourcefulness and enthusiasm of the First District Librarian. The unique educational activities of one of our West Coast districts, I have reasons to attribute largely to the appointment of a resourceful full-timed Educational Officer, who is given not only full freedom but also ungrudging facilities. Similarly, if any new scheme like a District Library Scheme is to prove a success, the first requisite is the selection and appointment of a well-trained, resourceful, enthusiastic librarian as the Library Organiser of the District. No District Authority should commit the blunder of initiating its scheme without this essential preliminary. If it does, it will be only attempting to prove that the scheme won't work.

If the appointment of the District Librarian should be the first step of the District Board, the first thing that the librarian himself should do is to get first-hand knowledge of the people whom he has to serve. It would be unwise and fatal to start with standardised notions about the requirements of the villagers. Experience in other countries has shown that villages apparently identical in type actually need different standards of books. The County-librarian of Nottinghamshire gives telling examples of this in her paper on "How to start a County Library Scheme",[1] which, by the way, is a very lucid exposition of the initial difficulties of a District Library Organiser. Her first precept is "First know your people and to do this it is essential to visit each centre before opening it".

The second step for the District Organiser is to enlist the aid of the District Educational Officer, the Deputy Inspectors of Schools, the Tahsildars, the Presidents of the Village Panchayats, the Co-operative Societies and the others interested in Rural Reconstruction Work. With their aid and by personal investigation, he should select the most suitable person as the local librarian for each centre. The village teacher, or the village munsif or the village accountant—whoever is most popular in the village—should be selected for the task. By example and precept, the chosen representative should be helped to work up the necessary enthusiasm. This inspiring of the local librarians is an all-important part of organisation. For this task we want an organiser, above all things keenly enthusiastic himself—a personality

(1) *Proceedings of the Second County Library Conference held on November 4th to 6th, 1924*, pp. 12-15.

of more than ordinary tact, patience and capacity for hard work. It often happens that there is a deadly faction in the village. It is advisable, in such cases, to have one local representative for each faction.

The next step is to advertise the library idea intensively throughout the area. The vernacular newspapers of the district should be asked to announce the facilities offered by the District Library as prominently and as frequently as possible. Attractive handbills should be widely distributed in as many ways as possible. First-class posters, with charming colours and catching legends, should be distributed profusely. A picture of the lovely poster, designed by the Carnegie United Kingdom Trust for use by the County-libraries of Great Britain, is given in the accompanying plate. It represents "a torch of learning on enamelled iron, 17 inches by 13, with a red cartouche bearing in white lettering the words, COUNTY LIBRARY".[1] Local festivals and fairs should be visited and an intensive campaign of propaganda should be launched on such occasions with the co-operation of zealous honorary workers. Look at this account of an American Fair. "All over an American Fair were found notices 'Come and hear our travel book-talk in the library stall at 3-0 P.M., this afternoon'. And a considerable

(1) CARNEGIE UNITED KINGDOM TRUST: *Fifteenth Annual Report*, p. 33.

number did come."[1] It requires enormous work to carry the gospel of the Second Law into every village and hamlet and to drill the national importance of the work of the District Library into the minds of the country-folk.

Last but not least, a variety of well-built, well-written, well-illustrated books should be promptly and regularly served. Both recreative and informational books should be sent. Some of the informational books should have a bearing on local industries and interests. The experience of the local-librarian of a village in Cambridgeshire is worth quoting. "Books bearing on local industries—agriculture and horticulture—are eagerly looked for, and in this connection I would refer to a method we have occasionally to adopt. We frequently get a book which we know will be useful to certain persons who have never made use of the library. In such a case we send the book to the probable reader with a message suggesting he would glance at it and, if he is interested, keep it for a week or two. In this way we have circulated several technical books which would otherwise never have been read. The difficulty in one such case was to get the book back again; the borrower had found it so useful in his daily work that he could not do without it. I have no doubt in my own mind that this gentleman is richer by many pounds already

(1) CARNEGIE UNITED KINGDOM TRUST: *Some Impressions of the Public Library System of the United States of America*, p. 84.

as a result of what he has learnt about fruit-packing, *etc.*, from a book I sent him at a venture. But we have made another friend and created another reader. I am beginning to believe that many farmers and gardeners do not realise that there are books in existence which deal exclusively with their interests and difficulties and it is our job to correct this notion".[1]

The circulation of lantern slides should be made part of the work of the District Library. In some districts, I have seen several lanterns, distributed by the District Board, simply rusting for want of slides. Not infrequently parts are broken and the gas jet is clogged with rust. In one place the lens was so hopelessly coated with oily dirt that, even after half-an-hour's cleaning, it could not be restored to its usual transparency. With no lack of co-ordination whatever, several lanterns are to be found in one and the same centre—one with the health-inspector, one with the school-inspector and another with the local school—but none in order and none with slides. The District Library can eliminate this wasteful duplication and, what is more important, circulate slides periodically. It may send round also gramophone records and picture collections. There are great possibilities again for educational work through travelling cinematograph shows, which may exhibit pictures to awaken interest in other countries, in

(2) *Proceedings of the Second County Library Conference held on 4th to 6th November*, 1924, p. 61.

nature, in manufactures, in industries, in marketing methods and in civic hygiene. It is good to enlist sympathy by first showing films based on the Ramayana, Mahabharata, Sakuntala and so on and alternate them with more utilitarian and informational films. In the initial stages, when the printed word can only be heard when read to by others and cannot be read by themselves by the vast body of illiterates, this side of a District Library Service will be not only essential but will also be a good incentive to make the villagers long for and submit to the rapid liquidation of their illiteracy, which, again should be one of the transitory features of the activities of our District Libraries for some little time.

It may be convenient to have the central repository of the District Library at the headquarters of the District. It should be designed to facilitate the work as much as possible. A stack-room, a packing-room and an office-room will suffice. At the beginning, one or two convenient and consecutive rooms in the ground-floor of the District Board Office may be sufficient. The staff must grow with the scheme. But, from the very beginning, there must be a minimum of one reliable assistant to do the routine work, which would otherwise occupy too much of the time which the librarian should spend on organisation. As the librarian will have to be constantly in the interior of the District, the assistant should be competent to be in charge on such occasions.

The transport will vary with the local conditions of the district. A district like Tanjore can exchange boxes of books quite easily with the aid of its net-work of railways and bus-lines. In a district like Kurnool the aid of bullock-carts and carriers may have to be invoked. But it may not happen for any District Librarian "to travel two days on a mule taking another mule to carry the books like one of our fellow librarians across the water", as pictured by Col. Mitchell.[1] An ideal method of transport is that of the library-van. It may be fitted with shelves to carry about a thousand volumes, from which the villagers and the village-librarians may make their selection on returning the volumes which have been read. The librarian may himself drive or accompany the van in its rambles through the district. It will also advertise the District Library Scheme in a very effective way. This is an economical form of transport and will eliminate the travelling charges of the librarian. The van may visit each centre once in three months. The local centres at which the exchange is to be effected may be any convenient places such as schools, temples, *mutts*, post offices, stores or homes. The accompanying figures show some of the exchange stations of American villages. The book-van-day is a *gala* day in these villages. The moment the librarian drives the van in, a swarm of men, women and children surround the van and

(1) *Proceedings of the Fifteenth Conference of the Library Association*, p. 79.

HOME USED AS LOCAL CENTRE.

STORE USED AS LOCAL CENTRE.

history fascinate them and for this reason one would have these books more profusely illustrated''.[1] Within two years of its existence the county-library of Cambridgeshire has disclosed varied reading interests. The librarian of Cottenham, another village of the same county records, ''There is the shoemaker who refuses everything but history and historical novels, who cannot believe that people exist in Wake's own Country who have not read Kingsley's *Hereward*; and the fruit-grower who insists on books on astronomy''.[2] Another county-librarian makes mention of a gardener devouring every book on Egypt which the village-librarian could procure for him and of a railway guard reading Sven Hedin's books of travel.

The cheer that the travelling library is bringing to the denizens of dreary villages is illustrated by a note[3] received by the County-librarian of Kent from a villager ''who lives eight and a half miles from a town and had been supplied with books to help her in her study of French literature'', the note ending with ''ever so grateful to you for help in constructing a happy little world for me''. Again we are told ''The parish of Esclusham Below

---

(1) *Proceedings of the Second County Library Conference held on 4th to 6th November*, 1924, p. 59.

(2) *Proceedings of the Second County Library Conference held on 4th to 6th November*, 1924, p. 61.

(3) *Proceedings of the Second County Library Conference held on 4th to 6th November*, 1924, p. 66.

in the Denbigshire which has a population of about 1,900 scattered over several mining hamlets, which has converted 263 of them into constant readers, issues about 7,000 volumes a year; and the local librarian cheerfully reports, "The Parish Council Members are jubilant over the progress made and *will go* to any length to ensure its future success".[1]

We cannot end this section more appropriately than by quoting the fervent wish for the progress of the Second Law of Library Science into the midst of peasants, uttered by the Dean of the New York State College of Agriculture. "It should scarcely be necessary to say that the educational system within a county is not complete until there exists one or more good libraries serving the entire population. For most rural counties, the county-library seems to be the answer. Until farm children and adults alike have convenient and regular access to book-collections suited to their varied tastes and needs, our national happiness and progress will fall short of their possibilities. The time is here when there should be a nation-wide movement to establish and bring into active use the library facilities accessible to all farm-homes."[2]

---

(1) *Proceedings of the Third County Library Conference held on 18th to 19th November, 1926*, p. 11.

(2) PELTON (Ralph A.) and BEAL (Marjorie): *The Library of the Open Road*, being No. 188 of the *Cornell Extension Bulletin*, pp. 34-35.

THE NORMAL AND THE ABNORMAL

The next antithesis to be considered—the Normal and the Abnormal—is of a more complex nature. There are abnormalities of all kinds. There is the temporarily abnormal sick in the hospital. There is the removable abnormality of illiteracy. We have the reclaimable abnormal in the prisoner behind the bars, while the blind and the deaf and dumb form the classes that are commonly described as abnormal. The *all* in 'BOOKS FOR ALL' embraces every one of them. The Second Law knows no exception. It can have no rest until it has arranged for the supply to EVERY ONE, NORMAL OR ABNORMAL, HIS OR HER BOOK.

A ROUND TABLE

The Patient.—Ah! this endless confinement to bed! Those endless eternal—blank—white walls! How I wish I could run away!

The Psychologist.—Soft, my friend, soft. Don't work yourself up into that mood. It will do you harm.

Our friend has just come to discuss with us the ways and means to remove that tedium.

The Second Law.—Cheer up, Sir, I have brought with me a trolly full of books. You will soon see it wheeled from ward to ward and bed to bed.

The Patient.—I can't stand the rattle of the trolly.

The Psychologist.—(Aside to Second Law.) Poor old fellow! Worn out nerves! The slightest scratch upsets him.

The Second Law.—Don't be afraid. My trolly is noiseless, being specially built for hospital use. A blind man cannot know that it is moving.

The Blind Man.—Oh!—You don't know how sharp our ears are.

The Second Law.—Even so, I am certain, you can't hear it.

The Patient.—So thoughtful of you. I am sorry for my temper. What books have you brought for us?

The Second Law.—Beautiful picture books, charming Art-journals, entertaining novels, inspiring poetry, a few hymns, *Tit-bits* and—

The Patient.—Ye—es. Your choice is wide enough. But, you have left *me* out.

The Second Law.—How?

The Patient.—You see, I have been a Professor all my life. I care for no reading which is not heavy.

The Second Law.—I would have no objection to give you what you want, but remember one danger. Suppose your illness takes a bad turn—God forbid—then the Doctor will throw all the blame on the stiff books I supplied, and, who knows, perhaps even cancel my visitor's pass!

The Psychologist.—You needn't have that fear any longer. Perhaps you don't know that I am here full-timed. Send all kinds of books. I shall take care to give EACH PATIENT HIS BOOK —I mean, what he can enjoy without detriment to his health. At any rate, I shall assume the responsibility and see that the Doctor does not throw the blame on you.

The Second Law.—I am ever so grateful. What can I send you, Professor?

The Patient.—Some *Croce* in Italian, if you please, ...

It is so kind of you to think of us, unfortunates.

I am tired; I can't sit up any longer. May I, with your permission, retire!

The Psychologist.—Yes, certainly.

Attender! the wheeled chair.

The Second Law.—Professor, pass my message on from bed to bed. When my librarian goes round with the book-trolly, each patient can tell him his requirement. Now that the Psychologist is here, I can send down anything they ask for.

The Patient.—Thank you, God bless you. Good-bye, for the present.

The Mother of the Dumb.—Fancy the old man's wish to grind his Italian even in bed.

The Illiterate.—What is that Groce, Madam?

The Blind Man.—Oh! You don't know that! It is Croce, not Groce. Croce is one of the greatest living philosophers. He is an Italian, and naturally he writes in Italian.

The Psychologist.—I am also in charge of the local jail,—I mean, as a Psychologist, I have also to attend on the prisoners.

The Second Law.—But, what can I do? It was only the other day that I sent my Librarian round with the book-van. That old Jailor there, was hard as flint. He growled, it appears, "What! Books for damned murderers!" It seems he even insulted my Librarian saying, "If you don't have a more decent way of earning your bread, take the earliest opportunity to break into a house, and I shall have a chance to give you some work.

The Jailor.—What? When was it?

The Second Law.—Some months back, I think.

The Jailor.—Thank God! it was not I!

The Psychologist.—All that is now an old story. That old jailor has now been retired. You do not seem to know how the recent reforms have humanised everything. That old biting sort of jailor is gone. They are now recruiting men of culture—men with sympathy, men who want to reclaim the criminals rather than keep them eternally in chains. That is why they want me there.

The Jailor.—I assure you, Madam, that you will ever have my heartiest co-operation in your philanthropic mission. On behalf of my predecessor, I tender you and your librarian, my most sincere apologies.

The Second Law.—Thank you, Sir, but I am so glad to hear of this change. I am most happy. One difficult problem that I had set for this conference is thus already solved.

The Psychologist.—Have you with you the list of books you sent the other day?

The Second Law.—Here it is.

The Psychologist.—It is all right, so far—as—it—goes . . . . . But you seem to have entirely forgotten the political prisoners.

They would like to have more serious books—Economics, Politics, Metaphysics, Sociology and so on.

The Second Law.—Will they allow such books inside the prison?

The Psychologist.—Certainly, why not?

After all, it is with the greatest reluctance that the Government consigns these men of culture to prison. It is more to vindicate the Majesty of Law, than to deprive them of their liberty. Sunday-players and Salt-law-breakers are usually the tallest intellectuals of a community. They go to prison only for technical offences, and the Government also is anxious that such men should be allowed a good supply of books and periodicals, lest their forced inaction should end in morbid melancholy.

The Jailor.—Yes. That is the correct policy. I shall post you this night a list of their requirements.

The Second Law.—I shall take it on hand immediately it arrives and see that the books reach you by noon, to-morrow.

But our service cannot be at its best, unless we get into personal touch with our readers.

The Jailor.—That is easily done. I shall put your Librarian on our weekly visitor's list. Will that do?

The Second Law.—Ideal.

The Blindman.—Ladies and gentlemen, I am glad you do all that for those who are shut in prisons. What about us who are shut in perpetual darkness? I hear that the last census revealed that we are no less than 479,637 in number.[1]

The Second Law.—Indeed, that is my next point for discussion.

I am aware that fifteen persons in every ten thousand are blind in your country.[2]

But, I have books for you also.

The Jailor.—What? Can the blind read?

The Second Law.—Yes, the Braille-books. The blind can read them with the tips of their fingers.

The Jailor.—It's news to me. Do they look like real books?

The Second Law.—Yes, only they are very bulky. The Bible forms 38 volumes measuring 10 inches by 13½ inches by 2; while a novel by Scott or Dickens makes

---

(1) *Census of India*, 1921, Vol. II, Part II, *Tables*, p. 141.

(2) *Census of India*, 1921, Vol. I, Part I, *Report*, p. 211.

from 8 to 10 volumes of like dimensions.[1] Further they are very heavy. Each Braille-volume weighs 5 lbs.[2] Still, as the blind cannot go to the library, they are usually sent by post and the post office charges only a nominal rate.

The Illiterate.—Are the letters simple? Can we learn them?

The Psychologist.—Why should you go to that. You have your sight and you can learn the ordinary script.

The Braille-books are not written in the usual script. The letters are made of raised points arranged in accordance with a code.

The Jailor.—When was it invented?

The Second Law.—Long ago. Nearly a century ago. In fact the first book for the blind produced in the United Kingdom was in 1827.[3] The first complete edition of the Bible in Braille was produced in 1890.[4]

The Blind man.—What! a century back! Where can we get them?

---

(1) THE CARNEGIE UNITED KINGDOM TRUST: *First Annual Report*, p. 13.

(2) PUBLIC LIBRARIES COMMITTEE: *Report on Public Libraries in England and Wales*, p. 142.

(3) *Encyclopædia Britannica*, 14th Edn., Vol. III, p. 721.

(4) *Encyclopædia Britannica*, 14th Edn., Vol. III, p. 723.

The Second Law.—Most of the countries have now established a National Library for the Blind. England had it founded as early as 1882.[1] America had it shortly thereafter. Germany, in 1894[2] and—

The blind man.—What about us here?

The Second Law.—The movement is spreading. It has recently come to China and it may reach here at no distant date.

The blind man.—Till then?

The Second Law.—England and America will gladly serve you.

The blind man.—Have they enough volumes?

The Second Law.—Oh, yes. In England alone, the stock exceeds 100,000 volumes.

The Jailor.—A hundred thousand volumes for the blind!

The Psychologist.—Books are the main solace, you know, which those afflicted with blindness possess.

The Jailor.—Are they popular?

The Second Law.—Yes. The borrowers of the British library for the blind exceed 10,000, while the annual issue has gone beyond 50,000. It was only the other day that the Queen gave away prizes

---

(1) *Librarian's Guide*, 1928-9, ed. by Mark Meredith, p. 66.

(2) *Minerva Jahrbuch*, 1930, Vol. I, p. 1387.

to the blind children who used the libraries most effectively.

The Illiterate.—What kind of things do they read?

The Psychologist.—All kinds of things of course. The requirements of the blind do not differ materially from those of others. The standard of intelligence is as high, and certain of the faculties are not infrequently more highly developed.[1]

The blind man.—Why, we have one among us here who is an expert in watch and clock repair. He is now having a roaring business and his sighted competitors use their eyes to gaze at his success in wonder and envy.

The Second Law.—There are now several blind boys who appear for University examinations and get their degrees.

The Illiterate.—Then, we are worse than the blind.

The blind man.—Yes, as the Lord said, "Having eyes, see ye not".[2]

The Second Law.—You can easily help yourself.

The Illiterate.—But, I can't read.

The Second Law.—If you go to the library, you can have books read to you. There

(1) PUBLIC LIBRARIES COMMITTEE: *Report on Public Libraries in England and Wales*, p. 141.

(2) St. Mark, VIII, 18.

are readers specially appointed for the purpose—

The Psychologist.—And, in the meantime you can learn to read and write.

The Illiterate.—I should love to. But can I?

The Psychologist.—The library has a club for the liquidation of illiteracy. Have yourself enrolled in it and in six months you can yourself read without help.

The Illiterate.—May I bring my wife with me? She too would like to learn.

The Jailor.—Yes. Your granny too!

The mother of the dumb.—Now, what about *my* child. He is deaf and dumb.

The Second Law.—He is no special problem for me, provided he can read and write.

The mother of the dumb.—He cannot, that is my trouble.

The Second Law.—Then send him first to my sister, "EDUCATION FOR ALL". She will readily equip him with the power to read and write. Perhaps our friend the Psychologist may be able to give you more information.

The Psychologist.—It is now quite easy to teach the deaf and dumb. I shall arrange for it.

The mother of the dumb.—After he learns, can you give him books?

The Second Law.—With great pleasure. I am here for that.

The mother of the dumb.—Have you ever come across deaf and dumb readers?

The Second Law.—Any number. Here is one of the latest reports to hand.[1] "Across the desk of one reader's adviser a young girl passed a slip of paper. Upon it were written the words:—

"I only went through the fifth grade. Can you tell me some books to help me upwards."

The girl was deaf and dumb. She sat down beside the adviser at her desk and they wrote their messages to each other on a large sheet of paper.

"How old are you?" wrote the adviser.

"Nineteen," she wrote in her turn, "I am a folder in a laundry. I like poetry, but I also want to know some facts.

. . . . .

The girl returned again and again for more books, encouraged by the knowledge that she could learn through her own ability to read."

(1) *Adult Education and the Library*, Vol. III, p. 20.

The mother of the dumb.—Sweet girl! I wish my son could have that solace, granted him.

The Second Law.—The very purpose of my existence is to give it to him.

All sing in a chorus:

There's room for all
Let not the mean
Or learned dean
Restrict the books
T' a favoured few.
We've Books for all.

Books for the rich
And Books for the poor
Books for the man
And Books for the dame.

Books for the sick
And Books for the fit
Books for the blind
And Books for the dumb.

Books for the bungler
And Books for the wrangler
Books for the burgher
And Books for the cotter.

Books for the lettered
And Books for the fettered
We've Books for all
For one and all.

A stranger slips in singing:

Books for all; yes, Books for all
If and only if you add
Books for the land
And Books for the sea.

The Jailor.—May I know, sir, to whom I am speaking?

The Stranger.—I am an ordinary sailor, sir. My vessel touched this port last night. As I was strolling along the street, your chorus caught my ear. The porter told me that you were having a Books-for-the-abnormal-Round - Table, and the old man was kind enough to let me in.

The Jailor.—I am sorry, you are too late. We are just breaking up.

The Sailor.—Did our claim engage your attention at all, sir?

We are the most abnormal people on earth, spending all our days on water, floating from end to end of this vast world.

The Second Law.—I am taking it up as a question by itself. You may rest assured that you won't be forgotten.

THE LAND AND THE SEA

While the antitheses between the rich and the poor, the male and the female, the town and the country, and the normal and the abnormal, have been, from the beginning, engaging public attention with varying results, the antithesis between the land and the sea seems to have, for long, suffered neglect because 'Out of sight's out of mind'. The sea-faring people spend most of their time away from their home and their requirements and handicaps are seldom realised by those that lead a settled life on land. Nevertheless, even in India, which is not very prominent in her maritime activities and enterprises, as many as 600,000 persons[1] spend more time on water than on land. Even if their case is brought to our mind, the problem of giving EVERY MAN AT SEA HIS BOOK bristles with difficulties. In the words of the Executive Committee of the Carnegie United Kingdom Trust, "conditions inseparable from life at sea combine in creating obstacles to an organised service. The impracticability of financial support from local rates; the constant changes, except in large companies, in ships' crews; uncertainties in the movements of tramp ships; the need for exchange facilities in many of the principal ports of the world—all these factors contribute to the difficulty of the problem".[2] Still the Second Law of Library Science insists that such difficulties are not insurmountable, and should be solved. In response to its insistence, England founded, in 1919, "the Seafarers' Education Service, which attempts to supply ships with books on an ambi-

(1) *Census of India*, 1921, Vol. I, Part II, p. 204.

(2) *Thirteenth Annual Report*, p. 31.

tious scale, as regards both organisation and choice of books . . . In May of that year the World Association for Adult Education called together representatives of the owners and maritime trade unions and the mission societies. A permanent commission was thereupon appointed to undertake the work of providing libraries as part of a complete educational scheme for seafarers".[1]

Experience soon showed that seafarers would read the best books and would treat them with respect. On long voyages especially, most of the books get into use and it is estimated that nearly 75 per cent of the crew take to reading, while hardly 10 per cent of those on land are inclined to do so. At the end of 1928, the total number of ships thus served was 1276.[2]

The problem of putting the supply of books to seafarers on a proper financial basis has been fully discussed by the Public Libraries Committee.[3] It starts with the message of the Second Law: 'BOOKS FOR ALL, WHETHER ON LAND OR ON WATER'—the seafarers have no less right than their compatriots on land to a service of books paid for out of public funds. The only question is whether the responsibility for meeting their needs should be met by the State exclusively, by co-operation between the State and the local

(1) PUBLIC LIBRARIES COMMITTEE: *Report on Public Libraries in England and Wales*, pp. 144-145.

(2) CARNEGIE UNITED KINGDOM TRUST: *Fifteenth Annual Report*, p. 44.

(3) *Ibid.*, p. 146.

bodies of the port-towns or by the latter alone. The members of the Committee do not regard the last alternative either as reasonable or as practicable. Nor would they recommend that the State should be saddled with the entire responsibility. On the other hand, they would suggest that the task should be divided evenly between the shipping companies, the seafarers themselves, the library authorities of the seaports and the State.

The Committee makes the following analysis of the library income of the Seafarers' Education Society during the first five years:—

	£
Shipping Companies ..	6,899
The Chamber of Shipping ..	500
The Maritime Trade Unions ..	590
The Carnegie United Kingdom Trust	2,385
Sundry bodies and individuals ..	390
Sale of literature, etc.	84
..	10,848

This analysis discloses the significant absence of the State and the Local Bodies. The Committee would invite their attention to the call of the Second Law and urge them to put in their quota, not necessarily as money, but perhaps better as books, the books on the shelves of the Central Library of the State and the books on the shelves of the Municipal Libraries of the ports.

The keepers of light-houses stand in need of books no less than the sailors themselves. The fate of most of the men confined in the solitude of light-houses is as hard as that of Robinson Crusoe in his desert-island. Or perhaps worse. While Robinson Crusoe had the freedom to wander about, even that freedom is denied to them. While the fate of the ships and their passengers as well as the prosperity of the merchants on land depend on their vigilant and selfless services, it is but reasonable that the call of the Second Law on their behalf should be heard with the greatest willingness. While shore light-houses may be served by the District Libraries or the Municipal Libraries, as the case may be, there should be a special central organisation for catering to the needs of isolated rock light-houses and light-ships. The total number of light-houses and light-ships that are thus regularly served with books in Great Britain and Ireland is nearly 300.

THE ADULT AND THE CHILD

But the struggle of the Second Law takes the most puzzling phase when it has to negotiate the antithesis between the adult and the child. It has been, for long, held by all—and it is even now being held by some—that the child has no right to any books other than text-books and that it is only n'ver-do-well's that will "waste time in extra-reading". On the other hand, it has been—and by some even is—at the same time believed that one who has completed formal schooling has already made the closest possible approach to the omniscience that books can supply. One has only to witness, from the Cauvery Bridge at Kumbakonam, the surface of the Cauvery water bestrewn and bedecked with the printed pages of torn books, cast away by the candidates coming out of the College-Hall, after the last of the University Examinations. This casting off is meant by many as a ceremony to symbolise that they have passed the stage of books.

This belief that the educated adult does not need books any longer can really be traced to what may be called 'the Camel theory' of education—that before we start on the journey of life we can be given all the mental food necessary to carry us through the whole way. It does not recognise that maturity has its educational aptitudes, aspirations and urgencies. But this theory, that education has primarily to do only with the training of children, has, however, little basis in psychology and gets little support from practical experience. Of course, children must be educated. But an educational system, that does not recognise the perpetual need of the adult for the tools of education, is a mere futility. In any dynamic democracy, that is constantly evolving newer and better order of things, the definite task of Public Education is that of constantly educating the adults to participate intelligently in this new order of life. Adults must first learn how to live the new order before they can teach it. It is the unfortunate neglect of this factor that has led to the clock of our educational curriculum being blindly, but harmfully, set back every now and then, at the instance of powerful politicians, who insist on having their fingers in every pie, but who, in the plenitude of their ignorance, would know of no curriculum other than what they were themselves drilled through, in their own far-off boyhood. Out of the practice of living must come the understanding that can translate this kind of living into education for the children. Hence, even though a man has as many degrees as a thermometer, even though he be graduated with the highest honours, he is grossly uneducated, or will soon become so, if he stops his reading and lets his brain grow rusty from the day of his convocation onwards. Education really begins at the cradle and is completed only at the grave. All the educated adults are therefore comprehended in the 'ALL' in 'BOOKS FOR ALL'.

Persuading the graduate adult to submit himself to the sway of the Second Law is only one side of this phase of the struggle. The Second Law has an equally up-hill task to do, to convince the University that her interest in the education of her *alumni* should not end on the day she confers her degrees on them. Although she has no right to force on them any more of formal teaching, the duty of continuing to educate her *alumni* through the books of her library is cast on her. One of the achievements of the Second Law of Library Science is the driving home of this new duty, in which progressive Universities and their libraries are beginning to take an increasing part. The Second Law would even offer a threat to the University saying, "You cannot retain the interest and the loyalty of your graduates, unless you strengthen this new service to them through your books. There must be this higher intellectual bond. Nay, viewed from the national point of view—and after all it is the National Exchequer that maintains you—such service to *alumni* is essential if the money spent on under-graduate education is not to be thrown away for lack of proper follow-up work after graduation".

This brings us to the new orientation which the Second Law has brought about in the methods of instruction. It tells the Universities, "The best thing that you can do for your raw under-graduate is to awaken in him a zest for thinking and the habit of reading. Remember, education does not end in your class-room. I have to begin where you leave. It is easier for me to keep the reading undergraduates reading, than to catch them when they are men and women and start them afresh to read. In return, I have no objection to your relying upon me, more fully in your class-room teaching; indeed, I am quite prepared to be by your side in your daily task and take the under-graduate by hand and walk alone with him when he leaves you behind." Similarly it tells the schools, "The hope of the future lies in the child-ren of to-day. Remember that a large proportion of children walk straight from your care to mine. There is no University for them. Hence, it is imperative, that you should give them the widest opportunity in your school-library to form the correct reading-habit. You know that the child, who forms a deep love of reading in the school, is more likely to continue that reading-habit in after-life. Hence, reinforce the library-work at school so that I can reinforce the library-work of the future". In its attempt to scale over the perplexing antithesis between the adult and the child, such is the reconciliation and understanding that the Second Law is achieving between the old and the new instruments of education, *viz.*, the Schools and Colleges, on the one hand, and the Library on the other.

Thus the struggle of the Second Law of Library Science was largely due to the unlimited democracy and universality of its appeal. The vagaries of Nature may militate against the rule of democracy in many spheres of life. No political or ethical creed can equalise the differences of physique, temperament and intelligence any more than the differences in height or colour. But, the Law "BOOKS FOR ALL" has proved to be more than a match to her mischievous whims. She may blind the eyes of some; she may tie up the tongues of others; she may cast the lot of still others in solitude; she may subject the majority to the grind of poverty. And yet, the Second Law would treat them all alike and give to EACH HIS OR HER

BOOK-VAN-DAY IS A GALA DAY FOR CHILDREN.

the ONE, in company with all the others.[1] This last act of Sambandar would, in its expression of universal brotherhood, serve as a symbol of the Second Law of Library Science.

சீர் பெருகு நீலநக்கர் திருமுருகர் முதல் தொண்டர்
ஏர் கெழுவு சிவபாதவிருதயர் நம்பாண்டார் சீ
ரார் திருமெய்ப் பெரும்பாணர் மற்றெனையோர் அனைந்துளோர்
பார் நிலவு கிளை சூழப் பன்னிகளோடுடன் புக்கார்.

அணிமுத்தின் சிவிகை முதல் அணிதாங்கிச் சென்றார்கள்
மணிமுத்த மாலை புனை மடவார் மங்களம் பெருகும்
பணி முற்றும் எடுத்தார்கள் பரிசனங்கள் வினைப்பாசம்
துணி வித்த உணர் வினராய்த் தொழுதுடன் புக்கொடுங்கினார்.

ஆறுவகைச் சமயத்தில் அருந்தவரும் அடியவரும்
கூறுமறை முனிவர்களும் கும்பிடவந்த அனைத்தாரும்
வேறு திரு அருளினால் வீடு பெற வந்தாரும்
ஈறில் பெரும் சோதியினுள் எல்லாரும் புக்கற்பின்

காதலியைக் கைப்பற்றிக் கொண்டு வலம்கொண்டு அருளித்
தீது அகற்ற வந்தருளும் திருஞானசம்பந்தர்
நாதன் எழில் வளர் சோதி நண்ணி அதனுட்புகுவார்
போத நிலை முடித்த வழிப்புக்கு ஒன்றியுடனானார்.[1]

(1) *Cf.* SEKKILAR: *Periya Puranam*, II Kandam, verses 1250-1253.

[Sekkilar was a famous biographer of the Tamil country in the twelfth century.]

CHAPTER III

The Second Law and Its Digvijaya

In the last chapter, we witnessed the slow struggle of the Second Law, from trench to trench and barrier to barrier; in this chapter, we shall see the sweeping success of 'BOOKS FOR ALL', in its unimpeded *Digvijaya* or world-conquering expedition. The last chapter enumerated the varied vested interests that were found entrenched against the march of the Second Law; the present chapter will take us round the world in the wake of the majestic conquest of the message 'BOOKS FOR ALL'. While till now we witnessed the spread of the Second Law into the different strata and sections of society, we shall now witness the spread of BOOKS FOR ALL into the different continents and countries of the world. BOOKS FOR THE CHOSEN FEW had existed ever since books came to be written. But, BOOKS FOR ALL is a new concept. While libraries have existed from time immemorial, the 'Library Movement' had its origin only within the memory of some of our octogenarians. It is not our object, at present, to trace the history of libraries that were built either to hoard books or to serve books, at most, for a select few. Our attempt, on the other hand, will be to make a rapid survey of the growth of the modern Library Movement in as many communities as possible. It is not with stray individual libraries, however big, that we shall deal here; but, on the other hand, we shall have to deal with libraries in mass—with the out-burst of myriads of libraries, many of them though tiny little ones, throbbing with the life and radiant with the effulgence due to the possession of the democratic gospel of the restless Second Law.

AMERICA

The Second Law of Library Science dropped the seeds of the Library Movement all through the world. Some fell on stony places, some among thorns, and some into good ground. But the seeds, that fell on the fields of the New World, appear to have been the first to sprout. They seem to have already reached the fruiting-stage and appear to have even commenced to scatter fresh seeds, far and wide. As the first gardeners of this new family of plants, the Americans have had an opportunity of doing not a little pioneering work. They have exercised this unique opportunity with unique success. The energy, the enthusiasm and the resources of the New World came to be placed unreservedly at the disposal of this newly-sprouting species, the Library Movement. New grounds were constantly prepared, new transplantations were frequently made, new species were boldly cultured, new classifications were carefully ventured, new techniques became necessary and were invented, and new votaries were easily found in ever-increasing numbers. A canny Scot, who had made a mountain of dollars, freely scattered his wealth in the cause of this Movement. This concatenation of circumstances is by far the luckiest that has ever occurred. The result has been that America has come to be rightly regarded as the land of libraries. If we ask the nations of the world what they feel uppermost about their own Library Movement, most of them begin by saying, "We are following the lead of America. We are adopting American methods". Hence, it would be proper for us to commence our study of the *Digvijaya* of the Second Law with a brief survey of its exploits in this, the first home of the Library Movement.

1876 appears to have made a distinct epoch in the progress of the Library Movement in America. That was the year in which the American Library Association was founded. Speaking at the Fiftieth Conference of that Association under the caption *Seed time and harvest*, Mr. R. R. Bowker, one of its surviving founders, said, "Half a century ago there came together in New York three young men of ideas and ideals, brain seed which finds rich harvest in this assemblage, in the American Library Association, and in the development of the Modern American Library system, whose methods, this International Conference indicates, have found their way around the world".[1] On October 4,

---

(1) *Bulletin of the American Library Association*, Vol. XX, p. 303.

1876, these three young men secured a gathering of 'ninety men and thirteen women', who formed "the American Library Association, in which Mr. Melvil Dewey, the first Secretary, proudly enrolled himself as No. 1 and to which he gave the motto "The best reading for the greatest number at the least cost". At the Second Conference held in 1877, the attendance fell to sixty-six, and in a later one even reached as low as thirty. However, with the exception of the next two biennial conferences and the gap in 1894, the American Library Association has been holding conferences every year, reaching the thousand mark in 1902 and the two thousand mark in 1926. The membership roll which began with 103 names has now swelled to 11,833. Again, in 1850, America had only 644 libraries, of which many were open only to a select few. But to-day, there are no less than 6,500 libraries—all of which keep their doors open for all.

Can we infer from such astounding figures that the Second Law has seen the end of its mission in America? The American Library Association was not sure of an answer to this question and hence, with the aid of a small grant from the Carnegie Corporation of New York, it engaged, in July 1925, an experienced special officer to make a survey of the situation. The definite questions that were put to this special officer were[1]:—

(1) AMERICAN LIBRARY ASSOCIATION: *Library Extension, a Study of Public Library Conditions and Needs*, p. 19.

(1) How many of the people of the United States and Canada have access to public libraries?

(2) How many are still without public library service and where do they live?

(3) How far have public libraries grown since the American Library Association was founded?

(4) How far off is the goal of universal library service?

The Second Law was vitally interested in the report of the special officer. The survey was done with the utmost rapidity possible and the report of the officer saw the light of day in July 1926. What were the findings of the survey on the four fundamental questions? Here is a summary:—

(1) About 64 millions or 56 per cent of the people live in library areas.

(2) About 50 millions or 44 per cent of the people are still without public library service and, of these, 3 millions live in towns and the remaining 47 millions live in rural areas.

(3) Since the American Library Association was founded, one of its purposes, as set forth in its Charter of 1879, *viz.*, "Promoting the library interests of the country . . . by disposing the public mind to the founding and improving of libraries", is being steadily

worked out. About 6,000 new libraries have been brought into existence. In place of the 2 million volumes, 70 million volumes have come to occupy the shelves of the public libraries. About 240 millions of volumes are being issued annually and a sum of about 90 million rupees[1] is being spent per year on public libraries.

(4) The goal of universal library service has been reached only half-way. Apart from 44 per cent of the people being without library service, the existing number of volumes is entirely inadequate. It gives only six-tenths of a book per head of population. The number of volumes issued per year amounts only to 2 per capita and the amount annually spent on public libraries is less than a rupee per capita of the whole population. This meagre supply, giving such poor averages, is all turned to one half of the population leaving the other half in the cold.

The Second Law protested that such inadequacy and the consequent inequality of library opportunity are too undemocratic and it asked, "The problem of providing public library service

(1) Here, and elsewhere throughout this book, all references to foreign money are given in terms of their rupee-equivalent.

for the 50 million people, now without it, is large enough to challenge the best thought and effort you are capable of. You had the proud privilege of initiating the Library Movement in the world. Are you going to suffer that proud position to be lost?" "No, I shall buck up", said America and the American Library Association straight away charged[1] its Standing Committee on Library Extension with the task of making "an organised effort toward the goal of *adequate public library service within easy reach of every one in the United States and Canada,* and directed it to carry on this effort . . . in the closest co-operation with the League of Library Commissions, and all other interested agencies, through any or all of the following or similar methods:—

(1) Field agents for assistance in the establishment of State library extension agencies, county libraries, and local libraries and the improvement of existing libraries.

(2) Publicity especially through rural social agencies and educational medium.

(3) Free and wide distribution of publications to encourage library development.

(4) Surveys of library conditions and needs, to develop state-wide or local library programmes.

---

[1] (1) *Bulletin of the American Library Association,* Vol. XX, p. 339.

(5) Study and compilation of library laws, drafting of model legislation.

(6) Encouragement of demonstrations and experiments, especially in the State and county fields.

(7) Encouragement of private subsidies as an aid to library extensions.

(8) Further study of library extension problems."

A brief account of the activities of this Library Extension Committee[1] in 1929 may give an idea of the earnestness with which the challenge of the Second Law has been taken up. If the amount appropriated by the Committee can be taken as an index, it may be stated that it was as much as half a lakh of rupees in addition to several subventions granted by the Carnegie Corporation for specific purposes. It held a conference in Chicago and ran a Summer Institute in the University of Wisconsin, as a refresher course for field workers. On the side of publicity, it had many popular articles published in farm journals, like *American Farming, Prairie Farmer* and *Southern Planter*, in women's magazines like *Farmer's Wife* and *Women's Home Companion* and in educational periodicals like, *Illinois Teacher, School Life* and *Texas Parent-Teacher*. The total number of pieces of printed matter distributed free among the people was 75,670, in addition to considerable mimeographed matter. Six exhibi-

(1) *Bulletin of the American Library Association*, Vol. XXIV, pp. 207-228, Annual Report of the Committee.

tions were held and several talks were given in group conferences. It helped in the enactment of permissive legislation in five States and library bills were drafted for five other States. It secured financial aid from a charitable endowment for founding fifteen new country libraries and for strengthening thirteen existing ones.

If the original home of the modern Library Movement has need for such publicity, for so many conferences and for such an expenditure "to dispose the public mind to the founding and improvement of libraries", what should be the need for similar work in our own country, where the Library Movement is still only a name. Not only we have no Carnegie Corporation at our back, no angel with his *Akshayapatra,* to give unending financial help, but, on the other hand, we have the demon of inertia, which seems to be a clever *Kamarupi.* This monster takes as many different shapes as Proteus. It is now a snob scoffing at library-publicity as vulgar, now a cynic trying to trace all public service to some ulterior personal motive, and again a misanthrope cursing that no good can ever come to us; it appears as jealousy or as benumbing philosophy. Such an atmosphere is not congenial to the growth of Library Movement. Relief can come, perhaps, only from the State. Once the prestige of State action clears the atmosphere, the Library Movement may get a chance to properly dispose the public mind and find its further food in the natural soil of public opinion.

MEXICO

A step to the south takes us to Mexico. Here, the seeds of the Library Movement appear to have been lying on barren soil until the Revolution of 1910 created aspirations for popular culture. The earlier efforts, which were made to see that culture and education might not be the close preserve of the upper classes, did not however prove effective until a Ministry of Public Education was created by the Act of April 1917. This Ministry was charged by the President with the task of bringing about the much needed "social transformation". Accordingly, it attempted, for the first time, to construct a bridge across the cultural gulf between the classes and the masses. Before long, it discovered that the only suitable bridge was that of Public Libraries and established a Department of Libraries in September 1920. Finding that the majority of the people were illiterate, the ministry had to adopt rapid methods for the removal of illiteracy, with the aid of what were known as "cultural missions".[1] The work of the Department has been already so successful, that Mexico has now about 1,500 popular libraries, 1,000 school libraries, 800 industrial libraries and 500 rural libraries. It sent out in 1927 nearly 700,000 volumes to the libraries in the rural areas. The amount appropriated varies according to the condition of the public treasury. It was nearly Rs. 700,000 in 1923 but only about Rs. 60,000 in

---

(1) McLEAN (Robert N.): *That Mexican*, p. 106.

1927. The number of readers crossed the million mark in 1927. The technical section of the Department is maintaining a union catalogue of the book-resources of the whole country and runs a bibliographical magazine entitled *El libre y el pueble.*

The difficulties that confronted the Ministry of Education in this mission of 'social transformation' were not a few. "Mexico is a country of many races, many climates and many opinions. It is likewise a land of castes and social orders . . . Great distances and slow communications make it very difficult to mobilise public opinion . . . The inferiority complex of the Indian face to face with the European . . . hinders the progress of national integration."[1] Such a variegated Mexico is now being integrated by the Ministry of Education through the agency of the school and the library. The libraries are maintained, some by the Federal Government and some by the State Governments. Their stock of books aims to satisfy everybody's taste and to meet everybody's needs. It includes, not only books of the ordinary educational type, but also industrial manuals, agricultural handbooks and books on 'Home-Management', in accordance with local requirements. Lecturers equipped with cinema reels and lantern slides are sent even to the remotest villages to attract the people to the libraries. Children's rooms are opened to induce the reading habit and love of

(1) SAENZ (Moises) and PRIESTLEY (Herbert I.): *Some Mexican Problems,* pp. 55-57.

books, even before habits become rigid. Thus, Mexico has demonstrated what can be done by a handful of officials, working with enthusiasm and devoting all their energy to a task full of obstacles, if they have at their back a willing popular ministry.

In 1926, the Second Law induced another *Akshayapatra* bequeathed by Carnegie—The Carnegie Endowment for International Peace—to go to the help of the veteran Library Association of the neighbouring United States, saying "Why should you not occasionally cross the southern line and help the new plant that is sprouting in the Mexican fields? I shall bear the cost". The American Association zealously seized this offer and appointed a *Committee for Library Co-operation with the Hispanic Peoples* to devote its undivided attention to this brotherly act. This Committee began its work with great seriousness and with the aid of a subvention of about Rs. 3,500 received from the Carnegie Endowment, sent an influential deputation of American Librarians to attend the Second Annual Library Congress held at Mexico city in April 1928. This friendly visit was reciprocated by a Mexican Commission which attended the West Baden Conference of the American Library Association. This Commission utilised its sojourn as fully as possible to inform itself thoroughly of the American library methods. They visited several libraries, large and small, and no effort was spared to make their visits as informing and helpful as possible. One interesting outcome of a visit to the Library of Congress was that the librarian of the latter announced that a complete set of the Library of Congress printed catalogue cards would be deposited in the Mexican National Library. As the Library of Congress had no appropriation from which the cost of packing and transmitting this invaluable bibliographical tool could be met, the Carnegie Endowment for International Peace gave a sum of Rs. 5,000 for the purpose, in addition to the Rs. 10,000 it had granted to cover the expenses of the Commission.

This exchange of visits acted as a fillip to the growth of the Library Movement in Mexico and the problem of keeping up proper standards of administration became very acute on such a rapid growth of libraries. To meet this situation the Carnegie Endowment readily voted a sum of about Rs. 12,000 towards the cost of printing 5,700 copies of Dr. Ernest Nelson's *Los Bibliotecos en los Estados Unidos,* for free distribution among the libraries of Central and South America.[1] This is a carefully written hand-book, describing the methods of library management prevalent in the United States. Mexico gave it a cordial reception as a helpful source of information. In fact, the demand for copies was so great that a second edition had to be issued in 1929. Thus the Second Law saw the Library Movement grow vigorously from day to

(1) CARNEGIE ENDOWMENT FOR INTERNATIONAL PEACE: *Year Book,* 1920, pp. 68-69.

day among the Mexican people. As a result of its successful growth coupled with the spread of rural schools, "a Mexico different from the one that existed before the revolution is being forged".[1] When the nation shall finally come of age, the students of its history will find that not a small part of the credit for its maturing should fall to the mission of the Second Law of Library Science.

CENTRAL AND SOUTH AMERICA

The Library Movement in the remaining countries of Latin America is still in its infancy. It is only now that the ideas about the necessity of spreading education among the masses are getting broadened in most of these countries. The rich men and women in Latin America have not yet realised the need for or the wisdom of bequeathing money either for libraries or for other educational purposes, "their donations going rather to religious and charitable bodies".[2] Hence, the cost of nurturing the Library Movement has to be met by the Governments themselves.

However, the message of the Second Law of Library Science is being slowly spread in all the 20 Republics constituting South America. The American Library Association's *Committee for Library Co-operation with the Hispanic People* is extending to these Republics also the same co-

(1) TANNENBAUM (Frank): *The Mexican Agrarian Revolution*, p. 426.

(2) SHEPHERD (William R.): *Central and South America* (Home University Library), p. 193.

operation as it is showing to Mexico. At the 1929 Conference held at Washington, and attended by all the South American ambassadors, the ambassador of Colombia stated, "Before the Committee on Library Co-operation with the Hispanic Peoples lies a field destined to yield an abundant harvest . . . Those, who are acquainted with the problem of literary Commerce, recognise after careful study that the United States is destined to be the book centre for the Southern Continent . . . The South now more than ever needs to read."[1]

Another important organisation which is trying to bring about a uniform spread of the Library Movement in South America is the Pan American Union, which was organised on a permanent basis by a convention unanimously adopted by the Sixth International Conference of American States, held in 1928. One of the functions of this Union is "to assist in the development of . . . cultural relations, . . . between the American Republics," as specified in the sixth Article of the Convention.[2] This Union, which is housed in a palace presented by Carnegie, works in close co-operation with the American Library Association and the Carnegie Endowment for International Peace and much good is expected from its work in the propagation of the message of the Second Law of Library Science in all the twenty nations of South America.

(1) *Bulletin of the American Library Association*, Vol. XXIII, p. 315.

(2) *International Conciliation*, 1928, p. 346.

A LUCKY ALLIANCE

It can be seen from the above that an outstanding factor that has characterised the expedition of the Second Law in the New World is the incessant help rendered by that constant ally, Carnegie, and his benefactions. It is extremely doubtful whether the New World could have carried away the palm in the world's library race, but for the phenomenal service rendered by Carnegie to the mission of the Second Law. Hence, it may not be out of place to devote some space to Andrew Carnegie himself, before we take leave of the New World.

The son of a Scottish handloom weaver, who used to come home at night in utter despair with the distressing news, "Well, Andra, I canna get nae mair work" and of a shoemaker's daughter seeking to improve the family fortunes by keeping a "sweetie shop" at Dunfermline, Andrew Carnegie began life at 13 on Rs. 13 a month as a bobbin boy in a cotton factory of the United States,[1] and finally "emerged from the mephitic glooms of Pittsburg and scattered largesse over all the earth,"[2] as a God-sent ally of the Second Law of Library Science. It has been pictured by A. G. Gardiner that there were two Andrew Carnegies in one body and with one soul—the business man making millions and the philanthropist spending millions—without any

(1) JOHNSON (Allen) *Ed.*: *Dictionary of American Biography*, Vol. III, p. 500.

(2) GARDINER (A. G.): *Pillars of Society*, p. 88.

conflict whatever between the two, each coming into action on the word of command and vanishing when his task was done. "Business!" and up sprang the Iron-king keen as a razor; "Humanity!" and up sprang the Philanthropist bursting with benevolence. While his remarkable business capacity, his tireless industry and his clear provision enabled Andrew Carnegie to amass a fabulous fortune, his own "*Gospel of Wealth*"—first formulated in the *North Atlantic Review* of June 1899 in the words "This, then, is held to be the duty of the man of wealth: To set an example of modest, unostentatious living, shunning display or extravagance; to provide modestly for the legitimate wants of those dependent upon him; and, after doing so, to consider all surplus revenues which came to him simply as trust funds, which he is called upon to administer in the manner which, in his judgment, is best calculated to provide the most beneficial results for the community, the man of wealth thus becoming the mere trustee and agent for his poorer brethren"[1]—this, his own '*Gospel of Wealth*', made him give away, in Raghu's fashion, practically all he saved, "for the improvement of mankind".

The amount he gave for public benefactions was as much as a hundred crores of rupees. A large share of this colossal sum was put into the hands of the Carnegie Corporation of New York created by an Act of the State of New York, em-

(1) *A Manual of the Public Benefactions of Andrew Carnegie*, p. i.

bodied as chapter 297 of the laws of 1911, "to promote the advancement and diffusion of knowledge and understanding among the people of the United States, by aiding technical schools, institutions of higher learning, libraries, scientific research, hero funds, useful publications, and by such other agencies and means as shall from time to time be found appropriate therefor."[1]

Although he stated in his letter of gift that "no wise man will bind trustees for ever to certain paths, causes and institutions,"[2] he disclosed his mind by adding the rider, "My desire is that the work which I have been carrying on . . . shall continue during this and future generations".[3] It is well known that the work which the public associates with Carnegie's name is the work he has done as an ally of the Second Law and of the Library Movement generally. Indeed it has been said that when he put his fingers into his waist-coat pocket one might expect he was going to fetch out a library."[4] Probably, deep in his own mind, his innumerable library gifts took precedence over all others in importance. There was only one genuine remedy, he believed, for the ills that beset the human race

---

(1) *A Manual of the Public Benefactions of Andrew Carnegie*, p. 210.

(2) *A Manual of the Public Benefactions of Andrew Carnegie*, p. 207.

(3) *A Manual of the Public Benefactions of Andrew Carnegie*, p. 206.

(4) *Proceedings of the Carnegie Rural Library Conference, held on November, 2 and 3, 1920*, p. 12.

and that was enlightenment. "Let there be light" was the motto that, in the early days, he insisted on placing in all his library buildings. He sincerely believed that the light can be made to reach all only by providing BOOKS FOR ALL. It was this sincere belief in the message of the Second Law that made him such a staunch supporter of the Library Movement and brought about such a lucky alliance between him and the Second Law.

By an Amending Act of 1917, the Carnegie Corporation of New York was further "empowered to hold and administer any funds given to it for use in Canada or the British Colonies for the same purposes . . . as those to which it is by law authorised to apply its funds to the United States".[1] The first result of this broadening Amendment was for the Carnegie Corporation to carry the gospel of the Second Law into Canada. But, in 1928, finding that the whole American atmosphere was well charged with the message, BOOKS FOR ALL, the Carnegie Corporation wanted to carry that message into the Eastern Hemisphere as well. Prompted by this desire, looking eastwards from its home in New York, it surveyed the immediately visible regions of the Old World. First it espied a tiny little red spot standing out from the mainland of Europe. It was the United Kingdom. But finding that the canny Scot had made a separate and exclusive settlement for the land of his birth, its eyes began to sweep the Atlantic coast in search

(1) *A Manual of the Public Benefactions of Andrew Carnegie*, p. 210.

of another red spot. How one wishes that India had an Atlantic sea-board! At last, it spotted out a real red region at the southern end of the dark continent. That very moment, it urged a special commission to jump Hanuman-like across the vast Atlantic, and come back speedily with a definite scheme to usher in the era of the Second Law in that important southern outpost of the British Empire.

SOUTH-AFRICA

Accordingly, the Carnegie Library Commission, consisting of one American Librarian and one Scottish Librarian, landed at Cape Town on August 20, 1928. It toured the Union for three months and found it in complete possession of the Second Law's rival, *viz.*, BOOKS FOR THE CHOSEN FEW. No doubt it found some 211 libraries. But they were all screened "by the fine meshes of a £1 subscription sifter". The result was that readers were so few that the shelves showed little empty space even when every reader had his full quota at home and that the libraries were crying out for additions to shelving, whereas, if the Second Law had been heard, relief would have come through a considerable number of books being constantly in the hands of people and also through the larger percentage of books getting worn-out and discarded. Not only were the poorer Whites kept out of the benefits of the libraries by this £1 sifter, but the Blacks and the Browns, that formed the majority of the population, were utterly denied the use of books. The Commissioners describe this big blockade on the path of BOOKS FOR ALL in quite unmistakable terms:—"The South African is willing—perhaps has no other way out—for the native to cook his food, care for his children, keep his household in order, serve him in a personal way, carry his books to and from the library, but he would feel that an end of his regime were at hand if this same servant were permitted to open these books and read therein".[1]

The commission found that all the evils that follow from the negation of the first two laws of Library Science were abundant in the Union of South Africa. The person selected as librarian was usually "some local person, with the generally accepted qualifications of a love for books or the need for a job". The laymen constituting the library committee invariably arrogated to themselves the capacity to discharge "all of those executive functions" which are usually considered "as the reasons why librarians are trained, employed and paid for". Under such circumstances, "Librarianship is usually not held to be a profession; it is merely a custodianship". The ridiculous result of the prevalence of such a conception of librarianship is seen in the following experiences of the Commissioners: "For example, in one fair sized town where, as invariably, we were received with unimpeachable hospitability, tea was served in the midst of our deliberations—served

(1) FERGUSON (Milton J.): *Libraries in the Union of South Africa, Rhodesia and Kenya Colony*, p. 10.

by the librarian and her assistant who, their duties nicely performed, retired and were seen no more. In other places the librarian was not even introduced—not, be it insisted upon, through any intent of discourtesy on the part of the Committee".

Again the Commissioners found the library buildings "poorly planned, highly inconvenient and utterly unattractive". They also observe that "Fittings are made . . . seemingly with no knowledge of plans elsewhere found practicable. Shelving too often starts two feet from the floor and runs to the ceiling, thus making ladders a necessity". The same books were stocked in every library, all but unread. This tendency for every library to buy every book which its readers may occasionally require, with utter disregard of library co-operation and co-ordination, led to a sad waste of money, tied up capital in unproductive books and made it impossible for the people to have important special books which could have a direct bearing upon their success in opening up an undeveloped country.

College libraries were found to have suffered most, from the absence of a strong championship of the Second Law. The Commissioners have recorded "The Universities of Pretoria and Grahamstown have fewer books than one could reasonably expect to find in a good high school in America. . . . The quite ambitious University of the Witwaterstrand at Johannesburg offers the unique example of an institution of higher learning without library and without librarian . . . Classification, Cataloguing and those aids in the use of books which are to-day considered an essential part of a college library are either lacking or indifferently done. Every staff is almost hopelessly undermanned and quite generally with no one who has had library training. . . . The books are kept under lock and key".

Such a lengthy extract from the findings of the commissioners has been given because it seems to describe the Indian conditions with great accuracy. The hope that the commissioners' strictures on such conditions may, perhaps, open the eyes of those that have to do with the management and maintenance of libraries in India is the only justification for such a long digression. Switching back to the main purpose of this chapter, let us enquire how the Carnegie Commission has prepared the ground for the easy and certain progress of the Second Law in the Union of South Africa.

The Commission's trips about the country made it possible to convey the message of the Second Law to the Library Committees, especially to school authorities, to government officials and, in short, to every person and organisation that could be induced to stop and listen. With rare exceptions, the people concerned recognised the faults in their scheme and often expressed astonishment that they had never noticed them before. When the work of the Commission culminated in the Conference at Bloemfontein on November 15-17,

1928, the dead weight of "BOOKS FOR THE CHOSEN FEW" was buried without tears and without discussion and the only business that had to be transacted was to work out details on the assumption that the Law "BOOKS FOR ALL" was to be given possession of the land and, in fact, a scheme was finally forged with the usual Carnegie touch.

(1) The Union Government was urged to recognise the need for encouraging all school-children in the habit of reading books by giving them guidance in the use of books and to recognise the provision of library facilities as a legitimate charge on the public revenue of the State, so that the educational services founded by the State may prove effective and give a fair and lasting return on the amount spent on them.

(2) The Union Government and the Carnegie Corporation should each contribute an annual sum of Rs. 1,70,000 up to a specified period, after which the Corporation is to withdraw step by step and finally turn to other lands, leaving the entire responsibility on the shoulders of the Government.

(3) The National Library Scheme should consist of one main centre, six secondary centres, several minor centres and

innumerable distributing stations scattered throughout the country—in village schools, police stations, post offices, Y. M. C. A.'s and so on.

(4) Representations should be made to the South African Railways and the General Post Office to assist in the development of free library service by free transportation of books.

(5) Books should be served free to one and all, irrespective of the colour of the skin.

(6) A Library Association should be formed to maintain proper professional standards and to propagate the Library Movement.

(7) A suitable library legislation should be undertaken to place the sway of the Second Law on a permanent footing.

(8) And last but not least the Commission would recommend that "it is highly desirable for a director or an organising director to be on the ground" immediately to plan the proper working of the scheme in association with a National Library Board.

The Commission emphasises the grave importance of the last mentioned initial step with the words "Whether the funds of the Corporation and of the Union are to be wasted or whether they are to become golden seeds which shall produce nourishing crops year after year will depend very largely upon these first principles of library culture".

Before we leave the Union of South Africa, the present conditions of the Indian book-world call for a special mention of a step of far-reaching importance taken by the Carnegie Corporation at the instance of the Commission. The Corporation gave a grant-in-aid of about Rs. 26,000 to an existing native press to enable it to increase the quantity as well as to improve the bibliographical quality of the books in the indigenous Bantu languages.

The Carnegie Commission has made similar recommendations to prepare the way for the entry of the Second Law into the Rhodesias and the Kenya Colony. But, we may skip over the remaining parts of Africa. Nor need we linger long over worn-out Greece which greets us in her faded glory, as we cross the Mediterranean Sea.

EUROPE

But the outburst of enthusiasm that has characterised the post-war reception of the Second Law in every other important country of Europe is quite unmistakable. This has been due, not a little, to the grim light that the fiery furnace of the Great War threw on the fatal results of providing unequal opportunities for self-education, under the spell of the antiquated twins, EDUCATION FOR THE CHOSEN FEW and BOOKS FOR THE CHOSEN FEW. The democratic ideals and the social aspirations that were generated by that upheaval led to the banishment of these two mischief-makers in company with some of the crowned heads of Central and Eastern Europe. The new mental stir of the newer nations just liberated from age-long repression seems to have spread into the older and the neutral countries as well. They seem to have all vied with one another in making the quickest preparations possible for the reception of the Second Law of Library Science in their midst. New Acts were forged or old Acts were amended to carry out its message with the least possible delay. 'BOOKS FOR ALL' was one of the cries that rent the European sky in the decade that followed the Treaty of Versailles. But the manner in which the Library Movement worked its way varied from country to country.

BULGARIA

The vehicle, that it adopted in the first country that we reach as we proceed north from Greece, is of special significance to India. Bulgaria seems to show us how to put new wine in old bottles. She had in her possession a peculiar old institution called *Chitalista,* which "is a sort of library combining the activities of a Theatre, Movies, Social Hall (Community Social Hall) and library".[1] This time-honoured institution, which is held by the people in great affection, is the agent selected to distribute 'BOOKS TO ALL'. The innumerable lectures it organises on subjects of current

(1) *International Handbook of Adult Education,* p. 41.

interest, such as Hygiene, Agriculture, Sociology, Science, Religion and so on, lead to the popularisation of books, especially among the young. The Minister of Education who is a great library enthusiast had a law enacted in 1928, which has resulted in rapidly increasing the number of *Chitalistas* which were already as many as 1984. He further appointed a library-organiser and had her trained in England and America. She has a place in the National Council of Education.[1] The expert knowledge and the unbounded enthusiasm of this library-organiser are proving to be fitting lieutenants of the Second Law in its expedition through Bulgaria.

RUMANIA

Bulgaria's northern neighbour, Rumania, has also adopted a similar plan. When the time came to house the Second Law, she easily adapted her *Astras* and *Atheneums* for the purpose. These old institutions seem to have readily taken to the modern library idea as ducks to water. The *Astra,* which is but a short name for "The Association for Rumanian Literature and Culture", conducts courses for illiterates, organises study circles and maintains libraries. It has to its credit as many as 3,000 libraries. The financial handicap experienced by the Ministry of Education has led it to rely largely upon such old institutions and on private benefactions for the spread of the message of the Second Law.

---

(1) RUSSELL (William F.): *Schools in Bulgaria,* p. 25.

The financial handicap has also led the Ministry of Education to take another interesting step, which seems to be worth adopting in our country, where, in province after province, the Finance Member raises the bogie of financial commitments, the moment the question of a Public Library Bill is raised. The Rumanian Ministry of Education seems to have attempted to hit two birds at one stroke. The 8,000 and odd school libraries with over a million of volumes, which came to be established during the last few years, have been thrown open to the Public at large. The economy in administration and the intensive use of the book-resources that will result from such a step will afford great financial relief to most of our provinces for many years to come.

Another great lesson that the experience of Rumania teaches us is the futility of and the wastage involved in having a scheme of compulsory education, without making any provision side by side to supply the books that are necessary to keep up and give exercise to the literacy that is purchased at a heavy cost. In spite of the Cuza Constitution of 1866 having had a section on free compulsory education, the census of 1899 disclosed "that 78 per cent of the inhabitants above seven years of age could neither read nor write, the number of women illiterates reaching 90 per cent".[1] Such was the havoc of relapse to illiteracy due to the

(1) MITRANY (David): *The Land and the Peasant in Rumania*, p. 509.

absence of library provision. Hence, it can be seen that it is only the most reckless custodian of Public Finance that will say, "I have just enough money to spare for compulsory education but none for library provision".

YUGOSLAVIA

The three new nations of Central Europe which form the western neighbours of Rumania have taken to the modern library movement with great avidity. In each of these countries, the Ministries of Education have, from the beginning, understood their primary duty to lie in the removal of illiteracy and the provision of public libraries to keep up the literacy so acquired. In Yugoslavia, for example, a special Department has been established in the Ministry of Education to develop this new instrument of popular education. The Department has already organised more than a thousand village libraries[1] and nearly 700 courses for illiterates, in which hundreds of men and women are learning to read and write. The collections in such village libraries contain not only books intended for recreation but also those that relate to 'Household Work', so that the villagers may, by reading them, lead a happier, cleaner and brighter life.

HUNGARY

In Hungary, things have not yet taken a final shape. She is yet too poor to provide BOOKS FOR ALL, as she has not yet fully recovered from

(1) *International Handbook of Adult Education*, p. 476.

the consequences of the war, the revolution and the dismemberment of the country. Still, the Second Law is making its best efforts even there. The Minister of Education inaugurated in 1923 an elaborate enquiry into the needs and the means of effective popular education. As a result of this enquiry, an Adult Education Bill has just been drafted. The third chapter of the Bill deals with the library movement. It makes it obligatory for villages and towns to found libraries. Provision is also made for such places, as are too small and poor to maintain a library of their own, to be aided by travelling libraries maintained by the County Councils and aided by the State.

CZECHOSLOVAKIA

But the greatest success has attended the expedition of the Second Law only in Czechoslovakia. As soon as she escaped from the clutches of Austria—a name that meant to her "every device that could kill the soul of a people, corrupt it with a modicum of material well-being, deprive it of freedom of conscience and of thought, undermine its sturdiness, sap its steadfastness and turn it from the pursuit of its ideal"[1]—the teachings of one of her "awakeners", Palacky, rushed to her mind. One of his teachings was "Through education alone could the way of salvation be found",[2] and education was interpreted not merely as putting the children in school but as a life-long process.

(1) MASARYK (T. G.): *The Making of a State*, p. 15.

(2) *Ibid.*, p. 18.

Such an education meant the provision of BOOKS FOR ALL and hence "With all the problems of a new nation to face, Czechoslovakia made public library service compulsory in cities and villages by the Act of July 1919. Very small communes were given ten years of grace. By 1929, there was very nearly universal library service".[1]

The provisions of the Act were drawn up with the greatest regard for practical details. It provided for a graded system of libraries. Communes with more than 10,000 inhabitants should have a trained librarian, should have all the departments of a public library and should keep them open on all days. In smaller communes, a few of the departments may be dropped, the library may be closed on a few days of the week and a librarian who has undergone only a rapid one-month's course in library science may be employed. In small parishes, the village teacher may administer the library with the aid of a practical handbook supplied by the Ministry of Education.

The finances of the libraries are to be ordinarily found from special local rates. The poorer communes, however, are to be aided by the Ministry of Education by a free supply of suitable books. The Ministry should also maintain a School of Library Science for the creation of a competent library corps to enforce the rule of the Second Law and arrange for the periodical inspec-

(1) *School Life*, Vol. XV, p. 113.

tion of the libraries for the maintenance of proper standards. As the result of such a carefully framed Library Act, the number of libraries has risen from 3,400 in 1920 to 16,200 in 1926. There is, on an average, one library for 894 inhabitants and 44 books for every 100 inhabitants. 7·1 per cent of the population have become constant readers, the average number of books read by a reader in a year being 18·3.[1]

The area of Czechoslovakia is comparable to that of the Tamil Nadu, while its population is about two-thirds of that of the Tamils. Hence a comparison between the two countries cannot be said to be invidious. Czechoslovakia does not regard an annual public library expenditure of about Rs. 15,00,000[2] extravagant. In fact it works out to be only a little short of 2 annas per capita. The great importance that she attaches to libraries can be seen by comparing this amount spent on libraries with the total annual expenditure of the State, which is about Rs. 10,00,00,000.[3] Now, the annual expenditure of Madras is nearly Rs. 17,00,00,000.[4] One is curious to ask what is the total public library expenditure of Madras. Is it, at least, Rs. 1,00,000? Whereas Czechoslovakia spends nearly 1·5 per cent of her revenue on public

(1) *School Life*, Vol. XIII, p. 129.

(2) *Ibid.*

(3) *Statesman's Year Book*, 1930, p. 775.

(4) *Ibid.*, p. 127.

libraries, Madras does not set apart even ·05 per cent of her revenue for library provision.

Another feature in which Czechoslovakia resembles our land is in the heterogeneity of its people. They are made up of several races, which speak different languages. But she has shown that these features need not be regarded as standing in the way of our carrying out the mandates of the Second Law. She has, in fact, met the situation by a generous provision in the Library Act, that any minority community, that is at least 400 strong in a commune, should be provided with a special public library of its own, whose managing committee should be made up solely of members of that community. The interests of the communities, whose strength falls short of this minimum, are to be borne in mind by the main library of the commune, in its book-selection.

Another interesting matter in which the Czechoslovakian Government sets us an example lies in the interest with which it fosters the creation of books suitable for library use. Mr. T. G. Masaryk, the first President and, in a sense, the maker of Czechoslovakia, created a fund of about Rs. 4,00,000 for the institution of a quasi-public organisation *"in close relation to the central offices of the State"* for the direction of the cultural activities of the nation. It has been appropriately named the Masaryk Institute and has been functioning from April 1925. One of its activities is the provision of "books such as are suitable for libraries under advantageous conditions . . . Through specially drawn-up questionnaires it studies the psychology of the reader, and the power and influence of the printed word", and "interests itself in finding good books for the young, for school libraries and for youth in general. It publishes a critical monthly, *Unor*, specially devoted to literature for the young; issues lists of good books for youthful readers and organises every year exhibitions of suitable reading matter for young people"[1]. This is a fine example of all that will be done to further the library movement, by a State which sincerely believes in the message of the Second Law.

POLAND

Now, a further step to the North takes us into Poland—the persecuted Poland—which regained its full freedom only after the Great War. The moment Poland recovered political independence in 1918 and "the reunited Polish nation regained control of its destinies, the cause of education became one of the principal concerns of society and of the reborn Polish State".[2] At the initial stages many voluntary bodies like the Society of People's Libraries, and the People's School Association, came into prominence and carried the torch of library movement with willingness and enthusiasm. The

---

(1) *International Handbook of Adult Education*, pp. 62-63.

(2) KANDEL (P. L.) *Ed.*: *Education Year Book*, 1926, p. 321.

former is responsible for the establishment of about 1,300 libraries, while the latter has to its credit about 500 stationary libraries and about 800 travelling libraries. Local authorities too are taking their part. The city of Lodz, for example, has one adults' library and five children's libraries. These libraries are also centres of educational work carried on systematically by popular lectures and readings illustrated by music and pictures. In many of the children's libraries, self-government and self-management are being introduced.

The State has, by now, realised that such voluntary enterprises are too inadequate to meet the library needs of the country and that the mandate of the Second Law can be properly carried out only by legislation. A Library Bill, that has been recently drafted, makes it obligatory for every commune to establish a library, the smaller communes being served by travelling libraries provided by the central library of the District. The necessary funds are to be got by a special library rate. The Union of Polish Librarians, with its headquarters at Warsaw, is doing its best to further this legislation. When the Bill is passed into Law, about 15,000 libraries will come into existence[1] and the Second Law will establish its permanent sway in Poland.

SOVIET UNION OF RUSSIA

A step to the East lands us in Russia—that vast territory which stretches across the entire breadth

(1) *International Handbook of Adult Education*, p. 349.

of two continents. As a certain amount of scepticism seems to lurk in the minds of people about recent happenings in Soviet Russia, it may be well to begin the description of the Second Law's great achievements in that land of mystery, with an illuminating quotation from the honest expression of opinion of an impartial observer—Professor Paul Monroe, Director of the International Institute, Teachers' College, Columbia University—based on his experiences of a recent sojourn among the Russians. His description of the manner in which the Law 'BOOKS FOR ALL' is spreading into the remotest corners of Russia is contained in a section entitled, *The village culture centre, cottage library or the people's house,* in a paper he has contributed to *International Conciliation.*

"The village and rural population, not much interested in theory and not well informed, is the most difficult to reach. One instrument invented for the education of the peasantry is the 'cottage library' or culture centre, or People's House. A building is set aside for the culture use of the little community. In this are to be found a few books, many pamphlets, newspapers and posters. Much of the population education is carried on by posters, issued by the central government as well as by other agencies. These relate to all sorts of subjects: care of children, nature of diseases and especially of infections; propaganda against the fly, mosquito, hookworm, and other infections or carriers of infection. There are posters on the use of farm machinery, on the selection of seeds, on methods of land fertilization and cultivation, such as deep plowing; posters on anti-alcoholism and anti-religion, on the subject of foreign relations, and on all communistic doctrines. These cottage libraries always are used for the gathering of peasants in the evening. . . . Many of these culture centres have radios and the broadcasting from Moscow is excellent.

"Most of the centres contain a small stage for dramatic performances and serve as centres of recreation. The dramatic performance is one of the approved methods of instruction as well as of amusement.

"The cottage libraries are conducted by committees, each having charge of one specific activity. In such work is found also one of the chief educational agencies for improving the condition of the adults. One very popular form of performance is the dramatization of the news of the week by selected groups.

"In this centre also meet the various committees that have charge of the various interests of the village and its government; health, agriculture, schools, roads, relations with the county or district government, communistic education and propaganda, young communist organizations, etc.

"The question of the extent of the welfare and educational activities arises again in connection with these institutions as it does with the schools. I can only give my own experience. In the district of Leninakan, 2,000 miles from Moscow, which I visited, there are 201 villages. The district government reports that in 65 of these it has established culture centres; that 65 other villages have established such centres of their own volition; leaving about a similar number yet unreached. I personally visited six villages. All of them had schools; all had cottage libraries."[1]

As a matter of fact, as soon as the New Russia emerged from the October Revolution, the spirit of "EDUCATION FOR ALL" rushed into it with eagle speed in company with the Second Law of Library Science. Russia drank deep of the Pestalozzian conception of social education as "the polishing of one link of a large chain, which unites all humanity into a single whole; and the errors in the education and guidance of men consist for the most part in that separate links are isolated from the chain and one begins to philosophise over them as if they alone existed and as if in the quality of rings they did not represent the property of the whole chain".[2] Lenin proclaimed at the 1921 All-Russian Congress of Workers for Popular Enlightenment, "You must remember that an illiterate uncultured people cannot conquer". It was held "Unless the masses are enlightened, a rigorous heightening of their economic welfare is impossible, co-operation is impossible and a

(1) *International Conciliation*, 1929, pp. 590-591.

(2) Quoted in PINKEVITCH (Albert P.): *The New Education in the Soviet Republic*, p. 32.

genuine political life is impossible". Hence, the first fact to which the energy of the new government was turned was the alarming illiteracy and ignorance of the people. "According to the census of 1920, sixty-eight per cent of the inhabitants of the Soviet Union were illiterate. . . One of our primary tasks has consequently been the abolition of illiteracy. By 1933-34, the ability to read and write should be the possession of every citizen of the Soviet Union". In the words of the President of the State University of Moscow, such was the resolve that was made.[1]

Thus the immediate education of the adult population became a most important part of the work of the Commissariate of Education. The work involved the creation of "centres for the liquidation of illiteracy; political-cultural clubs and reading rooms (Lenin Corners); workers' and peasants' houses; permanent and itinerent libraries; self-education centres and magazines . . . propaganda work (including tableaux, plays, etc.) for special campaigns . . . Quick learners help the slower; semi-literates the illiterates . . . As soon as they can read a little they are encouraged as semi-literates to go to the local cottage reading room (Isba) or club, and then to the library. After six months of such work, a school is set up to prepare abler persons for a Rabfac".[2]

---

(1) PINKEVITCH (Albert P.): *The New Education in the Soviet Republic*, pp. 374-375.

(2) GOODE (W. T.): *School Teachers and Scholars in Soviet Russia*, pp. 61-63.

The tenth anniversary of the October Revolution was made an occasion to take stock of the achievements of EDUCATION FOR ALL and BOOKS FOR ALL in a decade's expedition in Russia. It was found that "approximately ten million persons were taught to read and write . . . The number of stationary libraries increased from 4,640 to 6,414, of urban moving libraries from 3,054 to 25,579, and of village moving libraries from 3,167 to 4,343 . . . In the Russian Republic in 1926, there were 7,250 circles in which 120,000 persons were studying".[1] The latest year-book on hand makes mention of 46,759 schools for illiterates and 50,000 travelling libraries.[2]

This phenomenal spread of the Library Movement has resulted in such a wide-spread love of reading that a reading room is not infrequently found even in the lobbies of cinemas, where the audience waits for the next performance. To satisfy the craving for reading, that is evinced by those that are just emerging from the grip of illiteracy, "a monthly journal is published under the title *Down with illiteracy;* the extensive use of illustrations and diagrams throughout the text makes it possible to put elementary articles on political and economic subjects before those who

(1) PINKEVITCH (Albert P.): *The New Education in the Soviet Republic,* pp. 380-381.

(2) SANTALOV (A. A.) and SEGAL (Louis): *Soviet Union Year-book,* 1929, pp. 479 and 487.

are just beginning to master the technique of reading''.[1]

The activities of the Publication Department of the Soviet Union illustrate the part that the State should play in the regeneration of a country like ours where more than half a century's divorce between the intelligentsia and the mother tongue has crippled the latter and has hence left the masses in utter ignorance of the recent transformation of the scientific, economic, political and cultural world. The Soviet Union has evolved a novel institution of what are called *Village-Book-Correspondents.* ''These correspondents have arisen in answer to a realisation on the part of the peasants of the part played by books. It is the mission of the book correspondent to keep the State Printing Office informed as to the types of books which have been most useful to the peasantry, most of whom are just beginning to read the illustrations which have proved most effective, the subjects on which books are needed, etc. This is only the beginning of the work of our book correspondents in the spreading of literature in the village.''[2] The systematic preparation of a literature for children is also in the first stages of progress.

---

(1) HARPER (Samuel Northrup): *Civic Training in Soviet Russia*, p. 273.

(2) *Weekly News Bulletin* of the Russian Society for Cultural Relations.

This intimate and active interest that the Soviet State is taking in the production of the necessary books to facilitate the supply of EVERY PERSON HIS OR HER BOOK in accordance with the requirements of the Second Law stands in sharp contrast to the conditions obtaining in our own land. The Madras Library Association found that grave difficulties were experienced by its Tamil Book Selection Committee as a result of the dearth of Tamil books dealing with current thought. The Council of the Association stated, "The present state of our country demands imperatively that books of an informational nature should be circulated in large quantities by our libraries. But, as has been remarked, there are very few such books in Tamil . . . No doubt, the law of supply and demand will govern the solution of this problem also. However, the Committee feels that the establishment of an appreciable number of public libraries would strongly create the necessary demand.

"The Council would also appeal to the Government and the Universities of the Province actively to foster the creation of the necessary supply during the initial stages. This is a legitimate and primary duty of the State which is responsible for the general welfare of the citizens and of the Universities one of whose main functions is the dissemination of knowledge. At any rate, the difficulties at the initial stages are too great to be overcome by any agency other than the State and the Universities. The experiences of other countries in similar circumstances go to confirm this view".[1]

The Universities may excuse themselves saying that the extension, rather than the dissemination, of knowledge was their primary duty and that, as they had not yet fulfilled even that primary duty owing to their absorption in the constant turning of the examination wheel, there was no near prospect of their developing an extension side. The Finance Minister of the Government, who seems to have been scared by the probable year-to-year profit and loss account of such an adventure, was unwilling to be convinced and pronounced that "The connection between the responsibility of the State for the general welfare of its citizens and the fostering of the publication of suitable books for their use is more rhetorical than convincing".[2]

Under such circumstances, the Second Law of Library Science will have to do a good deal of lobbying in Ministerial chambers and academic cloisters and first educate the highplaced and the learned with its experiences among other progressive nations, before it can hope to supply EVERY INDIAN HIS OR HER BOOK.

FINLAND

Let us now move westwards and have a look at Finland and her hospitality to the Second Law.

(1) MADRAS LIBRARY ASSOCIATION: *Second Annual Report*, pp. 21-22.

(2) *The "Hindu"* (Madras), October 23, 1930.

One might hastily exclaim, "What can that cold, far-off, sparsely-populated little-known land have to teach us." Finland is no doubt far off. In fact, she is largely confined to the Arctic circle. This no doubt makes her bitterly cold. She does not even see the sun for several days in the year. She is also very sparsely populated. With an area nearly as large as that of our province, she has barely three-fourths of the population of our District of Malabar. But, if she is little known, it is not her fault. She does not prevent us from knowing her. But "No one who knows anything of the Finns will deny that they are the best-educated nation in the world. Neither Germany nor America can claim an equality with them in this respect . . . The love of learning thus fostered has remained a prominent feature of Finnish character unto this day and is in part responsible for the progress of the people. There are very few of the lower classes that cannot read".[1] Indeed, we are told that in 1920, only 0·7 per cent of persons who had completed their 15th year could neither read nor write.[2]

Even in the centuries of her subjugation under a foreign yoke, Finland had seen the wisdom of following the Second Law of Library Science. But, till she regained her independence in 1917, the Finnish language had been superseded by a

(1) YOUNG (Ernest): *Finland; the Land of a Thousand Lakes*, pp. 208-209.

(2) *The Statesman's Year-book*, 1930, p. 837.

foreign tongue. It was only after the Great War relieved her from this handicap, that the national language regained its legitimate place and that there was "a marked increase in the number of books adapted to the needs of the agricultural and working classes and now there is no dearth of scientific and other educational literature"[1]. Again, till she got her freedom from her foreign masters, the few libraries, that were separated by long distances, had to be linked together only by the voluntary efforts of the Library Society of Finland. But by an Executive Act of 1921 and later by the Library Act of April 1928, the State has now taken upon itself the furtherance of the Library Movement.

This Act has brought all the libraries under the direction of a State Library Board presided over by a member of the Ministry of Education. The executive of this Board is termed the State Library Bureau and is managed by the Library Director. This Bureau does library propaganda, trains librarians, publishes bibliographical tools and improves library methods in all possible ways. Due to its fostering care, the 537 rural communes of Finland are now served by nearly 1,000 libraries. Of her 38 towns and 18 boroughs, nearly 80 per cent have public libraries of their own. Her chief town, Helsinki, which has a

---

(1) YOUNG (Ernest): *Finland; the Land of a Thousand Lakes*, p. 210.

population of 227,375, lends out more than 700,000 volumes in a year.

The Library Act provides for a library rate, which usually amounts to about 6 pies per capita. But an important feature, which is of interest to us whose central taxation is disproportionately high, is that of the "half-grant-system". The State gives a grant of 50 per cent of the expenditure on *books, salaries, rent, etc.*, in addition to special building grant.[1] The amount of library grant thus disbursed in 1928 was nearly Rs. 70,000. It can be realised that this State-grant is not as small as it looks if we remember that the population served is less than that of one of our districts.

NORWAY

We may begin our study of the progress of the Second Law in the Scandinavian Peninsula with a short review of the reception accorded to it by Norway. Although the Government of Norway has been subsidising libraries from 1830, it is only in the present century that her library provision has reached the level demanded by the Second Law. She has now about 60 municipal libraries and over a thousand rural libraries.[2] There is a Library Office attached to the Ministry of Education. Its chief function is to disburse the State grant and see to the maintenance of proper standards in the libraries. It also maintains a few travelling

(1) *International Handbook of Adult Education*, p. 122.

(2) *Bulletin of the American Library Association*, Vol. XX, p. 257.

libraries and particularly the circulating library for seamen which has deposit-stations in all the Norwegian ports. Mention has already been made (*vide* p. 85) of the part played by one of these deposit-stations in a fishing village of the North Coast in advancing a neglected fisher boy to a Professorial Chair.

SWEDEN

The eastern half of the Scandinavian Peninsula bears a more marked testimony to the advent of the Second Law of Library Science. The history of the Swedish libraries illustrates in a splendid fashion the transformation that will come over an old library system as soon as its message vitalises it. Here is an authentic account of the effects of its advent as given in a responsible handbook published by the Swedish Government in 1914. "The old parish libraries which had long existed in many places were rummaged in 1900. It was found that they either consisted of the decayed remnants of originally good collections, or that books were in good condition, but hardly ever used. . . . State aid to the people's libraries was first resolved on by the Ricksdag in 1905 . . . In the Ecklesiastik-departementet there are since 1913 two *library experts* (*bibliothekskonsulent*), who report to the Department, advise the general public as to books, etc., and superintend the State-aided libraries".[1]

(1) GUINCHARD (J.): *Sweden (first part)—Land and People*, pp. 383-384.

Thus the Second Law has been successful enough in Sweden to entrust the furtherance of the Library Movement to the State itself. Of the two *library experts*, one is in charge of the public libraries and the other of the school libraries. The expert in charge of public libraries has brought about a thorough reorganisation of the library system by the introduction of 'Open-access', by the establishment of children's departments, by the modernising of library buildings and by the steady raising of the professional equipment of the library staff. The advantages accruing from the modernisation had such a good effect on public opinion that the year 1929 saw the easy passage of a Library Act through the legislature. This Act "provides for a reorganisation of the service and a program of district (lan) library organisation corresponding to the American County Libraries . . . The Government will give 10,000 Kroner[1] annually to each district (5,000 if the district establishes a library, 2,500 if its librarian is trained, and 2,500 additional if its reference collection is adequate). The library adviser expects to organise two libraries each year, and to cover each of the 24 districts in 12 years".[2] Apart from this new district library scheme, Sweden has already got about 8,500 libraries including the 1,299 school libraries, which receive annually a sum of about Rs. 15,00,000 from the Local Bodies and in addi-

(1) The Indian equivalent is approximately Rs. 7,500.

(2) *School Life*, Vol. XV, p. 113.

tion, a State grant of about Rs. 3,75,000, while the annual issue exceeds 7 million volumes.

On the side of school libraries, there has been an equally great activity. Education has been planned more and more in such a way that it is directly linked up with the school libraries. Special instruction in the use of the library and its tools is given to the pupils. The School-Reform of 1928 requires increased self-activity on the part of pupils in close association with libraries and this has already caused an increase of grant to the school libraries. In the place of the 279 school libraries of 1913, there were 1,299 school libraries in 1927. In the place of the three hundred thousand volumes lent in 1923, two million volumes were lent to pupils in 1927. It would be educative if corresponding figures are worked out for Madras.

DENMARK

Of the trinity of Scandinavian countries, it is Denmark that has benefited most by providing EDUCATION FOR ALL and BOOKS FOR ALL. With the aid of a system of schools consciously directed to the upbuilding of industrial resources —particularly the unique system of Folk High Schools—and of a carefully co-ordinated system of progressive public libraries, Denmark, though endowed by nature with comparatively little agricultural wealth, "is now producing immense crops and making herself felt in the markets of the world . . . (and has happily) stopped the city-ward tide of the rural population and built up a rural social life wherein many of the social problems confronting rural communities in other lands have been cleared away".[1] This successful demonstration on the part of Denmark should open the eyes of our provinces in good time to the one sure remedy against the devastating "city-ward tide of the rural population" that is already setting in.

There is another lesson that Denmark can teach to those that are anxious to fulfil the exacting demands of the Second Law, with the maximum possible regard for national economy. Her library system is characterised by the most complete scheme of co-ordination possible. The national library chain begins at one end with the two reservoir State Libraries—the Royal Library and the University Library—at Copenhagen. They are, by mutual consent, specialising in the Humanities and the Sciences respectively. The next link in the chain is the group of 80 town-libraries, of which 27, placed at railway junctions, act also as central libraries or secondary reservoir libraries. And at the other end of the chain we find nearly 800 village libraries scattered throughout the country. The system of inter-library loan along this chain makes all the book resources of the nation available for a reader, no matter where he may live, and reduces the duplication of books to a minimum consistent with actual demand. This wonderful co-ordination is one of the results of the

(1) SANDIFORD (Peter), *Ed.*: *Comparative Education*, p. 439.

Library Act of 1920, which, in a sense, nationalised the libraries of the country and placed their development and supervision in the hands of a State Library Director assisted by a strong Library Inspectorate.

The same Act entrusted the care of the town libraries to the respective municipalities and that of the village libraries to the parish councils of the respective communes. The library funds made up of the local rates are supplemented by a State-grant, which is equal to the local contribution in the case of the smaller libraries. The State Library Director disburses the grants, prescribes the standards of equipment and work, gives bibliographical advice and arranges for the professional training of librarians. The State grant paid in a year amounts to about Rs. 7,00,000 and the money found from local rates and other sources amounts to nearly Rs. 12,00,000, thus bringing the annual library expenditure of the nation to about Rs. 19,00,000.

There are more than a million volumes in all the libraries taken together and the annual issue is nearly five million volumes. Care is taken to induce the library habit even in the school stage. In fact, "at each school there is a lending library, which is more and more appreciated by the children".[1] Thus the Second Law of Library

(1) BROCHNER (Jessie): *Danish Life in Town and Country*, p. 28.

Science is being entertained by the Danish people in an ideal manner.

GERMANY

Going south into the Republic of Germany, it is highly educative to spend some time over the wonderful organisation of the Scientific Libraries of Prussia, which were in existence even before the advent of the Second Law. This organisation was actuated by a desire to provide EVERY SERIOUS STUDENT AND RESEARCH WORKER HIS BOOK. It is characterised by the same thoroughness of detail, which is visible in the unique scientific "Handbuchs" that Germany alone, of all the countries, publishes in such large numbers.

The centre of this organisation is the Prussian State Library, Berlin. Its stock of two million volumes is added to, each year, by about fifty thousand new volumes, while the number of periodicals current is about 20,000. The basement area of the Library building, which is in thirteen storeys, is nearly 200,000 sq. ft. The classified catalogue is in more than 1,000 volumes, while the alphabetic index runs through 3,000 volumes to which about 90 are added annually. The staff is 320 strong, of whom 76 are specialists in different branches of Science, engaged in classifying the books and helping the readers in finding their references.

The libraries of the ten Prussian universities and four technical high schools, which are similar in organisation but smaller in scale, work in close co-operation with this Central Library. By mutual agreement they specialise in different branches of knowledge so that the library finances of the State as a whole are pooled together effectively and made to secure as many different publications as possible. This feature should be of special significance to us, where even the different departments of one and the same university tend to fritter away their meagre library allotments, by each department insisting on the purchase of a copy of one and the same book for its exclusive use, even though it may be required only occasionally.

The State Library maintains a Union Catalogue of the resources of all the Scientific Libraries of Prussia and an Information Bureau which helps the worker in any part of Prussia to get the materials he wants, through his local library from any library whatever in the State. It cannot be denied that such a carefully built system of scientific libraries has been one of the factors that have contributed to the enormous output of scientific work in Germany.

But, it can be easily seen that such libraries can serve only a select scholastic and professional few—the intellectual aristocracy, so to speak. While they serve their purpose in an admirable way, they fall short of the ideal preached by the Second Law, *viz.*, "Books for the wrangler and books for the bungler". The modern Library Movement of Germany is only some thirty years old, while it assumed a phase, acceptable to the

Second Law, only after the revolutionary social changes which came in the wake of the World War. The Union of German Republic Librarians, founded in 1922, is carrying on a strenuous propaganda on behalf of the Second Law and is trying to bring home to the Local and State Administrations the need for strengthening this new instrument of Universal Education to make democracy safe.

By far the most outstanding contribution of Germany towards the fulfilment of the requirements of the Second Law is a piece of work that is being carried on by the Leipzig Institute. This Institute for Readers and Reading owes its foundation to the persistent efforts of W. Hofmann, who has been pleading that a mere collection of books on the one side and a crowd of unaided readers on the other will not constitute a modern Public Library, which should help EVERY READER TO FIND HIS BOOK readily. He emphasised that the human agency capable of establishing contact between the right book and the right reader at the right time and in the right manner, forms a necessary third factor. To equip recruits for this work is no ordinary task and it is not every recruit that will have the requisite scholarship, temperament and personality for this advanced but necessary form of library service. Hofmann pointed out that an intimate knowledge of the psychological basis of reading is as important as a knowledge of books. The purpose of the Leipzig Institute is to give the necessary training to the library staff in this work—the reference work as it is called.

Even the most advanced workers stand in need of this kind of personal service while it is still more so with the common people and the students. When proposals for this vital side of library service are made, laymen, who have spent their youth in the pre-Second-Law days, would find slogans like *spoon-feeding* and *mothering* to turn down such proposals. Many Hofmanns are needed in our country to convince our library authorities of the imperative need for such personal service and to knock out of their heads the anti-deluvian notion that semi-literate attenders who can just read the backs of books and hence need not be paid more than *Maistries* or head-peons can constitute an adequate library staff.

ITALY

Going south, we may skip over Austria, which is not different from Germany for most academic purposes, and enter Italy. Although Garibaldi had the foresight to see the need for libraries and founded several people's libraries, most of them soon fell into disuse. It is only in the present generation that they have been revived and largely multiplied in number. For example, in the place of the four libraries Milan had in 1905, it has now got twenty. During the last decade several travelling libraries (nearly 2,000 in number) were also instituted to serve the rural areas.

The Italian Federation of Public Libraries founded about two decades ago has been doing yeoman service to the cause of the Second Law. It has induced the formation of several libraries, promoted the publication of books suitable for popular use, persuaded private benefactors, political associations, Local Bodies and the State to render financial assistance to the libraries and arranged for the professional training of librarians.

In recent years the Fascist Government has begun to take direct interest in the furtherance of the Library Movement. Its Institute of Fascist Culture has begun to finance the publication of books for popular use and to distribute them freely to the poorer libraries. The Government has also appointed a Director-General of State Libraries to re-organise the library system of the country. It has also established a Library School at Florence in addition to the schools maintained by the Universities of Padua and Bologna.

FRANCE

Moving westwards, we need not linger long over France, since in spite of her having many valuable collections, the library system as a whole is disorganised and poorly developed from the point of view of the Second Law. It is only in the last two or three years that some effort is being made to introduce some suitable reforms. The dismal note struck by the President of the Association of French Librarians, in the concluding paragraph of the note he sent to the Semi-centenary

Conference of the American Library Association proves clearly that there is much scope for work for the Second Law. He says, "On the whole, France does not lack scholarly libraries, which offer an infinite variety of intellectual resources, but which need active efforts to increase their effectiveness. Public reading facilities need to be organised in more democratic fashion and to reach town and country workers—in a word it is necessary to multiply "Libraries for all".[1]

BELGIUM

Going north, we meet Belgium which nearly equals our Kerala country (*i.e.*, Travancore, Cochin and Malabar taken together) in area as well as population. The Second Law stepped into Belgium with the enactment of the Destree Library Law in 1921. But already its expedition into that little country has achieved much. Even in 1928, Belgium had as many as 2,154 libraries, which house on the whole 3,615,494 books. There were 517,822 readers, who used 7,518,630 volumes.[2] A measure of the achievement of the Second Law can be got by comparing these figures with those of the 1,200 libraries issuing only 2,650,000 volumes in 1921. What work still remains for the Second Law may be seen from the fact that out of the 2,675 Belgian Communes 946 are still without Library Service.

---

(1) *Bulletin of the American Library Association*, Vol. XX, p. 202.

(2) *The Statesman's Year-book*, 1930, p. 677.

HOLLAND

A further step to the North would take us to the Netherlands. Her library system is quite out of the way in its organisation. Historically, the 'Society for Public Good' founded in 1784 and commonly known as the '*Nut*' spread its branches throughout the country and had an organisation for lending books so that the public of most of the towns began to establish libraries by subscriptions and donations, without waiting for the Local Bodies to take the initiative. It is such privately managed libraries that are usually known as Public Libraries in the Netherlands. These libraries which are about 100 in number get monetary help from the Local Bodies and the State, after they are once firmly established. The Central Public Library Association, with headquarters at the Hague, is an influential body, on whose recommendation the Department of Education usually disburses its grants. Some of these Public Libraries send supplies to rural areas and in return get additional grant-in-aid from the county authority. One defect of this system is that the income of a library is not steady but inconveniently fluctuates from year to year in accordance with the number of subscribers and the financial position of the State and the Local Bodies.

THE UNITED KINGDOM

Crossing the English Channel, let us land in the British Isles and examine how the expedition of the Second Law has been faring there. Though the seed of the Library Movement sprouted with the Ewart Library Act of 1850, the growth of the seedling was extremely slow for a long time except for the slight encouragement given to its support by the Queen's Jubilee collections. But the twentieth century saw it manured by Andrew Carnegie in a generous but judicious manner. This made the sickly unpromising seedling bloom forth suddenly in all its strength into a *Kalpaka* tree, shedding its fruits uniformly into every nook and corner of the United Kingdom, while the State was watching from a distance with a smile of complacence at this good luck of the nation.

The following table[1] will show the effect of the appearance of that lucky ally of the Second Law on the English soil:—

Years.	County Library Authorities beginning to function.	Other Library Authorities beginning to function.	Total of Library Authorities beginning to function.	Remarks.
Prior to 1850	0	1	1	
1850—1859	0	22	22	
1860—1869	0	17	17	
1870—1879	0	43	43	
1880—1889	0	73	73	Queen's Jub.
1890—1899	0	139	139	Carnegie's entry.
1900—1909	0	132	132	
1910—1919	0	27	27	
1920—1927	57	26	83	Carnegie County Library Scheme.
TOTAL ..	57	480	537	

(1) PUBLIC LIBRARIES COMMITTEE: *Report on Public Libraries in England and Wales*, p. 240.

It can be seen from this table that 71 per cent of the Library Authorities were coaxed into activity only by Carnegie's gift.

The following speech of Sir William Robertson, Vice-Chairman of the Carnegie United Kingdom Trust, will show that the entire county library scheme was due solely to the initiative of that Trust:—

"We made it quite clear—I happened to be one of the deputation and can speak from first-hand knowledge—that unless the Government were to endow the counties with powers to continue these schemes (the experimental county library schemes financed entirely by the Carnegie United Kingdom Trust), we would have to reconsider our attitude altogether and withhold the giving of encouragement to counties to continue this work . . . It was, of course, absurd to encourage a county to come along and run this scheme for two or three years and then that the whole thing should lapse; we therefore put it strongly before the Board of Education that, unless they brought forward an Act empowering the authorities to continue the work, the trust must curtail its activities. The result was the Act which enables you to go forward and continue the work which we have enabled you to begin".[1]

Again the characteristic passivity of the British Government in the furtherance of the

---

(1) *Report of the Proceedings of the Rural Library Conference*, 1920, pp. 12-13.

Library Movement and in the reception to the Second Law was pointed out by Viscount Haldane, the then Lord Chancellor, in his speech welcoming the delegates of the Second County Library Conference. He said, "Matters like Education, instruments like Libraries, we leave to take care of themselves . . . The State, of course, will have to take it up, but it does not take things up until it finds things going. Then it will say, "Here is a good thing, a popular thing; let us develop it and thereby attract votes to those who administer its affairs!" I am in hope that the Educational movement generally has got to that stage; the Library Movement has hardly done so, though I think that there are signs that it is getting near it".[2]

But whatever be the agency at work, the expedition of the Second Law has now attained the greatest success in Great Britain. The ideal BOOKS FOR ALL has been nearly reached. For example, 96·3 per cent of the population of England and Wales have now easy access to the books they want. Nearly 13 million volumes are to be found among the urban and county libraries, while the annual issue is approaching 80 millions. About 15 per cent of the population have become regular readers while the annual library expenditure for the urban and rural libraries taken together is about one and a half crores of rupees, which works out to nearly 10 annas per capita.

---

(2) *Report of the Proceedings of the County Library Conference, November 4th to 6th*, 1924, p. 10.

This is raised by a special library rate, whose median value for urban areas is about 2 pies in the rupee, while that for the rural areas is less than half a pie.

In fact, the expedition of the Second Law has already become such a complete success in the United Kingdom, that its Library Movement has now entered into the final phase of consolidation and co-ordination on a national basis.

AUSTRALIA

Taking leave of the island centre of the British Empire, we may begin our exploration of the East, by a peep into the island continent of the same Empire. This colony is emulating the mother country in its hospitality to the Second Law of Library Science, subject to the limitations due to the absence of Carnegie's alliance. There are about 1,200 libraries in the whole country aided by the Local Bodies or the State as the case may be. The book-needs of the widely scattered rural population are generally looked after by what are called County Institutes, of which there are about 230 to serve the two hundred and fifty thousand people who live in the country. With the aid of suitable subsidies from the State they are doing good work and have collected a stock of about 600,000 volumes, which are in constant circulation.

THE HAWAIIAN ISLANDS

From this mighty island, we shall pass on to a tiny group of islands in the middle of the Pacific.

The Hawaiian islands demonstrate the good old adage, 'Where there is a will there is a way'. The natural handicaps of Hawaii in providing BOOKS FOR ALL are many. Standing as it does at the cross-roads of the Pacific, it is a melting pot of nations. Its population is made up of Chinese, Japanese, Portuguese, Filipines, Spaniards, Germans, Russians, British, Americans and several others. This polyglot population is scattered over eight major islands and several tiny ones. Such linguistic and transport handicaps have not hindered Hawaii from coming up to the highest expectations of the Second Law of Library Science.

In fact, it has provided universal public library service of a very high grade through four county libraries, which serve through 246 delivery stations. The finances of the library system are provided entirely by the State, the annual allotment being about Rs. 3,00,000. The librarians frequently go round the islands and get into personal touch with the readers to enable them to understand their needs and to lead them on to a wider range of study. About 700,000 issues are made in each year. The intense reading habit that this implies can be realised if it is remembered that the total population of Hawaii is only 250,000. It is said that even the remotest island, which is inhabited only by fifteen men in charge of a cable station, gets its quarterly exchange of books.[1]

---

(1) AMERICAN LIBRARY ASSOCIATION: *Library Extension*, p. 80.

This is indeed a literal fulfilment of the Law "BOOKS FOR ALL".

JAPAN

Now it is time we approach the Asiatic continent. Before reaching the mainland, it is proper that we have a look into the progress of the Second Law in the Far-East Japan, which is fast approaching the front rank among the Powers of the World. The rapid progress that the modern Library Movement has made in Japan during the present century is at once the cause and effect of "her rapid transition into industrialism, of her newly acquired wealth and the effect of Western political ideas upon the masses" and of the successful way in which "the masses of the people are gradually being fitted to take their part in the expression of public opinion".[1]

After the middle of the last century, "when Japan broke with the policy of seclusion and looked upon the world, she was amazed to see floating on the opposite shores of China, a number of unfamiliar flags—the Tricolour, the Union Jack, and, nearest to her, the Double-headed Eagle".[2] She saw also visible signs of threatening encroachments on her shores. This led her to say to herself, "Change as the world doth change". She sent her best sons into the world to find out what she lacked and what she should do. When these

(1) BLAND (J. O. P.): *China, Japan and Korea*, pp. 176-178.

(2) NITOBE (Inazo): *Japanese Traits and Foreign Influences*, p. 15.

sons returned with their reports, she said, "Very well, mere sartorial revolutions and the indiscriminate bodily importations of impossible theories, made in Germany, France or America will not produce the necessary change. The only thing that can be effective is the slow but steady transmutation of the soul of every citizen, with a definite purpose and on a definite plan". Accordingly, an Imperial Rescript proclaimed in 1872, "It is designed henceforth that education shall be so diffused that there may not be a village with an ignorant family, nor a family with an ignorant member".[1]

After 'EDUCATION FOR ALL', thus ushered in under Royal auspices, had struggled to work its way single-handed for about a generation, it realised the need to seek the active aid of 'BOOKS FOR ALL". Accordingly, 1899 saw the issue of the first Library Law, authorising prefectures, towns and villages to establish public libraries. From time to time, the Ministry of Education issued informal instructions to the governors of the prefectures to encourage the establishment of Public Libraries. This has led to a rapid growth of libraries during the last thirty years, as shown by the accompanying graph. "In 1926-27 there were 4,337 libraries in Japan with 7,623,371 volumes."[2]

---

(1) SHARP (W. H.): *The Educational System of Japan*, p. 28.

(2) *Statesman's Year-book*, 1930, p. 1050.

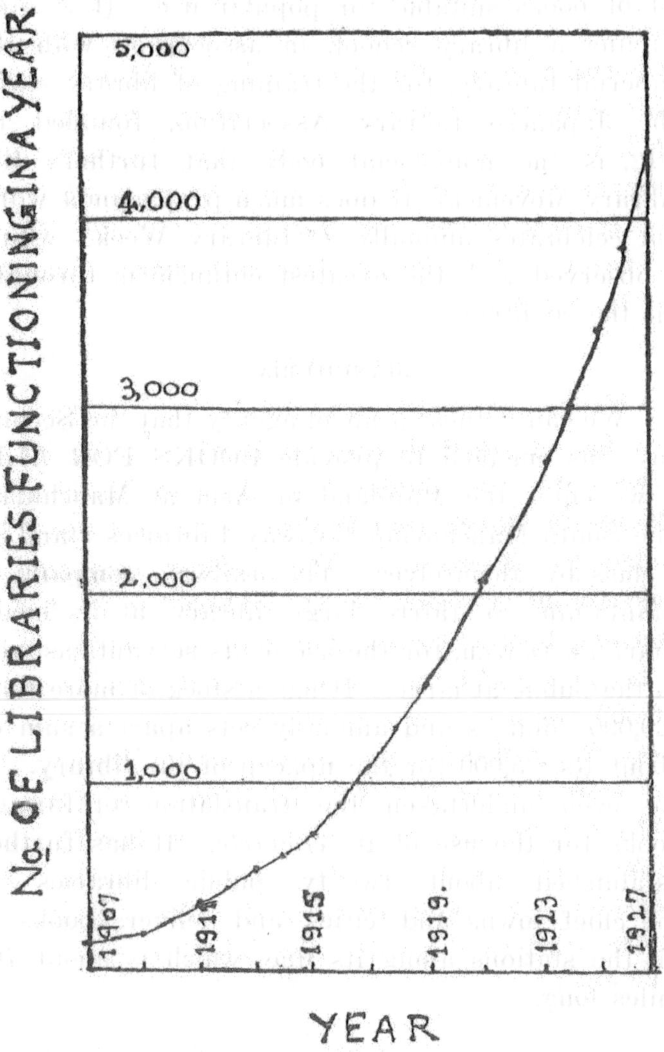
No. OF LIBRARIES FUNCTIONING IN A YEAR
5,000
4,000
3,000
2,000
1,000
1907
1911
1915
1919.
1923
1927
YEAR

The Ministry of Education issues a half-yearly list of books suitable for popular use. It is also running a library school, in association with its Imperial Library, for the training of library staff. The Japanese Library Association, founded in 1912, is the non-official body that furthers the Library Movement. It does much propaganda work and celebrates annually a 'Library Week', which is observed with the greatest enthusiasm throughout the country.

MANCHURIA

We can witness a novel agency that the Second Law has engaged to provide BOOKS FOR ALL, if we enter the Mainland of Asia at Manchuria. The South Manchurian Railway Libraries stand in a class by themselves. The railway company is maintaining a fairly large library at its headquarters, Dairen, for the use of its servants as well as the public at large. It has a stock of more than 120,000 volumes and annually sets apart a sum of about Rs. 25,000 for the upkeep of the library. It has even undertaken the translation of foreign books for the use of its *clientele*. It has further established about twenty public libraries in the chief towns and cities and delivers books at all the stations along its line, which is about 700 miles long.

CHINA

Coming to China, we find that the Library Movement has received a great impetus in the hands of the Republican Government. One of the Departments of the Ministry of Education is that of Social Education. This Department is in charge of Public Libraries and schools for illiterate adults. Another important agency that helps the cause of the Second Law in China is the National Library Association, founded in 1925. The Chinese Library Movement is being further fed by generous donations from America and from some Chinese merchants. While China has for long been sending most of her librarians to the New World to get their professional training, the Boone University has recently opened a library school under the auspices of its Faculty of Arts and its work is supplemented by several Summer Courses offered by other Universities.

INDIA

Scaling the Great Wall of China we do not find any trace of the Second Law as we wander through Turkistan, Persia and Afghanistan. In a paper on the libraries of Persia contributed to the Library Service Section of the First All-Asia Educational Conference of 1930, Mr. Herrick B. Young, the Librarian of the American College of Teheran, stated that the Library Movement "is yet to really begin in this ancient land. Requests from government departments who can organise their respective libraries and the interest with which the young Persian student is contemplating library service as a career give hope that such a movement is here in its first stages".[1]

But, as we enter our own country through the historic Kaiber pass, we find the Land of Five Rivers marked here and there with the fresh footprints of the Second Law. The ancient valley of the Sindhu has been the accredited cradle of many an Indian institution. As if to respect this ancient tradition, the Second Law seems to have chosen the Department of Public Instruction of the Punjab to be one of its first apostles in British India. It is indeed refreshing to hear, "Another recent development is the institution of village libraries. There are now over 1,600 such libraries attached to upper and lower middle schools. These libraries are maintained by the district boards with the assistance of Government grants, and are open not only to school boys and those who have passed out from the school, but also to village people at large, while the librarians are required to give lectures and talks to the people in general on topics useful to the countryside in addition to assisting literate people in the use of these libraries. For this purpose, in addition to ordinary books, pamphlets and magazines, supplied by the district boards, the best available literature on 'agricultural, co-operative and health subjects and other topics of special interest to the village community is supplied

(1) *The South Indian Teacher*, Vol. III, p. 537.

by the Rural Community Board which also provides the librarian's allowances."[1]

The influence of the Second Law seems to have even reached the neighbouring province. We are told, "Another important scheme, namely, the establishment of circulating and travelling libraries in districts was launched by the United Provinces Government during the period under review. In 1924, that Government decided to establish, as an experimental measure in 1925-26, circulating libraries in a few selected districts in accordance with the recommendations of a Committee appointed to advise Government on this and allied matters. Three districts were accordingly selected for this purpose in 1925-26 and the district boards concerned were given grants. The scheme was extended to one more district in 1926-27 and it is reported that the experiment has met with a fair measure of success".[2]

Indeed the Second Law seems to have secured the sympathy of even the Government of India. The Educational Commissioner with that Government was one of the earliest converts to the cause of 'BOOKS FOR ALL'. Whatever the coming reforms may do with the office of the Commissioner, let us hope and pray that the Provincial Ministers of Education will take early steps to realise his anticipation that "libraries will occupy a prominent

(1) *Report on the Progress of Education in the Punjab*, 1927-28, p. 66.

(2) LITTLEHAILES (R.): *Progress of Education in India*, 1922-27, pp. 268-269.

position in the field of education in the near future and that their influence will be exercised far and wide throughout the country''.[1]

While our Bengalee brethren have formed a Library Association to spread the message of the Second Law in their province, it must be stated that it is only in Baroda that it has been given the fullest facilities to provide BOOKS FOR ALL. In the words of the Dewan of Baroda, ''The Library Movement in Baroda is part of a carefully devised programme of mass education inaugurated and developed by His Highness the Maharaja Saheb . . . A scheme for free public libraries on a grant-in-aid basis was introduced in 1910, and to-day has grown up from humble beginning a net-work of prant, town, village and travelling libraries, which serve over 60 per cent of the population of the State.

''The centre of these activities is the library in Baroda with its adjuncts, the Oriental Institute, the women's library, the juvenile library and the visual instruction branch. Then come the district and town libraries, 45 in number with 19,000 readers and 222,000 books. Lower down in the scale are 661 village libraries with over 37,000 readers and more than 250,000 books; while villages which do not own libraries are served by the travelling libraries section which in 1926-27

(1) LITTLEHAILES (R.): *Progress of Education in India, 1922-27*, p. 269.

circulated 418 boxes with 13,400 books to 123 centres".[1]

Going further south, we see a few decaying remnants of a bumper crop of libraries that shot forth at the close of the last decade in the land of the Andhras but soon got strangled, partly as a result of the vicissitudes of the Political Movement with which they got intertwined.

But Madras has now a three-year old Library Association which has already succeeded in inducing the Local Government to give a chance for one of its libraries to develop as a central reservoir library. It has also succeeded in inducing the Districts of Chingleput and Malabar to make a small beginning of a District Library Scheme. It has published lists of books suitable for popular use and instituted a Summer School to prepare well-informed votaries to serve the Second Law and its sisters. It carries on a publicity campaign "to dispose the public mind favourably towards libraries and books". It has secured the happy co-operation of the premier University of the Province, whom it has induced to recognise the importance of the Library Movement first by arranging for a course of University Lectures on the Laws of Library Science and later by taking over the Summer School under its academic care.

With all that, it is doubtful if it can gather the momentum necessary to carry the Second Law

(1) DUTT (Newton Mohun): *Baroda and Its Libraries*, pp. 21-22.

through the colossal resistance confronting it. The causes that contribute to the resistance are many—political, economic, linguistic, financial, and so on. This resistance will readily melt away, if Madras can find a Carnegie, such as America and England had the good fortune to have. No doubt the merchants, the zemindars, the *Maṭhādhipatis* and the landed aristocracy can easily do for Madras what Carnegie did for Great Britain and America. But unfortunately, with some rare exceptions, their gospel of wealth appears to be still what we observed to be current in South America, "their donations going rather to religious and charitable bodies".

India belongs to the British Empire and may hope to have the benefit of the provisions of the amended charter of the Carnegie Corporation of New York. But, it is doubtful if India will catch the eye of the Carnegie Corporation in the near future. Nor have we the *Nuts* of Holland to so charm the people into a reading mood as to start their own libraries, without waiting for the initiative of the Local Bodies. No doubt we have old bottles like the Chitalishtas of Bulgaria and the Astras of Rumania. But the question is who can and will put the new wine into such old bottles.

All that the Madras Library Association can do is to be a willing ally and a publicity agent of the Second Law as the Polish Library Association was, if a more resourceful and influential body can put its weight on its side. If there is one outstanding lesson that the history of the Digvijaya of the Second Law brings out clearly, it is the responsibility of the Minister of Education in providing BOOKS FOR ALL. It is not America, it is not South Africa, it is not Holland, it is not England that points us the way to fulfil the mandates of the Second Law. It is the new Governments of Central and Eastern Europe and the old Governments of North-Western Europe that give us the clue. It is the example of the Ministries of Education of Czechoslovakia, Finland, Sweden, Denmark, Japan and Hawaii that should inspire our Ministry of Education.

We cannot end this rapid sketch of the World conquering Expedition of the Second Law of Library Science more appropriately than by praying, in all sincerity, for the speedy success of the Second Law in India as well and by reminding our Ministers of Education that the example of their brethren in the other progressive nations is but in close consonance with the precept of our ancient law-giver:

"To carry knowledge to the doors of those that lack it and to educate all to perceive the right!

Even to give away the whole earth cannot equal that form of service".

यो दद्याज्ज्ञानमज्ञानां कुर्याद्वा धर्मदर्शनम् ।
स कृत्स्नां पृथिवीं दद्यात् तेन तुल्यं न तद्भवेत् ॥
(मनुः)

CHAPTER IV

The Second Law and Its Implications

In the last chapter we had a ride round the world in the wake of the World-conquering Expedition of the Second Law. While in its camp, it would be an advantage if we investigate the full implications of its message and make a study of what it would involve if the Second Law is to be entertained on an adequate scale. The study of the implications of the Second Law will be easier if we consider it in the form 'EVERY PERSON HIS BOOK'. Of these four words, it is 'EVERY' and 'HIS' that keep the secret of the implications. Hence, it would be proper to devote some time to each of these words.

The consequences of putting the emphasis on 'EVERY' can be inferred from the common saying भिन्नरुचिर्लोकः— "Varied is the taste of the world" to which we may add "Varied are the requirements of the readers". The question to be considered is: What, then, are the obligations involved in an undertaking to provide *every* person his book? It may be convenient to examine them under four categories—(1) the obligations of the State, (2) the obligations of the Library Authority, (3) the obligations of the Library Staff, and (4) the obligations of the readers themselves.

THE OBLIGATIONS OF THE STATE

The obligations of the State centre round (*a*) finance, (*b*) legislation, and (*c*) co-ordination. Of these, the last obligation will be of help in reducing the first obligation to a minimum and the second is usually the means of defining the manner of discharging the other two.

FINANCE AND LEGISLATION

We may start from the axiomatic statement that a necessary factor for the maintenance of a library system, which can render satisfactory book-service to every member of a community, is finance. Finance seldom falls from heaven like Manna. It was only in pre-historic Israel that the Lord said, "Behold, I will raine bread from heaven for you, and the people shall goe out, and gather a certain rate every day".[1] For some reason best known to Himself, the Lord seems to have now given up such direct action and never says, "Behold, I will rain rupees from heaven for you; and the libraries shall go out, and gather a certain rate every day". Hence, each community has to find, all by itself, the finance necessary for the maintenance of its libraries. If it is lucky to have in its midst millionaires, who are guided by Carnegie's *Gospel of Wealth*, it may exempt many of its members from the contribution of their quota. If not, each member must put in his share and it is the business of the State to fix the levy and arrange for its prompt collection. It may either ask the Central

(1) Exodus, XVI, 4.

Government to collect and hand it over to the library auhorities or empower the Local Bodies to collect it themselves and spend it on their respective libraries, or it may distribute the burden between them in any proportion.

The moment the word, library-tax, is uttered, it appears to take the breath away from our ministers. When they regain their breath, they often give the standard excuse, "There will be a hue and cry. There will be down right opposition". One possible rejoinder for this may be "Do they give up collecting every tax which is opposed?" But, if they happen to be themselves unconvinced of the message of the Second Law and of the need for providing funds to get the benefit of that message, it may not be out of place to present to them the economic bearing of the message "BOOKS FOR ALL".

The people of any community are its greatest economic asset—worth in rupees several times more than all its material property. Everything, that conserves this human asset and helps to make it more productive and valuable, is of direct economic value to the community. Schools and libraries are two of the most important public institutions for improving the economic value of this human asset, even apart from its far more important spiritual value. This economic value of the people is a very real one, even though most of us never think of the vastness of this human wealth in terms of rupees, annas, pies. The data collected by the great life-insurance companies would lead one to an understanding of the tremendous economic value of human beings in the mass and the vast possibilities of increasing this value through the supply of BOOKS FOR ALL.

"Here are the conclusions of the Metropolitan Life Insurance Company on the economic value of the people of the United States, as based on the studies made by their technical staff The material wealth of the United States in 1922 was $321,000,000,000—an inconceivable sum. The economic value of the people of the United States that year was five times as great—more than fifteen hundred billion of dollars—over one trillion, five hundred billion of dollars. . . . And yet in all our discussions of taxation we are in the habit of giving vastly more consideration to material wealth than to human wealth. Studies such as those of the Metropolitan indicate the tremendous importance of schools and libraries in developing the economic value of our people, for it has been demonstrated many, many times that the average properly educated person is of much greater economic value to the community as well as to himself than an uneducated one".[1]

However, a knowledge of this tremendous value—the greatest natural resource of every community as well as of the country as a whole—is rarely realised by the general tax-payer. It is the

(1) *Essays offered to Herbert Putnam . . . on his thirtieth anniversary as Librarian of Congress*, p. 370.

business of the statesman, who is at the helm of affairs, to perceive it clearly and, instead of taking refuge under the unwillingness of the short-sighted tax-payer, to take a bold step forward. Then, he is sure to get encomiums showered on him or on his memory for such bold action, in the days to come. The statesman is put at the head of affairs just to inaugurate such far-seeing measures, not within the ken of ordinary men, and not merely to run the well-established machinery of administration. Few are the statesmen who possess this far-sightedness and courage of conviction.

As for the people who are served, if they get the books they want when they want them and if they are made to realise, by actual experience, that the libraries exist but to serve their interests, it will not be long before they rejoice to see the library item on their tax bill. Indeed the experiences of countries, where it is now held to be a worthy expenditure of public funds for the State to offer its citizens a free service of books, point to that conclusion. To give but one example, "In 1850 the Public Libraries Bill (of England) was carried by a majority of 17 only. In 1919, it was carried without a division".[1] Perhaps it may be instructive to trace, in greater detail, the slow but steady melting away of the opposition to the library-tax, as the advantages of public library

(1) PUBLIC LIBRARIES COMMITTEE: *Report on Public Libraries in England and Wales*, p. 23.

service began to reach the masses, although it had to be thrust down their throat, in the first instance.

Prompted among other things by a paper of Edward Edwards entitled "*A Statistical View of the Principal Public Libraries in Europe and the United States of North America,*" read before the Statistical Society of London on 20th March, 1848,[1] Mr. William Ewart gave notice for a Select Committee on the need for provision of public libraries, in the autumn of the same year. On the 14th February, 1850—after the receipt of the report of the Select Committee—the same gentleman moved the House of Commons for leave to introduce a modest and purely permissive "*Bill for enabling Town Councils to establish Public Libraries and Museums*" by levying a rate not exceeding one half-penny in the pound, on the general assessment of the town. In opposing this inoffensive permissive measure, which imposed an affirmative vote of two-thirds of the rate-payers for adoption of the Act in any Town, Mr. Buck proclaimed that "the additional taxation, which the Bill proposes, *at a time* when the nation is so generally *impoverished,* is considered a great grievance by the manufacturing as well as the landed interests of the country". Another, Mr. Goulburn, sided with the opposition pleading that "the poorer rate-payers, who would have either no time for reading or might live at a considerable distance . . . would yet have to bear

(1) *Journal of the Statistical Society of London,* Vol. XI, pp. 250-281.

their full share of the expense". Mr. Bernal chimed in with the remark that the Bill would "enable any Town-council, desirous of carrying into effect the views of any small section of the inhabitants, to tax the general body of rate-payers for an institution which might soon degenerate into a mere political club". Mr. Spooner "almost feared that, by the institution of lectures hereafter, these libraries might be converted into Normal Schools of Agitation". After this series of out bursts, a division was taken. The Ayes were 118, the Noes 101.

The opposition was pertinaciously continued at every subsequent stage and the patience of the promoters of the Bill was sorely tried. Several narrowing modifications were thrust into the Bill and six divisions had to be taken, until, at last, in a tattered form it received the Royal assent, on the 14th of August, 1850. A ludicrous mutilation, that the guerilla warfare of the opposition introduced into the Act, left the formation of the library to chance-gifts by precluding the purchase even of a single book with municipal funds, while the guardians of these funds were permitted, if they pleased, to incur any lavish expenditure for buildings and furniture. But it was felt that it bravely broke the ice and, however crude, contained the seeds of a wiser legislation for the future.

When, however, Mr. Ewart moved in 1854 for leave to introduce an Amending Bill, the opposition was much milder. Mr. Caldwell expressed his conviction that "the whole country was greatly indebted to the Honourable gentleman for the pains he had taken with this subject". Another Right Honourable gentleman was of opinion that "these institutions had been most beneficial" and added that his constituents "were extremely anxious for the extension of the principle". The active opposition was confined practically to the two old diehards, Buck and Spooner. The final division gave 64 Ayes and 22 Noes, although the maximum leviable rate was doubled. In 1866, by another Amending Act the majority necessary for adoption of the provisions of the Act was reduced from two-thirds to one-half.[1]

The peculiar power of the Second Law to gradually melt away opposition, provided a statesman with vision takes it up, is amply borne out by the fact that the 1919 Act, which altogether removed the hampering limit to the library rate and empowered any library authority to levy any rate it liked for library purposes, was passed, as we saw, without a single division. Indeed the opposition to Library Legislation resembles the arguments against the art of swimming. One might say that unless a man could float he could not swim and that unless he could first swim he could not float. And, yet, this arm-chair logic is stultified by the action of the man of faith, who, leaping and struggling, finds that he can swim.

(1) This sketch of the Library Legislation of England is taken from two books of Edward Edwards, *viz.*, *Memoirs of Libraries*, Vol. I and *Free Town Libraries*.

The power of the Second Law to melt away opposition is the direct result of the education imparted by the supply to EVERY PERSON OF HIS BOOK. We saw in the second chapter how a judicious supply of useful books, sent at a venture quite unasked to a fruitgrower in a village in Cambridgeshire, opened his eyes to the value of books. Certainly he would no longer grudge paying his quota to his county library service. And, after all, the creation of a favourable public opinion really consists in the creation and integration of such individual opinions.

Exactly similar has been the history and experience of all the nations that made an attempt at library legislation in the nineteenth century. But the nations that then adopted a policy of "wait and see" are like the man who postponed locking his stable door. They now attribute their backward position, in the economic rivalry of the world, to the delay they thus caused in the supply of BOOKS FOR ALL and are straightaway plunging into compulsory legislation. They seem to rely on the Mimamsa maxim न कदाचिदनीदृशं जगत् "Never was the world unlike what it is at present" and the similar dictum, न क्वचिदनीदृशं जगत् "Nowhere is the world unlike what it is here". Many countries are now fast following the lead of Czechoslovakia in straightaway putting into force a compulsory Public Library Act, with a definite time-scheme for the establishment of Universal Library Service.

Neither Madras nor any province of India should hesitate any longer to adopt a proper Public Library Act and to spend the little money that is needed to enhance the value of their human asset so as to bring it to the level it has attained in the other countries of the world.

A Departmental Conference

Present:—

1. The Development Minister.
2. The Finance Minister.
3. The Education Minister.
4. The Director of Public Instruction.
5. The Director of Public Health.
6. The Director of Industries.
7. The Director of Agriculture.
8. The Director of Rural Reconstruction.

The Second Law also was, by special invitation, present.

The Development Minister.—Gentlemen, with your permission, I shall first convey to the distinguished lady the most sincere welcome of our Government. It is significant that, unlike other distinguished visitors from overseas, she has spent a year amidst our commoners, before giving us a chance to show her the State's hospitality.

Coming to business, this conference is a direct outcome of the activities of our distinguished guest.

Her mission is to provide BOOKS FOR ALL. It is a problem bristling with difficulties.

The Education Minister.—Thanks to the propaganda of the SECOND LAW, I'm sure I can't face my constituency, unless something is done before the next election. My colleague referred to the difficulties. The main difficulty is that of Finance. I trust my other colleague will give his generous help in this all-important work of National Education.

The Finance Minister.—I shall be most happy, if I can be of any help in the matter. But, I don't see any way of finding money except by additional taxation. You know what that would lead to.

The Director of Public Instruction.—Now that finance has been mentioned, I may say at once that it is financially unsound—it is penny-wise and pound-foolish if I may use that expression—to spend annually 6·95 crores of rupees on the Elementary Education[1] of children and to plead lack of funds "for the establishment of suitable village libraries . . . to keep them literate and to extend the bounds of

(1) INDIAN STATUTORY COMMISSION: *Interim Report* (Hartog Report), p. 43.

their knowledge, after their formal schooling ceases''.[1] I don't know if the Minister for Finance is aware that not less than "39 per cent of the children educated relapse into illiteracy within five years of their leaving school''.[2] Is this economy of Public Funds?

The Education Minister.—There is no doubt that we must take a long view of things.

The Second Law.—Gentlemen, if I may interrupt you at this stage, I shall read out an extract from an address to the Efficiency Club by the Parliamentary Secretary to the Board of Education of the United Kingdom, "One of the principal considerations that weighed with Parliament in passing the Continuation School Clauses of the Act was that under the system as it existed at that time, the sums spent in elementary education between the ages of five and fourteen were to a great extent wasted—mark the words—by the absence of further provision for the children, and it is only when the continuation schools—I shall add

(1) LITTLEHAILES (R.): Educational Commissioner with the Government of India. *Progress of Education in India, Ninth Quinquennial Review*, Vol. I, p. 263.

(2) *Progress of Education in India, Seventh Quinquennial Review*, Vol. I, p. 122.

'and Public Libraries'—are in proper working order that we shall obtain benefit for what we are now spending on our elementary schools".[1]

The Education Minister.—I have read that address of Mr. Herbert Lewis with some care. I have made some notes from it; "The situation is full of difficulty. But may I remind you that there is a very great quantity of work to be done at the present time at a comparatively trifling cost?" Now, I shall implore my friend, who is generous enough to grant us seven crores to purchase literacy, to give us at least seventy lakhs, to begin with, to retain that literacy. Surely he sees wisdom in sanctioning a certain recurring percentage of the capital cost to the Department of Public Works to keep their buildings in good repair. I only want what amounts to a similar maintenance charge.

The Director of Rural Reconstruction.—I join the Education Minister in his appeal to his colleague. The library as an instrument of education has too often been neglected . . . What India wants to-day, besides the ordinary

(1) YAXLEE (Basil A.): *Working out of the Fisher Act*, p. 78.

school and college libraries, are small public libraries of which there are very few . . . These libraries, one of which should be found in each important village, will cater for the needs of both the English knowing and the vernacular reading public.[1]

My work in the village is largely handicapped by the absence of libraries. There is no means of keeping the ideas alive and making them grow in the people's minds.

The Director of Agriculture.—I may say the same about the work of my department.

All the valuable work we carry on at Pusa and Coimbatore are like pumping water into a huge city reservoir, which ought to be, but is not provided with distribution-pipes.

The Second Law.—I found practically all your publications used with interest, by the farmers at Reading.

The Director of Public Instruction.—There you are. Reading has a library. We don't have it. That makes all the difference.

The Finance Minister.—I am not so sure. You remember we had a Publicity Bureau, not long ago. That used to distribute

(1) LITTLEHAILES (R.): *Progress of Education in India, Ninth Quinquennial Review*, Vol. I, p. 263.

most of your publications free in tons to each village. That has demonstrated the inertia of our people, the unwillingness of our people to learn.

The Development Minister.—I am afraid I should ask my learned friend to refresh his memory with the recent Report of the Royal Commission on Agriculture. I would particularly invite his attention to the concluding sentence of the Commissioners—I quote from p. 90 of the *Abridged Report*, which in fact is identical with what occurs in p. 674 of the *Main Report*—"Our enquiry has convinced us that, *given the opportunity*—mark that word—the cultivators of India will be found willing and able to apply in progressive degree the Services of Science and of organisation to the business of agricultural production".

I quite agree, however, that these pamphlets of the Publicity Bureau went straight into the oven. But why?—

The Second Law.—Because a postman handing over a packet of printed slips is not like a librarian who establishes contact between books and people.

The Director of Agriculture.—I am obliged to the distinguished lady for putting her finger on the right spot. I was about to say, we spend several crores a year on preparing a grand feast of Agricultural Improvements, but we omit to invite the guests and we grudge to pay for service.

The Development Minister.—Surely, that white elephant of the new Imperial Council of Research may wait. My friend will perhaps get a better return for his money by placing that sum at the disposal of the Second Law of Library Science. We go on making things top-heavy.

The Finance Minister.—Its creation is due to the Royal Commission,[1] you quoted from.

The Director of Agriculture.—If you swear by one recommendation of that Commission it is difficult to see why another—perhaps a more vital—recommendation should be quietly passed over.

The Finance Minister.—What are you referring to?

The Director of Agriculture.—I shall read from the Report. I think, it is at page—.

The Second Law.—Page 672, please.

The Director of Agriculture.—Thank you. Right you are. Here is what they say.

---

(1) ROYAL COMMISSION ON AGRICULTURE IN INDIA: *Report*, pp. 48-58.

"Throughout our Report, we have endeavoured to make plain our conviction that no substantial improvement in Agriculture can be effected unless the cultivator has the will . . . to take advantage of the opportunities which science, wise laws and good administration may place at his disposal. Of all the factors making for prosperous agriculture, by far the most important is the outlook of the peasant himself". Now, what is the amount that the budget provides for this 'by far the most important' recommendation? Again, "This, in the main, is determined by his environment."

The Second Law.—I only demand a place for books in that environment.

The Director of Agriculture.—They proceed to lay down "We have no hesitation in affirming that the responsibilities required to effect this improvement rests with Government."

The Finance Minister.—My friend is discretely abstaining from reading the next sentence:

"The realisation of this important truth has led, in recent years, to a large increase in expenditure on the departments concerned with rural welfare".

The Development Minister.—Then I must certainly read out also the sentence after that. "None the less, we feel that its force is inadequately appreciated by the Government of India and by Local Governments and that the necessity that the rural problem should be attacked as a whole, and at all points simultaneously, is still insufficiently present to their minds. We cannot but think that the failure to grasp the full significance of the proposition we have laid down in some measure explains the absence of any co-ordinated attempts to effect that change; . . . in the psychology of the peasant without which there can be no hope."

The Director of Rural Reconstruction.—Certainly no hope. Every minute of my life I am realising the practical wisdom of these words. I often find the Agricultural Propagandist rushing through the village with his demonstration-van. As soon as he leaves the village, the effect of his demonstration disappears.

The Second Law.—If there is a village library—a live library with a live librarian—

that won't happen. To gather back the money sunk in the Agricultural service, to gather it for the uplift of the country, to convert the product into an available form, you must give EVERY PEASANT HIS BOOKS.

Certainly, it cannot be considered wise or economical to turn down the National Library Scheme on grounds of Finance.

The Director of Public Health.—The constant effort of my Department to obtain for the nation the best value for all it spends is equally thwarted by lack of public libraries.

The Second Law.—The United States of America considers the cost of her great library service as a valuable insurance premium for health insurance.

The Director of Rural Reconstruction.—I agree. One great lesson that my experience has taught me is this: Nothing is more certain than the fact that the physical advancement and health of mankind is dependent, not upon a physician's efforts, but upon the whole social evolution of the people. Now, these desired ends are not reached merely by announcing them, still less by leaving things to chance, drift or fate. There is need everywhere for an educated and enlightened public opinion. Only an educated people is an effective people in combating disease,[1] and people cannot be educated without an efficient net-work of Public Libraries.

The Finance Minister.—Is it suggested that the Public Library should concern itself with a work that is primarily the business of the Department of Public Health?

The Second Law.—Yes and No. No, if it relates in any way to the handling of disease; yes, in the dissemination of knowledge, that will save life and make the community more healthful and joyous in work and life.

The Director of Public Instruction.—I quite realise that we pay very inadequate attention to this side of education at school. Nor do we have a system of free libraries, where people may inform themselves of the laws of physiology and health.

The Director of Public Health.—That is why India's death-rate is double that of England and Wales. Her infantile mortality is about 4½ times that of New Zealand. In India the expecta-

---

(1) *Annual Report of the Chief State Medical Officer of the Ministry of Health (Great Britain)*, 1927.

tion of life at 5 is approximately 35 years as against 54 in Great Britain. Put in another way, of 100,000 boys born alive in Denmark more than half would be living at age 65, while in British India just about half would be dead at age 11.[1]

The Second Law.—Certainly it is no wonder, if we remember the wonderful library system of Denmark. 'BOOKS FOR ALL' is Denmark's motto and that has paid her—

The Finance Minister.—Does the distinguished lady mean to suggest that if we plant libraries here, the boy who dies at 11 will live up to 65!

The Director of Industries.—That remark is neither fair nor correct. All that she means is that public opinion, well and constantly fed on Public Libraries, would more than anything else support all sane movements towards better sanitation and protection from infectious diseases; and more wholesome views as to food and clothing, exercise and fresh air and sober-living,[2] which would, in the long run, increase the average life.

---

(1) *Annual Report of the Public Health Commissioner with the Government of India for* 1927, p. 233.

(2) GORE (John K.): *A World's War Against Disease*, p. 54.

The Director of Public Health.—The Honourable Minister will perhaps appreciate the view of the distinguished visitor if it is put thus: The correlation-coefficient between the provision of Public Libraries and the level of Public Health is positive and gets to be fairly large in course of time.

The Director of Rural Reconstruction.—The Public Library is in a better position than any other civic institution to diffuse knowledge to all classes in the community.

The Education Minister.—It should, therefore, be a positive aggressive dynamic force to make knowledge within its keeping count for individual and communal well-being.

The Director of Industries.—I say "Amen" to all that my co-directors say. Modern industrial progress without Public Library Service is like attempting to run a car without the axle.

The Finance Minister.—From the warmth with which words are flowing from the lips of my friends, I am afraid, I have to infer that they are under the illusion that I am quite oblivious of the value of books and libraries. I may tell them at once that *that* is not my difficulty. Our problem is to find ways and means to raise the necessary funds. As I said, I am at a loss—

The Development Minister.—Yes, that is what I feel too. It is better we put our heads together and solve the problem of Library Finance. Perhaps, the distinguished lady can enlighten us with what she might have observed in her extended travels.

The Second Law.—It is usually met in one or all of three ways: (1) Local rates, (2) Grant-in-aid from Government, and (3) Private benefactions and endowments.

The Education Minister.—The last category mentioned by the Second Law brings to my mind our vast Religious Endowments, which now appear to be hardly well used.

The Finance Minister.—That is an idea. Quite an enormous portion of the wealth of the country is tied up in these medieval institutions. Certainly we must modernise the form of these charities. At any rate, if it is done we need not feel sorry that a Carnegie was not born in India.

The Development Minister.—True. But, there may be legal difficulties in the way.

The Director of Public Instruction.—We may get it examined by the Advocate-General.

The Finance Minister.—And if necessary bring in suitable legislation.

The Second Law.—Such endowments can only give a start. But money for the annual up-keep should be found locally. Local responsibilities should be left on local shoulders.

The Finance Minister.—That will be very difficult to bring about.

The Second Law.—I shall only point out that the experience in other countries clearly proves that once people begin to enjoy the benefits of a well-conducted library service, they cheerfully vote to pay for that service.

The Development Minister.—Let us assume, for the present,—

The Finance Minister.—I am not so sure.

The Second Law.—If you will bear with me, I can prove, by *a priori* reasoning as well as the example in other countries, that the money you spend on libraries comes back to you in the long run tenfold. It would come back in the shape of economy due to the improved civic sense and habits of the citizens, in the shape of greater human-power due to the higher average life, in the shape of increased out-put of production due to greater skill in the workers, in the shape of better balance of trade due to more informed methods of marketing—

The Finance Minister.—That is all right. But—

The Education Minister.—There can't be any *but* in this matter. As the Right Honourable J. R. Clynes said once: "We spend enormous amounts of public money on a great many objects, and so much money has been expended on all manner of causes, and for all manner of purposes, that we cannot any longer say that we cannot afford the public money for any purpose of this sort. Indeed, we cannot afford any longer to save public money in this way and stop ourselves in regard to what is now one of the most important purposes of our public activity. I do not regard money, whether it be laid out privately or through the public purse, as an outlay completely spent without return, when we pay out in connection with any educational purpose. It is not expenditure in that sense, in the sense that it is money paid over and done with; it comes back in worthier forms. To the extent that we improve, say, the average man or woman educationally, there is improvement . . . The man who loves books, who likes to read, whether in the library or in the home, depend upon it, is usually a better man than the man who never troubles his head about books at all . . . It is a most serious thing for the future of any country to have a Democracy which is not educated, to have a Democracy which is dependent upon the penny newspapers or the penny pictorial, or whatever it may be, so that . . . the work has to be begun, and—no matter what discouragements you feel in the earlier stages of an effort of this sort, the greater the discouragement, the greater the energy in that purpose, or the immense usefulness of such purposes,—is bound to benefit the State as a whole . . . '"[1]

The Development Minister.—I was saying that, assuming that a careful levy of taxation is possible, we should like to have further advice from the Second Law regarding practical details.

The Second Law.—If you add to your brilliant galaxy of Directors a Director of Public Libraries, he will look after the details.

---

(1) *Proceedings of the Carnegie Rural Library Conference, November 2nd and 3rd,* 1920, pp. 66-67.

Perhaps, I may add that, even before your Director is appointed, you may get a modest library legislation brought into force.

The Development Minister.—That is exactly what I wanted. Will you mind staying a little longer, so that we may draft, at least, the main clauses of a suitable Library Bill.

The Second Law.—I anticipated this and hence I have already drafted a Bill for Madras with the assistance of some of your Directors and your Drafting Secretary. With slight modifications it can be used by other provinces as well.

The Finance Minister.—Have you a copy with you?

The Director of Public Instruction.—Yes. Here are enough copies.

The Second Law.—I am reminded of an extraordinary way in which an American State has made *crime* a source of Library Finance.

The Development Minister.—How can crime develop libraries?

The Second Law.—The Constitution of Michigan, ever since its inception in 1835 down to this day, has been having a provision whereby the proceeds from all penal fines collected for the violation of State Laws are set aside for library use; the amount thus appropriated being more than 15 lakhs of rupees per annum.

The Director of Public Instruction.—We had something similar here.

The Finance Minister.—Really! What is it?

The Education Minister.—I believe our friend refers to the *Fine-Hall* of one of our Andhra Colleges. You see, we had a resourceful Principal who accumulated all *fine collections* and built with it a general assembly hall, which is also used to house the college library.

The Director of Industries.—Another Principal, who is a friend of mine, has utilised all such *fines* for decorating the college walls, with a *Fine-Arts* collection.

The Development Minister.—Let us hear more from the distinguished lady about the working of that extraordinary provision in the Michigan Constitution.

The Second Law.—The penal fines collected in each county remain in the county and are distributed annually to the district libraries of the county according to the population. The largest amount of penal fines for libraries in one of the counties was realised when a number of officials and others were fined and some sent to prison in connection with a water-supply scandal, involving bribery in a conspiracy to tie up a city in a contract with a private concern. The city received its share of these fines and the library immediately invested several hundred dollars in books on every phase of water-purification, with the hope that they might contribute something to the city's unsolved pure water problem.[1]

The Finance Minister.—This is indeed a very illuminating instance.

Let us now adjourn for lunch. We may meet to-morrow at 11. That will give us some time to look through the Draft Library Bill, so that we may discuss it later with more intimate knowledge and greater facility.

* * * *

Extracts from the Draft Public Library Bill

PART I

CENTRAL AUTHORITY AND LOCAL AUTHORITY

1. *Central Authority.*—(1) The Ministry of Education shall be the Central Library Authority for the Province of Madras.

---

(1) *Essays offered to Herbert Putnam . . . on his thirtieth anniversary as Librarian of Congress*, pp. 373-374.

(2) A Bureau of Library Service shall be attached to the Ministry of Education and it shall be charged with the superintendence of matters relating to Public Libraries.

2. *Director of Libraries.*—The chief executive officer of the Bureau of Library Service shall be the Director of Public Libraries and he shall work under the general direction of the Minister for Education.

3. *Advisory Committee.*—(1) There shall be an Advisory Committee for advising the Bureau of Library Service on any matter referred to it by the Ministry of Education.

(2) The Minister for Education shall be the Chairman and the Director of Public Libraries shall be the Secretary of the Advisory Committee.

(3) The other members shall consist of (*i*) three elected by the Legislative Council, (*ii*) two nominated by the Council of the Madras Library Association, and (*iii*) two nominated by the Governor in Council.

4. *Local Library Authority.*—For the purposes of Public Libraries—

(*a*) the Council of the Corporation of Madras, as respects the city of Madras,

(*b*) the Municipal Council of every Municipal town with a population of over twenty thousand, according to the census of nineteen hundred and thirty-one, as respects its Municipal area, and

(c) the District Board of every District other than Madras, as respects its District (excluding the area of any such Municipality),

shall be the Local Library Authority.

5. *Library Committees.*—(1) Every Local Library Authority shall have a Library Committee or Library Committees, including also experts not necessarily members of the Authority, constituted in accordance with this Act.

(2) (a) All matters relating to the exercise by the Local Library Authority of the powers under this Act, or of any powers connected with libraries expressly conferred by or under any other Act, scheme, or order on the Local Library Authority, except the power of raising a rate or borrowing money, shall stand referred to the Library Committee, and the Local Library Authority, before exercising any such powers shall, unless in its opinion the matter is urgent, receive and consider the report of the Library Committee with respect to the matter in question.

(b) The Local Library Authority may also delegate to the Library Committee, with or without any restrictions or conditions as it may think fit, any such powers aforesaid, except the power of raising a rate or borrowing money.

(3) The Library Committee of a Local Library Authority shall be constituted in accordance with a scheme, made by the Local Library Authority, and approved by the Ministry of Education, which shall formulate a schedule of model

provisions with respect to the making of such schemes.

(4) Any such scheme shall, when approved, have effect as if enacted in this Act, and any such scheme may be revoked or altered by another scheme made in like manner, which shall have the same effect as an original scheme.

(5) A Library Committee may, subject to any directions of the Local Authority, appoint such and so many sub-committees consisting either wholly or partly of members of the Committee, as the Committee thinks fit.

6. *Power of Municipal Councils to relinquish powers and duties under the Act.*—The Municipal Council of a Municipality having any powers or duties under this Act may, at any time, by agreement with the District Board of the District, and with the approval of the Ministry of Education, relinquish in favour of the District Board any of their powers and duties under this Act, and in that case the powers and duties of the Authority so relinquished shall cease, and the area of the Authority shall, as respects those powers, be part of the area of the District Board.

7. *Provisions as to co-operation and combination.*—(1) For the purpose of performing any duty or exercising any power under this Act, a Local Library Authority may enter into such arrangements as it may think proper for co-operation or combination with any other Local Library Authority or Authorities and any such arrangement

may provide for the appointment of a Joint-Committee, for the delegation to that committee of any powers or duties of the Local Library Authorities (other than the power of raising a loan or borrowing money), for the proportion of contributions to be paid by each Local Library Authority, and for any other matters which may appear necessary for carrying out the arrangement.

(2) The Ministry of Education may, on the application of two or more Local Library Authorities, by scheme provide for the establishment and (if thought fit) the incorporation of a Federation for such purposes of any such arrangements as aforesaid as may be specified in the scheme as being purposes relating to matters of common interest concerning libraries which it is necessary and convenient to consider in relation to areas larger than those of individual Local Library Authorities and the powers conferred on Local Library Authorities by this section shall include power to arrange for the performance of any library functions by such federation as if it were a Joint-Committee.

Provided that no Local Library Authority shall, without its consent, be included in such a scheme establishing a federation and no Local Library Authority shall be obliged to continue in a Federation except in accordance with the provisions of a scheme to which it has consented.

(3) A scheme constituting a federation may, on the application of one or more of the Local Library Authorities concerned, be modified or

repealed by a further scheme, and, where a scheme provides for the discontinuance of a federation, provision may be made for dealing with any property or liabilities of the Federation.

8. *Inspection of Minutes.*—The minutes of the proceedings of the Local Library Authority, and, where a Local Library Authority delegates to its Library Committee any powers, and the acts and proceedings of the Library Committee as respects the exercise of those powers are not required to be submitted to the Local Library Authority for approval, the minutes of the proceedings of the Library Committee relating to the exercise of those powers shall be open to the inspection of any rate-payer at any reasonable time during the ordinary hours of business.

PART II

SCHEME AS TO POWERS AND DUTIES

9. *Schemes for comprehensive organisation of Public Libraries.*—With a view to the establishment of a national system of Public Libraries available for all persons capable of profiting thereby, it shall be the duty of every Local Library Authority, so far as its powers extend, to contribute thereto by providing for the progressive development and comprehensive organisation of Library Service in respect of its area, and with that object any such Local Library Authority from time to time may, and shall, when required by the Ministry of Education, submit to the Ministry schemes showing

the mode in which its duties and powers under this Act are to be performed and exercised, whether separately or in co-operation with other Local Library Authorities.

10. *Preparation and submission of schemes.*—(1) The District Board of a District, before submitting a scheme under this part of the Act, shall consult the other Local Library Authorities within its District (if any) with reference to the mode in which and the extent to which any such Local Library Authority will co-operate with the District Board in carrying out its scheme, and when submitting its scheme shall make a report to the Ministry of Education as to the co-operation which is to be anticipated from any such Local Library Authority and any such Local Library Authority may, if it so desires, submit to the Ministry of Education, as well as to the District Board of the District, for consideration in connection with the scheme of the District, any proposals or representations relating to the provision or organisation of Library Service in the area of that Local Library Authority.

(2) Before submitting schemes under this part of this Act a Local Library Authority shall consider any representations made to it by any persons or bodies of persons interested, and shall adopt such measures to ascertain their views as it may consider desirable, and the Local Library Authority shall take such steps to give publicity to their proposals as it may consider suitable or as the Ministry of Education may require.

11. *Approval of Schemes by the Ministry of Education.*—(1) The Ministry of Education may approve any scheme (which term shall include an *interim*, provisional or amending scheme) submitted to it under this part of this Act by the Local Library Authority and thereupon it shall be the duty of the Local Library Authority to give effect to the scheme.

(2) If the Ministry of Education is of opinion that a scheme does not make adequate provision in respect of all or any of the purposes to which the scheme relates, and the Ministry is unable to agree with the Local Library Authority as to what amendments should be made in the scheme, it shall offer to hold a conference with the representatives of the Local Library Authority and, if so requested by the Local Library Authority, shall hold a public enquiry in the matter.

(3) If thereafter the Ministry of Education disapproves a scheme, it shall notify the Local Library Authority, and, if within one month after such notification an agreement is not reached, it shall lay before the Legislative Council the report of the public enquiry (if any) together with a report stating its reasons for such disapproval and any action which it may intend to take in consequence thereof by way of withholding or reducing any grants payable to the Authority.

(4) If any Local Library Authority fails to submit a scheme to the Ministry of Education either within one year after it is asked to do so by

the Ministry of Education or before 1945, whichever date is earlier, the Ministry of Education shall lay before the Legislative Council a report stating any action which it may intend to take in consequence thereof by way of withholding or reducing any grants payable to the Authority.

PART III

PUBLIC LIBRARIES

12. *Duty to provide and maintain Public Libraries.*—(1) The Local Library Authority whose scheme has been approved shall, in accordance with and subject to the provisions of this Act, maintain and keep efficient all Public Libraries within its area which are necessary and have control of all expenditure required for that purpose and shall provide such additional Public Libraries as are, in the opinion of the Authority itself, necessary in order to provide for its area a sufficient number of Public Libraries.

(2) The Local Library Authority shall have power to appoint the necessary staff subject to the Regulations framed in this behalf by the Ministry of Education and placed before the Legislative Council.

(3) The Local Library Authority, for the purpose of providing sufficient Public Libraries for its area, may provide, by building or otherwise, library buildings properly fitted up and improve, enlarge and fit up any library buildings provided by it and supply books, magazines, newspapers,

maps, specimens of art and science, lantern-slides, cinema-reels and apparatus and other relevant materials and conveniences and shall have power to do or provide everything necessary for the efficiency of the Public Libraries provided by it.

(4) The Local Library Authority may discontinue any Public Library provided by it or change the site of any such Public Library, if it satisfy the Ministry of Education that the Public Library to be discontinued is unnecessary or that the change of site is expedient.

13. *Liquidation of illiteracy.*—(1) A Local Library Authority may take such steps as it may think fit for the liquidation of illiteracy among the adults of its area and, for that purpose,

(*a*) may associate with itself any committee on which the Local Library Authority is represented who will undertake to provide the means of such liquidation of illiteracy; and

(*b*) may aid that committee by furnishing such land, buildings, furniture, and apparatus as may be necessary, but, save as hereinafter provided, the Local Library Authority shall not incur any expense in respect of the staff required.

(2) Where the Local Library Authority shall resolve that any of the persons within its area seeking the benefit of its Library Service are unable by reason of illiteracy to take full advantage of the Library Service and shall have ascertained that funds other than public funds are not available or are insufficient in amount to defray the cost of the

liquidation of their illiteracy, it may spend out of the rates such sum as may be approved by the Ministry of Education for that purpose.

14. *Prohibition of fees in Public Libraries.*—No charge shall be made for admission to a Public Library provided under this Act for any library area or, in the case of a lending library, for the use thereof by the inhabitants of the area; but the Library Committee, if it think fit, may grant the use of a lending library to persons not being inhabitants of the area, either gratuitously or for payment.

PART IV

FINANCE

15. *Power to accept gifts.*—A Local Library Authority shall be competent and shall be deemed always to have been competent to be constituted trustees for any library endowment for purposes connected with Library Service, whether the endowment was established before or after the commencement of this Act, and shall have power to accept any real or personal property given to it as a library endowment or upon trust for any purposes connected with Library Service.

16. *Endowments.*—(1) Nothing in this Act shall affect any endowment or the discretion of any trustees in respect thereof. Provided that, where under the trusts or other provisions affecting any endowment the income thereof must be applied in whole or in part for those purposes of a public

library for which provision is to be made by the Local Library Authority the whole of the income or part thereof, as the case may be, shall be paid to that Local Library Authority, and, in case part only of such income must be so applied and there is no provision under the said trusts or provisions for determining the amount which represents that part, that amount shall be determined, in case of difference between the parties concerned, by the Ministry of Education.

(2) Any money arising from an endowment, and paid to a Local Library Authority for those purposes of a public library for which provision is to be made by the Local Library Authority shall be credited by the Local Library Authority in aid of the rate levied for the purposes of Library Service.

17. *Library Fund.*—(1) The expenses to be incurred by a Local Library Authority in the execution of this Act shall be met from the Library Fund, maintained by the authority.

(2) To this fund shall be credited:—

(*a*) The amount raised as library-rate, which the Local Library Authority may raise at such rate or rates as may be determined by it from time to time;

(*b*) The amount (if any) which the Authority may transfer to it from its general funds;

(*c*) The amount realised from endowments (if any);

(*d*) Any other amount that the Authority may receive for general library purposes;

(*e*) An amount, not less than the sum of the amounts appropriated from the above sources, for actual expenditure, in the preceding year, for the purposes defined by this Act, which the Local Government shall annually contribute subject to such conditions and limitations as may be prescribed in the Regulations framed by the Ministry of Education and placed before the Legislative Council from time to time; and

(*f*) Any special grant that the Local Government may give for specific purposes such as acquisition of land, construction of library building, or other specific purposes, subject to such conditions and limitations as may be prescribed in the regulations framed by the Ministry of Education and placed before the Legislative Council from time to time.

18. *Power to raise loan.*—(1) A Local Library Authority may borrow money for any of the purposes under this Act on the security of any fund or rate applicable for those purposes with the sanction of the Ministry of Education.

* * * *

PART V

ACQUISITION, APPROPRIATION AND ALIENATION OF LAND

* * * *

PART VI

ACCOUNTS AND AUDITS

* * * *

PART VII

INSPECTION, RETURNS, REPORTS, ETC.

27. *Inspection of Public Libraries.*—The Ministry of Education may by its officers, or by other organisation, inspect any Public Library for the purpose of ascertaining the character of the Library Service.

28. *General returns.*—A Local Library Authority shall make such report and returns, and give such information to the Ministry of Education, as the Ministry may require.

29. *Collection of information.*—In order that full information may be available as to the provision for Library Service and the use made of such provision, it shall be the duty of the Library Committee when required by the Ministry of Education to furnish to the Ministry such particulars with respect to the libraries as may be prescribed by Regulations made by the Ministry and placed before the Legislative Council.

30. (1) *Public Enquiry.*—The Ministry of Education may hold a public enquiry for the purpose of exercise of any of its powers or the performance of any of its duties under this Act.

The Ministry shall furnish a copy of the report of any enquiry so held to any Local Library

Authority concerned with the subject-matter of the enquiry, before taking action on it.

31. *Annual reports.*—The Ministry of Education shall annually lay before the Legislative Council a report of its proceedings under this Act during the preceding year.

PART VIII

BYE-LAWS

32. (1) *Power to make Bye-laws.*—A local Library Authority may make bye-laws for all or any of the following purposes relating to any Public Library which by virtue of this Act is under its control:

(*a*) For regulating the use of the same and of the contents thereof, and for protecting the same and the fittings, furniture, and contents thereof from injury, destruction or misuse;

(*b*) for requiring from any person using the same any guarantee or security against the losses of or injury to any book or other article;

(*c*) for enabling the officers and servants of the library to exclude or remove therefrom persons committing any offence against the bye-laws or otherwise.

(2) A copy of the bye-laws made under this section shall be submitted, as soon as possible, to the Ministry of Education for information. If the Ministry finds any reason for so doing, it may suggest a reconsideration of or amendments to such bye-laws.

(3) All offences under any such bye-law may be prosecuted and all penalties recovered in a Court of Law having jurisdiction over the Library Area.

PART IX

GENERAL CLAUSES, DEFINITIONS, ETC.

* * * *

CO-ORDINATION

The third obligation of the State—that of co-ordination—is really an attempt to reconcile two opposing factors, *viz.*, the necessarily limited nature of the finances of a community and the apparently unlimited finances required to provide EVERY PERSON HIS OR HER BOOK EVERY MOMENT. These two factors can be reconciled only by a judicious pooling of the resources of the community by a carefully articulated scheme of library co-ordination and co-operation, which should not be left to chance or to the sweet will of the libraries themselves, but should be actively fostered by the State in the interests of national economy. There are three types of co-ordination possible, at three different levels, which need different modes of action, *viz.*, (1) fixing a lower limit to the size of the ultimate Local Library Area, which is to be done by legislation; (2) fostering amity, specialisation and inter-library loans, which can only be done by informal suggestions made at periodical conferences; and (3) maintaining certain central agencies, which must be financed and managed directly by the State.

It would be futile to invest a small area, whose ratable assessment is not fairly high, with independent library powers. With its meagre income, no efficient library service will be possible. Obviously no building can even be considered; to talk of a staff with a scale of salary, that can attract and retain really able, professionally qualified men, would be absurd; book-purchase must be inevitably small. The little money of each such small library would be absorbed, almost completely, in the duplication of one and the same set of certain commonly required fundamental books. Hence, the State should fix a minimum ratable assessment or a minimum population as the qualification for an independent library area.

In Madras, we can have really efficient service only in cities with a population of 50,000 or over. There are, in the whole province, only 12 such cities, *viz.*, Madras, Madura, Trichinopoly, Calicut, Kumbakonam, Tanjore, Negapatam, Salem, Cuddalore, Cocanada, Conjeeveram and Coimbatore. Even if we agree to admit second-rate town libraries, it won't be wise to go to towns of less than 20,000 population. And there are only 40 other towns with such a qualification, *viz.*, Mangalore, Rajahmundry, Tinnevelly, Vellore, Guntur, Ellore, Palamcottah, Palghat, Vizagapatam, Masulipatam, Bezwada, Tuticorin, Bellary, Vizianagaram, Nellore, Dindigul, Srivilliputtur, Rajapalayam, Aruppukotai, Berhampur, Cannanore, Tellicherry, Adoni, Mayavaram, Kurnool, Saidapet, Tiruvalur, Srirangam, Chidambaram, Erode, Gudiatham, Sembiam, Mannargudi, Virudunagar, Tenkasi, Tiruvannamalai, Tennali, Vaniambady, Anakapallee, and Bodinayakanoor, in order of population. Thus, the province can have, at the most, only 52 Urban Library Authorities. All other areas should be served only by the 26 District Library Authorities that should be instituted. Such a District Library Scheme, with travelling library facilities, is the only means of securing satisfactory service with the small finances that can be made available.

Even with as few Library Authorities as 78 for the whole province, it may not be possible for each authority all by itself to find sufficient funds to provide for EVERY PERSON HIS OR HER BOOK. Even if funds are forthcoming, it will be highly wasteful to do so. While each Library Authority should own one or more (if demand justifies it) copies of certain ordinary books, it is not conducive to national economy, for each of them, to buy copies of costly or occasionally used books. In fact, it is necessary that the 78 Library Authorities should arrive at an agreed scheme of specialisation. In such a scheme, each Library Authority will have, for its share, the building-up of as complete a collection as possible of materials bearing on local history, local industries and other local interests. If Salem is predominantly a weaving centre and the Nilgiris a plantation district, it is desirable that the Salem Public Library should, in addition to books of ordinary use and frequent demand, specialise in textile literature and the Nilgiris, in plantation literature. If there are stray citizens of Salem interested in plantation, the Salem Public Library should borrow the books they want from the Nilgiris Authority and, in turn, if a person in Coonoor is interested in textile industry, his books should be got from Salem.

The need for such a scheme of specialisation and inter-library lending is being more and more felt in all the countries of the world. It is only a Central Authority like the State that can guide its gradual growth along profitable lines. Periodical conferences should be convened by the State, to discuss and formulate the necessary adjustments from time to time. Such conferences will also incidentally lead to a useful exchange of ideas on several other library problems, such as classification, cataloguing, binding, publicity methods and so on.

To bring out such a co-ordination and such a healthy and willing co-operation between the 78 Library Authorities, and to secure further National Economy there is need for certain type of direct State action. Such co-ordinating activities should be undertaken by the Ministry of Education through a Bureau of Library Service attached to it. One such activity is the maintenance of an Information Bureau, similar to the one we referred to as existing in the State Library of Prussia. It must have a Union Catalogue of all the libraries of the province and bring about a smooth exchange of books between libraries, as and when required, so that any student in any corner of the province can get HIS BOOK with the least possible delay, cost and worry. It must also maintain a Central Library of rarely used and costly books for lending to any library on request, so that the 78 Library Authorities may invest their book funds in oft-used books and books of local interest. It must also gather the 'dead' books of the several Library Authorities from time to time and arrange for the housing of just a sufficient number of copies in permanent custody for occasional use. While it would be impossible for each Library Authority to give shelf-space for all its 'dead' materials, it is not proper for each such authority to destroy them indiscriminately and independently, lest certain books should happen to have no representative copy whatever in the Province. It should further provide for the maintenance of certain types of special libraries, such as the Library for the Blind and the Seafarers' Library, which, by their very nature, cannot get localised.

While these activities are absolutely necessary, the Bureau of Library Service may, with advantage, interest itself also in co-operative cataloguing as the Library of Congress does; it may endeavour to publish bibliographical aids from time to time; it may be possible for it to so influence the publishing world as to improve the bibliographical standard of book-production; it may, as the Social Education Department of the Government of Soviet Russia does, collect data regarding the supply and demand of books and endeavour to promote necessary publications to create for EVERY PERSON HIS OR HER BOOK; it may also help, in various ways, the maintenance of proper standards of Library Service and be a sort of clearance house for library ideas for the whole province. It may publish a periodical bulletin to further such exchange of ideas and to keep the several libraries informed of each others' achievements and novelties, so as to excite healthy emulation.

Some of the co-ordinating functions proposed for the State in a National Library System will be equally applicable to other library systems as well. Take, for example, a University Library System. It is likely to have a Main Library and several Departmental Libraries in addition to the libraries in the constituent colleges. The chief executive of the University should exercise many of these co-ordinating functions through a carefully chosen Library Committee of academic and administrative interests, if the resources of the University are to be properly husbanded and wasteful duplication is to be avoided. The usually meagre library finances of the colleges may well be invested in a sufficient number of copies of text-books and other similar works in frequent demand.

Unless the University has an indefinitely long purse, it would be well advised to restrict the Departmental Collections to duplicate copies of important reference books, in daily demand by the members of the department and certain other oft-used books in the line of enquiry which is, for the moment, engaging the attention of its members. The departments should be encouraged and advised to draw all other kinds of books from the Main Library as and when need arises. In particular, it is doubtful if any University can be rich enough to purchase duplicate sets of Scientific Periodicals, whose number has already crossed the 25,000 mark. The executive of the University should try to invest its funds on single copies of as many different periodicals as possible rather than permit the departments to have each the luxury of a complete run of some of such periodicals, opened, perhaps, on half a dozen occasions in a term.

If the executive of the University attempts such co-ordination, it can certainly make its library allotment go much longer than otherwise and make a closer approximation to the ideal of the Second Law. Individual departments may not be able to take a comprehensive view of the University Library system as a whole and may, under the obsession of their immediate and isolated interests, each prefer to have duplicate copies of all kinds of materials ever at their elbow. While such an ideal arrangement may be worth having in theory, it is only the central executive of the University, which has to cut the coat according to the cloth, with prudence and a longer view of things, that can see the problem in its proper perspective and decide the extent to which an approximation to that ideal can be ventured.

At the same time, the executive should minimise the handicaps of the departments due to the curtailment of duplication, by judicious housing-arrangements. The orientation of the University buildings can be so made that all the departments virtually have the whole library system at their elbow. If the Second Law is borne in mind, and also from the point of view of the Fourth Law, it must be made possible to locate most of the research departments under the same roof as the library. Even if it is not practicable to accommodate *all* the departments in that way, the executive should at least be guided by the principle that the research departments have the first claim for all the available extra space in the library-buildings.

THE OBLIGATIONS OF THE LIBRARY AUTHORITY

While well-thought-out legislative and co-ordinating measures on the part of the State are necessary, they are not by themselves sufficient. The State action can find the money, and may, perhaps, be of help in providing the building. But the life, necessary to vitalise them, can only be supplied by the local Library Authority. This obligation of the Library Authority centres round two factors, (1) the choice of books, and (2) the choice of staff.

CHOICE OF BOOKS

Mention has already been made of one aspect of the choice of books, *viz.*, specialisation with a local bias. The ideal way of fitting a library to give EVERY PERSON HIS BOOK may be that of gathering together all the products of the printing press from its very inception to the present moment, from the first book printed by Caxton to the last book printed to-day. "Some idea of its size is given by Iwinski[1] who, in 1911, published the results of an elaborate statistical study of book-production. He estimated that there were then in the world twenty-five million 'different books'. We should, however, find need to correct this figure if we bear in mind that Iwinski limited his estimate to 'different books', and did not take into account different editions, reprints, issues, variant copies, etc., of the same book, neither did he include such occasional, fugitive, and ephemeral items as maps, charts, prints, proclamations, music, engravings, broadsides, news-sheets, newspapers, sermons, almanacs, etc., which would swell his estimate to an enormous extent."[2] With such a bewildering number of materials in print, it can be seen that every Library Authority should willingly co-operate with the other libraries in the country—perhaps even in the world at large—and accept a policy of

(1) IWINSKI (M. B.): *Statistique internationale des imprimis* in INSTITUT INTERNATIONAL DE BIBLIOGRAPHIE: *Bulletin*, 16, pp. 1-139.

(2) *Essays offered to Herbert Putnam . . . on his thirtieth anniversary as Librarian of Congress*, p. 114.

specialisation, if it is to help EVERY READER WITH HIS OR HER BOOK.

As a matter of fact, it may even be said that it is not so much to the size of the library as to the choice of its collections that the Second Law looks for the fulfilment of its message. It would insist that the essentially limited nature of the finance of a library makes it imperative that as much knowledge and judgment are required in the choice of books "as in the choice of a house or a wife, a wireless valve or a sparking plug. Roomfuls of books may be a mere accumulation, whilst a simple shelfful may constitute a library, the volumes having been selected and placed side by side to serve a definite purpose . . . A good general library might be regarded as a grouping of such special collections, properly co-ordinated so as to strengthen and amplify each other without wasteful overlapping".[1]

Another important aspect of the choice of books is that of going in for a large number of encyclopædic and other reference books. In the first place such books are usually costly and cannot be bought by individual citizens and secondly such books will usually furnish most of the information that is frequently sought by the majority of readers. With a good collection of such reference books, the problem of supplying EVERY READER HIS OR HER MATERIAL will be solved to a large extent. That this elementary fact has to be

(1) BAKER (E. A.), *Ed.*: *The Uses of Libraries*, p. 7.

stated explicitly may be seen from the following:—One of our big libraries managed to pull on for more than a dozen years without the *Encyclopædia Britannica,* while most of our schools have not yet realised the value of or the need for a set of the *Book of Knowledge.* Under such conditions, the task of fulfilling the mandate of the Second Law even to a limited extent is almost impossible.

A third point about the choice of books is that of knowing the readers and understanding and anticipating their needs. This can be done only by actual contact with the readers. Hence the Library Authority should allow itself to be guided largely by the librarian, who alone is in a position to observe and report. One possible danger may be due to the fact, that, under the present conditions of our country, the most influential members of the Library Authorities may be pursuing literary professions and hence may not either understand or be able to sympathise with the need that the ordinary persons may feel for books dealing with Arts and Crafts. If such literary members bear in mind the emphasis that the Second Law places on *"every"*, the narrowing effect of such a danger may be minimised.

CHOICE OF STAFF

Next to the choice of books, the choice of staff can make or mar the fitness of a library to give EVERY READER HIS OR HER READING MATERIAL. We have dwelt at length, in the First Chapter, on the need for a well-educated, technically trained, properly paid staff. Now we may add the need for an adequate staff. This problem will again turn up in a more serious form when we discuss the Fourth Law.

A Library Authority that is anxious to obey the Second Law and give EVERY READER HIS BOOK, should realise "that an enormous proportion of the general public, not excepting the more studious and intelligent, are not aware of all that libraries contain or that books contain, and even when they have some apprehension, do not know how to get what they are in need of. Few have the knowledge and skill required to extract the very best out of any kind of library . . . One of the most familiar experiences of all who have to do with libraries is to see people, hard up for information, going away empty handed after a protracted search for what is ready waiting, properly catalogued and indexed, and perhaps contained in ready-reference works staring them in the face on the open shelf".[1] If the Library Authority realises this, it will appreciate the need for an adequate competent staff to show every reader "how to use books as tools and libraries as workshops" and to make even the limited resources of its library yield to EVERY READER HIS OR HER MATERIAL.

THE OBLIGATIONS OF THE LIBRARY STAFF

This brings us to the next category of obligations, *viz.*, the obligations of the Library Staff.

---

(1) BAKER (E. A.), *Ed.*: *The Uses of Libraries*, p. 4.

There is a Tamil proverb which says that even though the desired boons may be granted by God, they may be held up by the ministering priest. Similarly, even though the State and the Library Authority might have duly discharged their obligations to the Second Law, its mandate may not be properly carried out unless the library staff discharge their obligations in an efficient manner. We are not referring here to the possible negligence or indifference of the Library Staff. They have been dealt with in the first chapter. On the other hand we refer only to what the Second Law would demand of an earnest staff, actuated by a sense of duty. The obligations of the library staff to facilitate the fulfilment of the Second Law centre round: (1) shelf-arrangement, (2) cataloguing, and (3) reference work.

The obligations of the Library Staff which centre round these points will appear in even stronger light, when we deal with the Fourth Law. Hence, we shall try to complete the study of the implications of the emphasis on *'every'*, by devoting a few lines to the obligations of the readers themselves.

THE OBLIGATIONS OF THE READERS

We have seen that hardly any library can afford to get duplicate copies of books. Hence EVERY READER can get his books only if each reader remembers that he is not the only person using the library. He should not forget that the Second Law pleads not only for his rights and privileges but also for those of others. It is usual to invoke the civic sense of people in some places by a placard with the legend "when you leave this place, see that you leave it as clean as you would like others to leave it for you". Each reader who uses a public library should be guided by a similar maxim. He should show as much consideration to the interests of other readers, as he would like that they should show to his own interests. While maxims like this are easily accepted in theory, it usually becomes difficult to observe them in practice, without the aid of some external help. While nobody is so obtuse as not to perceive the imperative need to observe *the rule of the road* if road-travel is to be safe, most people cannot resist the temptation to break it unless the policeman enforces it almost at every turn. Hence the readers should look upon the rigid enforcement of the rules of a library as an aid rather than as a hindrance. They should try to obey them as cheerfully as one obeys the directions of the policeman on point-duty.

LIBRARY RULES

One usual rule, to which readers often object, is that which fixes an upper limit to the number of volumes that can be taken home at a time. This limit may be fixed as three, or six or eight or any other number. Arguments may be found in favour of any particular number. Hence, whatever be the number fixed by the rule, it may appear to be purely arbitrary. But once that number is fixed the Second Law expects that every reader should deem it an obligation to respect that number without murmur. One should not go behind that rule and question on every conceivable occasion the propriety of the number chosen. When a member had in his possession one more book than the rules permitted, a librarian had reluctantly to write to him asking him to return the extra book. But he flared back writing, "I am afraid the rules of your library are too exacting for it to become popular and your notice reminds me of the methods of the income-tax department. I am, however, returning one book as desired". The librarian expressed his thanks for the last sentence and treated the rest of the letter as not written.

Every reader should realise that this rule is intended not to inconvenience the individual but to benefit the public in general. A library book at the house of one reader is necessarily withdrawn from use by others and the rule attempts to minimise this objection to lending by limiting home-use to as many volumes at a time as can be reasonably expected to be in active use. While six books used at one time by a reader, who must consult them all together, are performing useful service, even a single book that lies idle for a week on some one's private table is being wasted.

Another rule, which causes perhaps much greater vexation, is that which fixes a time limit for the return of books taken on loan. Experience all the world over has taught the Library Authorities that this rule cannot be enforced without a penalty for its infringement. The favourite penalty is a monetary fine of so much per day for the retention of a borrowed book beyond the period allowed. The idea here is not to make this fine a source of revenue. On the other hand the library tries to help the reader in every possible way to avoid paying such fines. It usually indicates the due date on a special date-slip attached to the first page of the book. It sends a reminder card as soon as it becomes overdue and every week thereafter until the book comes back. But the trouble about this, as about all fines for trivial misdemeanour, is that it comes to be regarded as payment for a privilege. The person who wants to keep a popular book an extra fortnight, thereby inconveniencing the next one on the waiting list, knows that it will cost him only a few annas to do so and he cheerfully pays it, unmindful of his civic responsibility. This is as bad as it would be if a motorist should take with him extra money for fines, to be able to pay for the privilege of rash-driving.

There are others that get irritated by the term 'fine' appearing in the library rules. They argue vociferously, "We are not criminals to be fined. We are gentlemen, I have never paid any fine either to my school or to any court of law. The payment of fine is most demeaning to me". There are still others who ask to be exempted on the ground, "I am a busy man. I can't always find time or remember to examine that date slip and return the book in time". Or "I am frightfully engaged in intensive research. I draw so many books at a time. Hence I can't afford to find out when each book is due". Very often, the fact in such cases may be that the book lies on the reader's private table unopened for days and days, others being deprived of their legitimate use.

Another rule that has been dictated by experience is that books of ready reference, rare books that cannot be replaced, heavy books that cannot be safely carried, Art books that are full of plates, which are, by nature, frail and easily destructible, should not be taken home but should be consulted only in the premises of the library. Dictionaries, cyclopædias, directories, year-books and such other publications are not intended to be and cannot, ordinarily, be read continuously. Further they contain such a fund of varied information that practically every person would require their use. The frequency of their use would be not only high but would also be evenly distributed throughout the day. If a reader appreciates the anxiety of the Second Law to give EVERY READER HIS CHANCE to use them, he would see the anti-social nature of confining them to his private study, where they are bound to be idle for most of the day.

The Art Books like Ananda Coomaraswamy's *Indian Art* or Ganguly's *Rajput Painting* or Hurlimann's *Indien,* not only have a delicate physique but are also very costly. Since libraries cannot find funds to buy copies of such books more than once, the Second Law requires that such books are carefully kept and used in the library itself, so that their life may be prolonged as much as possible, to give EVERY READER HIS CHANCE to use them. If a reader has the goodness to calculate the extra-cost incurred by him in using them in the library itself and compare it with the possible risk involved in their removal from the library and remembers his obligations to his fellow-readers, he will see the unreasonableness of desiring to break this restrictive rule.

Another important class of printed material about which severe restrictions are usually placed by all libraries is that of periodicals. The current numbers, which alone contain the latest phase of the progress of thought, are of vital interest to many a reader. One unfortunate trait that persons, engaged in narrow fields of work, develop either unconsciously or purposefully is to assert that certain periodicals are of interest to themselves only and hence would be best used, not while lying on the library-table, but on their personal study-table. It is difficult to argue this point. The Second Law would plead with them saying,

"Let the guiding fiction be, not that no body else would require it but that many others would require it. Sacrifice a little of the luxury of turning through the pages of a periodical coming hot from the press, while reclining on a lounge with the charming domestic setting. Do cultivate the habit of looking at a library as a place to go to,—'as a community centre',—and make it a point to drive to the library once in two or three days so as to look into the latest issues of even a larger number of periodicals, without at the same time depriving others of their chance''

The anti-social habit of segregating periodicals and perhaps forgetfully letting them lie for an indefinite period amidst the heap of unused books on private tables appears to be most prevalent in professional colleges and universities. Of course, plausible excuses and justifications may be forthcoming. But the Second Law would only ask them to look at the other side of the picture and calmly consider the little sacrifice that is required on the part of individuals to form a systematic habit of periodically going to a central place to use them and the immensely greater chance such a habit will give to an immensely large number of students and other readers, who perhaps are less influential and command less leisure and facilities but are no less interested in their use.

Those that short-sightedly revolt against the time-rule, fine-rule, reference-book-rule and periodicals-rule are not so difficult to handle. They at least call a spade a spade. But a much more intractable reader is one who concedes everything and says "Yes, your rules are all necessary. Every body should respect them if every body is to have the fullest benefit. But let *me alone* be exempted". This special privilege may be claimed on several grounds. One may say "I am a member of the Municipal Council (or whatever body it may be) that manages the library. Hence, I should be shown special considerations. One special consideration that I elect to ask is exemption from all library rules". Another may say in a crisp form, "Wherever I go, I am given special privileges". They would appear to measure the happiness of their life by the number of occasions on which they get preferential treatment, in suppression of rules and regulations.

Instances like this may be multiplied *ad infinitum.* But suffice it to say that the criterion of the Second Law in giving special privileges is not the reader's social status, official position or love and delight in special treatment, but the capacity to fully and genuinely utilise such special privileges, which by their very nature should affect the ordinary privileges of other readers prejudicially. Hence the obligation that the Second Law would throw on the readers is to try one's best to conform to the Library Rules and ask for special privileges sparingly and only when it is absolutely impossible to have one's requirements fulfilled without them.

THE OBLIGATIONS OF THE LIBRARY STAFF

Now, we may shift the emphasis to the word "HIS" and trace the consequences. The first effect, that came to be realised as soon as the emphasis shifted to *'his'*, was to understand that the business of the Library Staff is not merely to dole out across the counter the books that are asked for. On the other hand their business is to know the reader, to know the books and to actively help in the finding by EVERY PERSON OF HIS OR HER BOOK. This phase of the work is known as "Reference-work". The first thing is to know the reader. We referred to the importance of it in the first chapter.[1] We also referred, in the third chapter,[2] to the only systematic way in which this power can be acquired and in which it is sought to be acquired in Germany by the work that is being carried on in the 'Leipzig Institute for Readers and Reading".

REFERENCE WORK

It needs to be emphasised that 'Reference work' cannot be done without special training and intensive experience. The laymen, who manage our libraries, seldom realise this obligation that the Second Law throws on the Library Staff but act on the assumption that any S. S. L. C.-holder will do for library work. But even they know that the holding of the S. S. L. C. does not qualify one to run a locomotive and that good manners and common sense are not all that is required for the practice of medicine. But since they regard library work as mechanically handing out books, the existence elsewhere of library schools, of degree courses in library science and of a Chair of Library Science in a University like Gottingen, is a puzzle to them.

(1) *Cf.* pp. 63-67.

(2) *Cf.* pp. 207-208.

They may be still more puzzled if they are told that libraries are now beginning to employ "readers' advisers" to whom readers may apply for aid in FINDING THEIR BOOKS. They may even object that such advisory service smells too much of school-mastering, whereas the adult learner must depend on himself. The reply that western countries give to such an objection would be "A man must digest his food in his own stomach, but that is no reason for refusing to cook it or for withholding knife, fork and spoon".[1]

Next to knowing the readers, the Library Staff have to realise that they exist for readers. They have to find out how much help could be given to EVERY READER TO FIND HIS BOOK without going beyond the limits of common sense and without becoming private secretaries or private tutors. The following extract from a book-mark with the legend *purposeful reading*, issued by Detroit Public Library, throws much light upon the way in which this obligation should be discharged by the Library Staff. It says that the library's *Educational Counsellor for Readers* will devote "his time to the more intimate discussion of books and reading with those who may wish to know of the book journeys of some one else. His position will be, not that of an instructor, but of a sharer of good things, who will likewise enjoy hearing of the pleasures of other adventurers. Further more

(1) BOSTWICK (Arthur E.): *The Public Library in the United States*, p. 51.

a large part of his time will be devoted to giving talks on books and other aids to readers wherever he may be called upon to do so by organisations interested in either general or specific intellectual pursuits"[1]

If the obligation, that the emphasis on the '*his*' in the Second Law throws on the Library Staff, is to be interpreted in such an ideal way, it can be easily realised that the necessary knowledge of books and book-collections should be very vast and thorough. While what may be learnt from the backs of books or what may be remembered by shape, size, colour, location and other associations may be of some help, they cannot be sufficient. When books are added in hundreds, week by week, however retentive may be the memory, one loses track of the accessions and the mind cannot hold all the titles.

Again it is a peculiar sort of knowledge that is needed to find for EVERY PERSON HIS BOOK. People at all levels will seek the help of the Library Staff to find their books. It may be a freshman that wants help to prepare for the scholarship examination; it may be a senior student who wants to lead a debate on *feminism;* it may be a professor who wants to settle a point in the phonology of the Dravidian vowel system; it may be a physicist who wants the book that will give him just enough and no more of *Matrices* to

(1) *Some Impressions of the Public Library System of America*, pp. 45-46.

understand Heisenberg's treatment of Wave Mechanics. Here are some typical topics on which queries were received in the course of one month. They will give some idea of the range and difficulty of the work:—

(1) The method of calculating the quantity of sun's heat that will fall in a year on the sides of a wall in the latitude of Madras;

(2) The advantages of pile foundations;

(3) Methods of utilising waste-products;

(4) The parts of Central India where iron deposits are said to be likely;

(5) Tamil-English equivalents of the names of plants;

(6) The vitamin content of the common Madras dishes;

(7) An authoritative account of the Hindu *Karma* theory;

(8) A readable book on *behaviourism;*

(9) The best book on 'Statistics' for teachers' use;

(10) Information about the coastal survey of Bombay and in particular about the silting up of the old harbours of the Kathiawar Peninsula;

(11) The number of electors and of those who actually polled during the last three general elections in each constituency;

(12) The quantity of monazite mined in the different countries of the world in 1929;

(13) A picture of a Roman Villa;

(14) An account of the conventions about flying corresponding to the Rule of the Road and a Code of Air-laws.

No person can depend on his memory to say what his library resources are on such a bewildering range of subjects. The Library Staff have necessarily to depend on certain recognised mechanical aids, to discharge their obligations in helping EVERY PERSON TO FIND HIS BOOK.

BIBLIOGRAPHY

The first tool consists of published bibliographies. The word *Bibliography* is a source of great confusion to many people. Murray's *New English Dictionary* mentions four different uses of this term. We are here concerned only with the fourth use given therein, *viz.*: "A list of the books of a particular author, printer, or country, or of those dealing with any particular theme; the literature of a subject".

One result of this aspect of the Second Law has been that hardly any subject is now unprovided with a bibliography. In addition to the select bibliography, that it has now become the practice to append to each book, there are several general bibliographies as well as those on specific subjects. John Minto's *Reference Books* published by the Library Association in 1929, is a good guide from which the important bibliographical books required for a library may be selected.

The obligation that the Second Law would impose on the Library Staff is that they should acquaint themselves with the scope and structure of such bibliographical books. It is only close and systematic study and frequent use that will secure for the staff the necessary facility in using them quickly and effectively. It is seldom that the arrangement is similar in different bibliographies. This makes the work of the Library Staff all the more arduous.

REFERENCE BOOKS

Another class of books of which the Library Staff should cultivate an intimate knowledge is that of ready reference books, such as atlases, dictionaries, directories, encyclopædias and year-books. There are now many such reference books in the field. In fact, most of the major subjects and even some of their minor sub-divisions have been provided with ready reference books. Many readers are not aware either of their existence or of the extent to which they furnish information. The requirements of the Second Law can be fulfilled to a remarkable degree, if the Library Staff have made a special study of the contents of such reference books. There can be nothing more embarrassing to a librarian than to say that he cannot find for a reader the information he seeks. But the frequency of such embarrassing situations can be considerably reduced if he acquires thorough familiarity with a representative set of reference books. Indeed, the percentage of readers that could be satisfied with the material culled by a skilful librarian from such publications is amazingly large.

CATALOGUE

A third obligation that the Second Law would impose on the Library Staff refers to the catalogue. Books are mostly of a composite nature. Very few of them really are of the 'monograph' type. While there may be a primary subject pertaining to a book, it generally deals with several other subsidiary subjects as well. It may happen quite often that the treatment which a subject receives in a book in which it occupies a subsidiary place is of just the kind that a reader requires. The chapter on Vectors—a sub-division of Mathematics —contained in Haas's *Theoretical Physics* is just the kind of treatment that many students of Mathematics may be seeking. Mrs. Manning's *Ancient and Medieval India,* which should naturally be placed in the division of Cultural History, contains chapters giving a clear synopsis and criticism of the outstanding works in Sanskrit Literature. It contains also a good exposition of the different schools of Indian Philosophy. Perhaps, the pages devoted to the theory of classification of biological sciences in J. A. Thomson's *Introduction to Science,* will be of utmost interest to students of classification. Many of the anthropological books contain much information of philological interest. They give not infrequently complete vocabularies.

The Second Law would throw on the Library Staff the burden of readily helping the reader to find HIS MATERIALS from all possible books housed in the library. This obligation can be discharged only by making the catalogue fully analytic and giving profuse subject cross-references. It would be impossible for any individual, however gifted, to carry all such information in his head. If the cross-references are not made sufficiently full, the library may have to turn away many readers unserved, while the materials sought by them are standing silently on the shelves.

CHAPTER V

The Third Law

We shall now pass on to a consideration of the Third Law. While it resembles the First Law in making its approach from the side of the books, it is in a sense a complement to the Second Law. While the Second Law concerned itself with the task of finding for every reader his appropriate book, the Third Law would urge that an appropriate reader should be found for every book. In fact, the Third Law is 'EVERY BOOK ITS READER'.

While the First Law revolutionised the outlook of the libraries, the Third Law would make that revolution as thorough as possible. It will be seen, further, that the implications of the Third Law are not less exacting than those of the Second Law. We shall devote this chapter to an account of the different devices employed by libraries to fulfil the requirements of the Third Law.

Perhaps a cynic may suggest the obvious device of having as few books as possible in the library. But such a device is ruled out by the extensive requirements of the Second Law; and its inconsistency with the Fifth Law will become apparent in a later chapter. The most prominent of the devices employed by libraries to satisfy the Third

Law is the *'Open Access System'*. The other devices relate to shelf-arrangement, catalogue entries, reference work, the opening of certain popular departments, publicity methods, and extension work.

THE OPEN ACCESS SYSTEM

By 'Open Access' is meant the opportunity to see and examine the book collection with as much freedom as in one's own private library. In an open access library, the reader is permitted to wander among the books and lay his hands on any of them at his will and pleasure. The powerful service that this system renders to the Third Law can be realised by those who have watched a library change from a 'Closed' to an 'Open Access' state. It is a matter of common experience that the change increases the number of volumes drawn for use. More important than that is the frequency with which readers 'make discoveries'. Not a day passes without some readers exclaiming with an agreeable surprise "I didn't know that you had this book!" It was only the other day that I found a student picking out Roland K. Wilson's *The Province of the State* from the shelf, where it had had about eight years' undisturbed rest prior to the introduction of the open access system. I asked the student who recommended the book to him. He said he did not know of the existence of the book and that he hit upon it by sheer chance, as he was browsing round in the Politics region. This chance occurs almost every minute in an open access library.

Here is another telling instance. The secretary of the local Teachers' Guild asked me for materials bearing on Secondary Education and Matriculation. I took him round the shelves to show him some of the presidential addresses of the Education Section of the British Association for the Advancement of Science. As I was pulling out the volumes and scanning the nature of the presidential addresses, the secretary, who was browsing round the neighbouring shelves, came back with a peculiar glee, exclaiming 'I have found out what I wanted'. He had a thin red quarto in his hand. It was Volume I, No. 1 of the *Universities Review.* An article in it entitled *The Dandelion and the Jack* contained just the idea he wanted. This red volume had been lying on the shelves for some months quite untouched by the hand of any but the peon on dusting duty. But for the introduction of the open access system, probably it should have remained like that for ages without ever finding its reader.

If there is faith in the Third Law, it is as absurd and as ineffective for a library to deny open access and simply offer to produce any book on request, as it would be for a busy store to lock up its wares in wooden cupboards and expect its wares to sell. The store, which is anxious to see every one of its things pass into the customers' hands, allows complete open access even to its tiny articles. Customers are allowed to come in crowds, browse round and handle any article. It looks on all people as potential customers and in its anxiety to find a buyer for every article, apparently lets the people loose inside its premises. Any visitor to that shop is sure to be convinced of the efficacy and the wisdom of that method. Exactly, the same method should be adopted by a library that wants to find a reader for every book on its shelves

It is a matter of common experience that the majority of readers do not know their requirements and that their interests take a definite shape only after seeing and handling a well-arranged collection of books. This factor came to be recognised only during the last 10 or 15 years in Great Britain. But in America, where the sway of the Third Law established itself even earlier, 'Open Access' had been brought into the service of that law even before the close of the nineteenth century. That a long view should be taken by the library authorities with regard to 'Open Access' is illustrated by the following extract describing the then new American tendency[1]:—

"As a rule the newer libraries are allowing a great amount of freedom in direct access to shelves on the part of all users of the library. Many of the more recent buildings have been planned so that the visitor may go directly to the shelves, and many of the older buildings have been remodelled to permit this practice. In almost every way this has been a gain. There has come with it no small loss of books. But that loss is insigni-

(1) *Popular Science Monthly*, 1904.

ficant in view of the greatly increased use of the libraries which has resulted from easy contact with books.''

Thus the sway of the Third Law has even convinced the Library Authorities of the wisdom of acquiescing in the unavoidable loss and sacrifice of a few volumes to increase the chances for securing for EVERY BOOK ITS READER. But let not this remark mislead one to infer that a heavy loss of books from year to year is a necessary concomitant of the 'Open Access' system. On the other hand, experience shows that the loss from theft is really negligible. A proper measure of the theft is the percentage of the number of books lost to the number of books issued in a year. Using such a measure, Miss Isabel Ely Lord, the Librarian of Pratt Institute Free Library, has demonstrated with elaborate statistics[1] that the theft in 'Open Access' libraries is not much greater than in 'Closed' libraries. She estimated the mean loss per year as "17 in every 10,000 circulated".[2]

Again where a theft occurs, it is almost invariably the act of some one or two deliberate and persistent thieves. "The general public are not thieves. Thieves from libraries are a class like burglars. One man commits a large number of burglaries and creates a great deal of trouble; but this does not prove that the whole population of a

(1) JANZOW (Laura M.): *The Library Without the Walls*, pp. 204-213.

(2) *Ibid.*, p. 207.

village or town is burglariously inclined. The benefit of open shelves is indisputable, and the probable loss of two or three hundred books per annum at a total cost of perhaps $150 may be considered small, if the salaries which would be required for one and possibly two more assistants, not to mention page-boys, etc., had to be paid".[1] Perhaps, we in the tropics may add that the loss is small when compared with the loss due to the perishing of paper and the ravages of insects, provided certain safeguards against thefts are introduced.

SHELF ARRANGEMENT

Even in an open access library, the chances for the fulfilment of the Third Law can be made or marred by the principle adopted for the arrangement of books on the shelves. Arrangement by size or (except in literature) by the alphabetic order of the author's name is as arbitrary as arrangement by the colour of the cover. Ordinarily, it is not the size of a book or its author (except in literature) that determines the kind of person that will use it. It is its subject-matter. Hence, it is by the subject-matter that the books should be arranged on the shelves if they are to be given a reasonable chance to find their readers. A well articulated classified arrangement of the books on a subject basis is what the Third Law would recommend. It can be easily seen that, if all the dozen books that the library may possess on, say, Alternating

(1) JANZOW (Laura M.): *The Library Without the Walls*, p. 187.

Currents are kept together and in close proximity to the other books on Electrical Engineering, there will be a much greater probability for each of them to be picked up by a reader than when they are scattered among perhaps a hundred thousand volumes, in accordance with the freak of the alphabet building up the names of authors.

The subject-matter of the book is not, however, the only factor that can arrest the attention of the visitors of the library. Psychologists tell us that[1] 'recency' is an important factor in securing attention. The Third Law would expect the library staff to exploit this factor as well, in the arrangement of books on the shelves and it is now a common practice in libraries to have a separate 'Recent Additions Shelf' very near the entrance. The soundness of the psychologist's dictum about 'recency' is usually well demonstrated by the rapidity with which the Recent Additions Shelf gets emptied. It is this shelf that invariably gives the maximum satisfaction to the modern librarian, who, under the influence of the Third Law, is greatly worried by the books that won't leave the shelves.

'Novelty' in shelf-arrangement is another means, not infrequently adopted to attract the attention of the visitors to books that need help in finding their readers. An occasional redistribution of the contents of shelves may help in establishing fresh contacts between men and books. Another usual device employed in this connection is the location of small attractive show cases with books in strategic positions of the reading-room and the stack-room labelled with catching legends like 'Books worth looking into', 'Books of the hour', 'Interesting books recently unearthed' 'Long-forgotten but useful books' and so on.

Another important factor in shelf-arrangement which has a decided effect on the chance of a book to get its reader is its easy accessibility or otherwise. Books within the comfortable reach of a reader of average height are much better used. I have experimented with an assorted set of books by placing them for a few weeks on the top-most shelf, which is 6½ feet from the ground, on the bottom-most shelf, which is only 6 inches from the ground, and on the intermediate shelves. The books found readers more frequently while on the intermediate shelves than while on the others. Shelves at a height greater than 6½ ft. are a standing defiance of the Third Law. The Third Law would insist that the top-most shelf of a book rack should be within the easy reach of a man of average height standing on the floor. Similarly, shelves broader than what is necessary to hold one row of books are great sources of temptation for the library staff to arrange two rows on them one behind the other, with the result that the books of the hind row are denied the chance to get their readers. A specification for a book rack of right dimensions possessing certain other features that are necessary in the light of the other Laws of Library Science is given in the appendix.

CATALOGUE ENTRIES

While well thought out shelf-arrangement is necessary, it is by no means sufficient to get for EVERY BOOK ITS READER. The catalogue also can be of immense help in this matter.

It even occasionally happens that a reader is more favourably impressed about the usefulness of a book when he sees its catalogue entry, although its size, get-up and other features might lead him to overlook it while examining the shelf. This may look strange but experience shows that it does happen. Perhaps, a recent occurrence may be cited as an example. A scholar asked one day for material on migration of population. He was taken to the shelf containing the books on the subject. There were at the most two dozen volumes. He turned them through and a little later he was helped to examine the catalogue cards relating to that class—particularly the red cross-reference cards. But, his attention was arrested by a couple of titles on the white main cards themselves and he eagerly said 'Where are these two books? I did not find them on the shelf'. But the books were actually there. They were thin unprepossessing pamphlets published by the National Research Council.[1]

---

(1) *Viz.*, Reprint and Circular Series:—

No. 48, *The Work of the Committee on Scientific Problems of Human Migration.*

After looking into them he found them so interesting that he felt thankful that he was taken to the catalogue, as he would have otherwise missed those two useful publications on account of their thinness and unimposing appearance. Here it must be remembered that the reader was one who was an experienced researcher, whose daily work should have involved the scanning of the shelves of libraries.

Apart from this general service of the catalogue to the cause of the Third Law, there are certain classes of catalogue entries which are specially conducive to the fulfilment of the Third Law. They are Series Entries and Subject Cross-Reference Entries. The Series Entry in the catalogue enters a book under the name of the *Series* to which it belongs, if it belongs to a serial publication. It occurs in the alphabetical index part of the catalogue. In the sequence of cards, all the cards with the same series as the heading are brought together, so that it discloses at once all the books that belong to the Series. Now, let us take, as an example, the *Home University Library Series*. There are books on several subjects included in this series. They are all written by recognised authorities in the respective subjects. Further the exposition is popular and the style, non-technical. Even non-specialists can benefit by a perusal of the volumes and do like to do so. If

---

No. 87, *Final Report of the Committee on Scientific Problems of Human Migration.*

a volume of this series gets only an author-entry, one who is not a specialist in the subject with which it deals may be scared away by the title of the book and by the name of the specialist, who is put down as the author. On the other hand, a specialist in the subject knowing as he will, that it is a popular book, may not go in for the book. Thus, the book may not get a reader at all. But, the series entry of the book will make the non-specialist reader at least go in for the book with eagerness. Instances of this nature may be easily multiplied. There may also be various other considerations that lead readers to pursue their study through books belonging to well-known series. Hence, a catalogue with a complete set of Series Entries may prove to be of great help in securing for EVERY BOOK ITS READER.

The Subject Cross-Reference Entry may be even of greater service. This entry will occur in the classified part of the catalogue. It will have a subject as its heading and mention the books placed under other subjects but dealing partly with the subject in the heading, stating whenever possible the particular pages which may be relevant. A book may be cross-referred in this manner from several subject headings. For example, it has been found necessary to prepare ten cross-reference cards for More's *Shelbourne Essays*. It is extremely doubtful if it is likely to get its legitimate quota of readers from among the students of Metaphysics, if its excellent essay entitled *The*

Pragmatism of William James is not cross-referred from "Pragmatism".

The experience of the *Essays and Studies* published by the English Association gives another practical demonstration of the service that cross-reference can render to the Third Law. These volumes were adorning the shelves for years with but an occasional sojourn into readers' hands; somehow the name of "English Association" and the look of the books had led the majority of students to regard these *Essays and Studies* as too high-browed to be of interest to any but the severest specialist. The Third Law had a very hard time of it in finding readers for them.

But from the moment the individual essays were cross-referred from appropriate headings, the volumes would seldom stay on the shelves. For example, the cross-reference from the heading "Shelley, criticism" to the essay on *Platonism in Shelley* in the fourth volume of the set, began to draw to it a continuous stream of borrowers. It went out on loan on 23rd December, on the 2nd January, on the 21st January, on the 25th January, on the 4th February, on the 13th February, on the 12th March, and so on without any rest. It was such a triumph for the Third Law, that the Second Law was hard put to it to find this book for every reader that asked for it. In fact, the demand for the book could be met only by restricting the loan for a shorter period than usual and regulating the issue by registration in advance.

Another interesting example of the extraordinary power of subject cross-reference in finding for EVERY BOOK ITS READER is the case of the ponderous composite volumes constituting the *Complete Works* of Count Rumford. A cross-reference card with the heading "Coffee" to pages 615-660 of the fifth volume containing an essay entitled *Of the excellent qualities of Coffee and the art of making it in the highest perfection* made all the difference in the career of that volume. Instead of being an inert victim to the piercing ravages of silverfish, it began its unending series of triumphant marches to the residence of one reader after another.

Even with books that are generally popular a careful cross-reference entry can increase their circle of readers. For example, Will Durant's *Mansions of Philosophy* began to attract a newer and wider circle of readers as soon as its tenth chapter, which is on *The Breakdown of Marriage*, got a cross-reference card with the heading "Marriage".

These few instances are sufficient to illustrate the importance of cross-reference in increasing the use of books. The Third Law would therefore urge the library authorities not to plead the bogey of economy and shortage of funds when the proposal for the necessary staff for cross-referencing work comes up before them. We shall have occasion to go in detail into the profit and loss account of cross-referencing work when we discuss the Fourth Law. But it is enough to state here that, if the authorities have any faith in the Third Law, they should provide for a profusion of cross-references. They should provide the necessary technical staff to have the contents of every one of the books of the library analysed threadbare and brought to the notice of every possible class of readers by means of appropriate cross-references.

REFERENCE WORK

Thus, open-access, classified arrangement and analytic cataloguing are three of the necessary devices employed for getting for EVERY BOOK ITS READER. But such mechanical devices are seldom sufficient. It is doubtful whether open-access can achieve all that it can for the Third Law if the library staff interpret open-access to mean "Provide the books and keep out of the way of the readers as much as possible". In such a case, several of the books and not a few of the readers may have to share the fate of the beast between hay-stacks. Again, it is doubtful whether the card catalogue, by itself, will ever become the guide, philosopher and friend of the ordinary reader of a library. The inherent difficulties of an analytic catalogue are many and serious. It may be safely said that an average analytic card catalogue will always be in need of an interpreter.

The mechanical organisation of a library—however desirable—can never be carried to the point of dispensing with personal service. The requirement of the Third Law defies and transcends machinery. It will always require the provision of human beings as "canvassing agents" for books. It is imperative that certain members of the staff should be set apart solely to assist the reader in the use of the catalogue and in the choice of books. Their business should be to interpret the books to the readers and to canvass readers, so to speak, for the books. The provision of such a staff—the reference staff as it is called—is one of the effective devices employed by modern libraries to carry out the mandate of the Third Law.

The Reference Department of a library is expected to serve the reader in the way in which large traffic companies serve travellers in giving them illustrated folders of the new places they would like them to visit. The staff on Reference Duty have exceptional opportunities to mingle with the passing throng of readers. This direct contact with the readers brings with it opportunities to observe their tastes and wants, their actions and reactions and their likes and dislikes. As a result of such direct contacts, an experienced Reference Librarian instinctively relates readers to books and conversely a book frequently suggests a reader to whom it will appeal. He knows his community and is familiar with its mind, spirit and dominant interests. He seeks to have his finger on the pulse of his public and is ever on the wait for an opportunity to find a reader for every book. In the hands of a competent Reference Librarian, a library is like a kaleidoscope. His skill consists in turning its facets in such a way that they can all be seen and that each facet may attract those for whom it has interest. This is the kind of service that the Third Law expects from the Reference Staff.

In recent years, the eagerness to serve the cause of the Third Law seems to have led some of the libraries of the New World even to undertake house-to-house surveys. A card is provided for each house to record the number of members, their respective occupations, their reading interests and whether they are already library borrowers. A cabinet of cards of this nature gives a useful picture of the social life and the intellectual interests of the residents of the locality. It is the business of the Reference Staff to spot out potential readers from the records of such a survey and try to convert them into actual readers.

THE OPENING OF POPULAR DEPARTMENTS

This brings us to the problem of converting potential readers into actual readers. The first step in this problem is to attract such potential readers to the library. One method that is ordinarily used for this purpose is to provide the library with a Newspaper Room and a Magazine Room. They generally occupy a disproportionately large floor area and yet they are tolerated on account of their value in this respect. It is a matter of common experience that the Magazine Room attracts a larger crowd than the library proper and that the

News Room is even more crowded than the Magazine Room. The library staff would go into these popular rooms at intervals, get into touch with their patrons and try to lead some of them on to the stack-room and the reading-room. Thus, apart from the Newspapers and Magazines furnishing direct reading matter, they are also coming to be used as regular baits. Such an exploitation of the craving, which humanity seems to have for news of an ephemeral nature, is one of the methods regularly adopted by libraries to increase the chance for EVERY BOOK TO GET ITS READER. The Third Law would depend on the law of probability, according to which the chance for EVERY BOOK GETTING ITS READER would increase with the increase in the number of persons visiting the library. Once this desire of the Third Law came to be recognised, one obvious corollary was that libraries should adopt all the recognised methods of publicity.

PUBLICITY

Apart from the insistence of the Third Law, the libraries stand in need of publicity for other reasons as well. It is no wonder that, when the library has been extending its scope, changing its outlook and altering its very character and functions, there should not be adequate understanding among the public as to what has been going on. For some, the library is still medieval, to others it is principally a purveyor of entertaining novels. Surprise is continually expressed when the public discover the width of its service and the catholicity of its interests. "I didn't know that you had Music books?" "Are you open on holidays? I didn't know that." "I didn't know that your catalogue is so analytic." Such expressions as these, no doubt, interest and please the librarian; but they are also a disquieting indication that a knowledge of the service he offers has not yet spread over the entire public. They make it evident that well considered publicity, is as necessary for the public library, as for a commercial firm, in order that the public may know of its existence and of the varied service that it offers.

In a paper on *Library Publicity Methods* Miss Wildred Othmer Peterson, Director of Publicity of Des Moines Public Library, says,[1] "Publicity, the art of influencing Public opinion, in all its varied forms holds a large place in the world of men to-day. It has proved its value to the business world for, had it not, certain firms in this country would not spend as much as a million dollars a year for publicity. If publicity is important to them is it not also important to Libraries? The only differences, however, are that librarians, in a great many cases, need to be educated to the importance of publicity and that libraries do not have the millions to spend. Every library now directs much time and thought towards publicity. The press lends its powerful

(1) RANGANATHAN (S. R.), *Ed.*: *The First All-Asia Educational Conference, Papers offered to the Library Service Section*, p. 429.

aid and even such agencies as Moving pictures and Radio are enlisted."

Library publicity has, in fact, become a special branch of the art of publicity. Books are written about it, and in the United States, there is a publicity committee of the American Library Association, with a paid publicity officer. This Committee holds what is known as the *Publicity Round Table* at each of the annual conferences of the Associations. "State-wide publicity" is said to be the key-note of the *Publicity Round Table.* The extraordinary methods that California adopts to popularise its library system and to attract its inhabitants to its libraries in as large a number as possible are indicated in a paper discussed in the Fifty-Second Annual Conference of the American Library Association held in 1930.[1]

Broadly speaking, library publicity falls into two classes—general publicity and individual publicity. General publicity is of the type "Eat more fruits" and "Buy more *khaddar*" without mentioning any special fruit-merchant or khaddar-merchant. Such general publicity in the library sphere may try to emphasise

"(1) The value of books and reading; the superiority of the book as a source of opinion, information, inspiration, education, over other forms of print;

(1) *Bulletin of the American Library Association*, Vol. XXIV, pp. 458-462.

(2) The library as a public institution, publicly supported and administered;

(3) The all round service of a live library, emphasising reference service, adult education and other less known aspects....;

(4) Some accepted library standards, as, ... book circulation per capita, book ownership per capita...'"[1]

Such general publicity would fall within the sphere of central organisations like the Madras Library Association or the State Department of Public Libraries if such a department is established. Even in countries like America and England, "the need of organised, centralised, library publicity" is being emphasised and provided for. Continuous publicity is carried on through press-notices, magazine articles, radio-talks, public lectures, demonstration tours, attractive sign-boards, periodical and itinerant exhibitions and the free distributions of leaflets and bulletins. The Japanese Library Association arranges for a country-wide celebration of a book-week in November. Such general publicity should be the predominant part of the library publicity in India, under the conditions that obtain at present.

In addition, individual libraries should see that their service is constantly brought to the notice of the public in an effective way. It is worth while for large libraries to have a special publicity assis-

(1) AMERICAN LIBRARY ASSOCIATION: *Library Extension*, p. 102.

tant. It should be the business of such an assistant or of the librarian himself, if such an assistant does not exist, to adopt all the recognised methods of attracting the public to the library, so that every potential reader may be converted into an actual one, thereby increasing the chances for the fulfilment of the Third Law. In organising its publicity campaign, a library should bear in mind the general principles of publicity, such as continuity, variety, novelty, clarity and personal appeal.

Perhaps the cheapest and the most easily available medium for library publicity is the Press. The library should keep itself in touch with the local newspapers. The newspapers would generally be willing to allow some space in the general news column and the local news column for information about the library. It is desirable that the librarian or the publicity assistant should frequently consult the editors and try to conform to their instructions in the matter of style, length, periodicity and other details, so that the matter sent by the library can be directly passed on to the compositors, with the least editorial labour possible. It may be useful to publish certain types of information such as recent additions, statistics of readers and issues and similar data on definite days of the week or dates of the month, so that the public may know when to look for them. They will act as systematic reminders to the public. It is not uncommon that the number of visitors to the library is slightly greater on the 2nd or 3rd of each month, as a result of the monthly statistics appearing in the local news column on the evening of the 1st. In addition to such systematic statements, the library should seek to appear in the press at odd intervals, whenever an opportunity offers itself for announcement such as, changes in the issue method, changes in the arrangement of books, changes in the hours, receipt of free gifts of special collections, improvements in the amenities to the public, participation of the library in exhibitions and conferences and occurrence of events about which special bibliographies may be prepared. The library staff may also be encouraged to contribute occasionally readable articles bearing on the humourous side of library experiences. It may be desirable to send to the newspapers occasional reports or extracts about the outstanding events in the libraries of other lands. Such publications sometimes rouse the curiosity of the public and induce them to take greater interest in their own libraries.

Next to the Press, mention may be made of the issue of printed or typed handbills and news-sheets. A good duplicating machine is a great necessity for libraries to use this form of publicity. It would be cheaper to use such a machine than to print. Recent additions, special bibliographies, notifications about changes of methods, descriptive notes about the personal service offered by the Reference Staff, and several such announcements can be issued in this manner both to those who are already on the members' list and to those who are yet to be attracted to the library. Although a little more costly, unlike the Press method of publicity, this form does not depend on the co-operation of outside agencies. It would also give ample scope for the resourcefulness of the library staff. It would be an advantage to keep a chronological and a classified file of such materials for future guidance.

A more costly mode of publicity adopted by some libraries is that of publishing a printed periodical, *e.g.*, *The Readers' Index* of the Croydon Public Library; *The Bulletin* of the New York Public Library; *The Harvard Library Notes* of the Harvard University Library; *The Bulletin* of the John Rylands Library, Manchester. Such library periodicals seek:—

"(*a*) to interest the public in the library as an institution,

(*b*) to keep the public informed of all the library's activities and facilities,

(*c*) to relate books to the existing tastes and interests of the public,

(*d*) to relate fresh topics to those about which borrowers already read,

(*e*) to arouse fresh interests,

(*f*) to keep the reader in touch with methods that can be followed up in books, and

(*g*) generally to stimulate—in an attractive "gentle" way—education, vocational and other, and culture."[1]

(1) McCOLVIN (Lionel R.): *Library Extension Work and Publicity*, pp. 179 and 180.

These periodicals usually contain an annotated list of recent additions as well as of books of topical interest, special articles dealing with the varying forms of the activities of the library and illustrated accounts of matters of local interest which are capable of being connected with the library. Such periodicals have usually to be distributed free, if they are to serve their purpose. The cost and labour involved are generally prohibitive unless it is possible to secure a sufficient number of advertisements.

Another recognised form of publicity that may be adopted by libraries is to arrange for occasional exhibitions. Some of the libraries of California are said to have provided themselves with window space for book displays. By a judicious variation in the selection and arrangement of display material, stay-at-home books are helped to find their readers.

The radio is another medium that may well be harnessed for library publicity. American libraries are said to be already utilising this medium with remarkable success. For example, "Several libraries in Iowa broadcast occasional talks, while the libraries at the Iowa State College and Des Moines have had regular programmes for the past several years. Two of the public libraries, Des Moines and Davenport, although 175 miles apart, are co-operating in a weekly broadcast, of 15 minutes duration, giving book and magazine reviews and general information concerning books and authors . . . letters expressing interest and requesting information have been received from listeners as far distant as 750 miles''.[1] However, the report presented to the 1930 Conference of the American Library Association by the Committee on Library Radio Broadcasting expressed the view ''The consensus of opinion seems to be that the value of library broadcasting as conducted at present remains to be proved. While there are obvious advantages there are also many difficulties that remain to be surmounted''.[2]

Some libraries advertise their services by means of posters. In fact there is no direct form of publicity that the libraries do not adopt. Here is an account of one ingenious and extreme form of advertisement, which has the flavour of the marketing methods of a business concern. ''During the annual fair which lasts for eight or ten days . . . to give publicity to the California county library system the large electrically lighted county library map of California and Sacramanto county used at the A. L. A. Conference in Philadelphia is maintained in a prominent place in the Agriculture Building. To emphasise this publicity the county libraries financed the making of thousands of county library fans bearing on one side the county library sign and on the other information regarding California county libraries. Each day a county

(1) *South Indian Teacher,* Vol. 3, p. 431.

(2) *Bulletin of the American Library Association,* Vol. XXIV, p. 464.

librarian and State Library Staff member passed out fans to multitudes of adults. The fans served to suggest many questions by the visitors and gave an opportunity to explain the county library system and to illustrate from the electrically lighted map points that needed clarifying visually. People from the counties of California which are without any county library . . . were among the interested recipients of this novel bit of publicity."[1]

But by far the simplest and the least expensive method of publicity is direct personal talk. This method can convert many persons into regular readers, if the library has on its staff one or two members with the necessary personality and power of speech to address gatherings of probable readers. It has been found from experience that if such addresses are to be effective too much time should not be spent on vague and general subjects like the benefits of reading or the services of a library in general. After a very short preliminary reference to topics of such a nature, one should rapidly descend to particulars and dwell in detail upon the specific services that the library in question can render to the members of the gathering. It may be serviceable to present comparative statistics of membership and book-issues. At the same time one should not be carried away by enthusiasm to promise to serve more than what the limitations of staff and stock would permit. The reactions of

(1) *Bulletin of the American Library Association*, Vol. XXIV, p. 459

such unfulfilled promises will do more harm than good to the Third Law.

The accompanying table and the figure showing the growth of issue in the Madras University Library illustrate the result of such personal appeals.

Year.	No. of Vols.
1914	.. 5,100
1915	.. 11,600
1916	.. 11,600
1917	.. 14,000
1918	.. 15,000
1919	.. 15,300
1920	.. 22,236
1921	.. 27,920
1922	.. 24,975
1923	.. 22,339
1924	.. 20,075
1925	.. 27,629
1926	.. 42,336
1927	.. 70,914
1928	.. 79,756
1929	.. 99,600
1930	.. 1,13,321

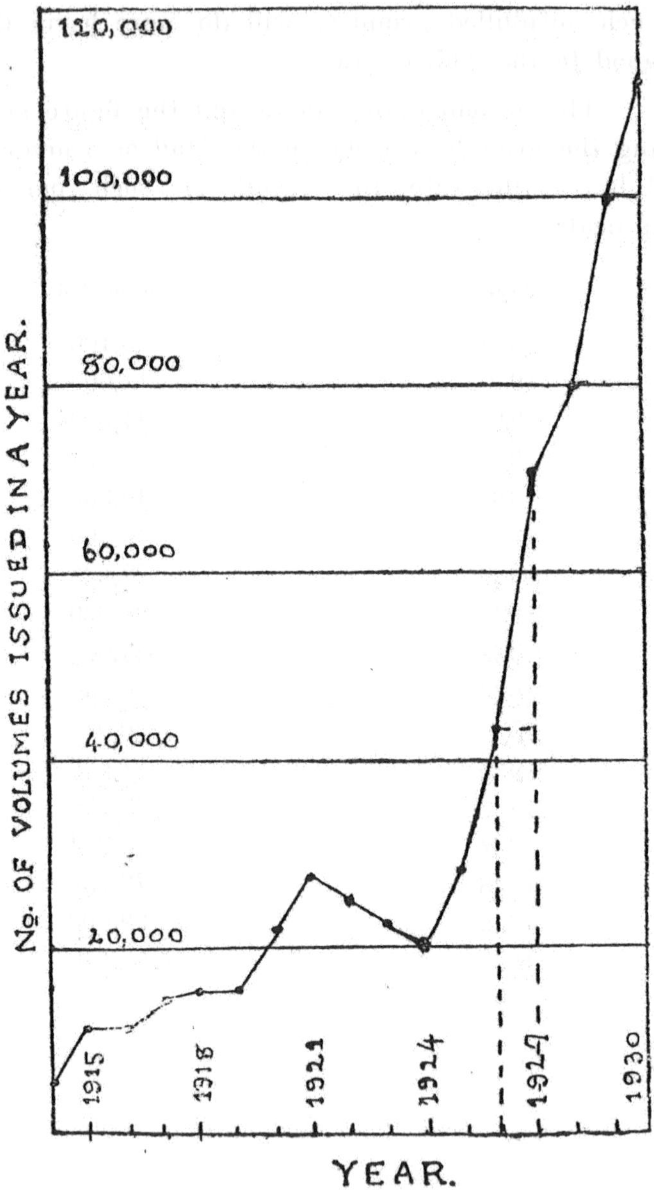
120,000
100,000
80,000
60,000
40,000
20,000
No. OF VOLUMES ISSUED IN A YEAR.
1915
1918
1921
1924
1927
1930
YEAR.

In the year 1927, several visits were made to students' hostels and small groups of undergraduates were addressed whenever an opportunity occurred. Professors of colleges who took interest in the matter were requested to mention in their lecture hours the services offered by the library. That these quiet personal appeals had the desired effect may be seen from the steep ascent of the graph during the year 1927. In later years as the increase of staff could not keep pace with the increase of work in the Reference Section and in the Counter Section, it was found necessary to suspend this publicity campaign, though with great reluctance. But there is ample need for reviving and keeping up the campaign if the interests of the Third Law are to be properly served.

EXTENSION WORK

Apart from such methods of pure publicity, libraries are nowadays developing certain new types of work which, in addition to their being directly educative or recreational, lead also to publicity as an important secondary product. Such new lines of activity may be referred to as "the extension work" of libraries. The object of extension work may be said to be an attempt to turn the library into a social centre whose function is the encouragement of reading. Its aim is to make readers of non-readers, to create and stimulate the desire for good reading and to bring book and reader together. Libraries that have come under the influence of the Third Law value these aims highly and take to extension work with great zeal.

One form of extension work that is very urgent in our libraries of to-day is the institution of the 'reading system'. As a result of the high percentage of illiteracy that prevails, the present generation of illiterate adults can be made to have the benefits of library service only by arranging to have books read to them at stated hours either by paid readers or by honorary readers who are actuated by a spirit of social service. We have seen in the third chapter, how this 'reading system' coupled with the formation of clubs for the liquidation of illiteracy has even converted many an illiterate adult into eager literate readers in post-war Russia. There is no reason why libraries, with this extension side properly developed, may not provide a sure solution of a similar problem in Adult Education in India as well.

Owing to paucity of books on current thought in the South Indian Languages, this form of extension work may have to be carried even further. To induce and maintain the interests of the illiterate workmen in books and in hearing books read, it would be necessary to read to them, not only books of a religious or recreational nature, but also books of useful knowledge dealing with their daily avocation and leading to increased efficiency in their work. In the absence of such books in the mother tongue and in the absence of any prospect of such books being printed, the only practicable course would be for the library to prepare a manuscript translation of suitable books from English and have the manuscripts read to them. It must be possible to find, among the English knowing local residents, persons willing to do the translation as a piece of social service. If each library in a district undertakes the translation of one or two books in a year and all such manuscript books are systematically exchanged between the different libraries, an appreciable region of knowledge can be provided for in a reasonable time. If no competent non-commercial agency like the State or the Universities would undertake the initial supply of such books on useful knowledge, this seems to me to be the only practical way of cutting the vicious circle of the law of supply and demand. But this extreme phase of extension work is only a strictly temporary expedient, for which there will be no need as soon as a market is created for the publishers to step in.

A second form of extension work that the libraries may pursue is that of organising reading circles. Persons pursuing particular subjects for profit or pleasure may be brought together by the libraries, so as to form a reading circle. Each such circle may have a leader and not less than two and not more than five other members. The library may give special facilities for such reading circles in the matter of books, periodicals and meeting places. For this purpose a library should have a suitable suite of small seminar rooms. Such reading circles are usually effective agencies in thoroughly exploiting the resources of the library in their respective subjects of study and hence their formation gives unusual satisfaction to the Third Law.

One of the necessary conditions for such institutions becoming popular is the fostering of a feeling of mutual cordiality and helpfulness between those who offer service and those who are served, together with a disposition to self-sacrifice. To this end, the library should strive to reduce formality to a minimum and make everyone feel at home. As a natural extension of this attitude, a modern library even goes so far in its effort as to make personal and social contacts and not infrequently offers meeting place for local learned organisations in an attempt to make them, as constituent parts of the general public, feel that it desires to function as an intellectual centre for the locality. Such meetings offer opportunities for the exploits of the Third Law.

The possibilities of this form of extension work can be inferred from "the following statement of a small English town library, of societies meeting there regularly—The British Legion, Cage Birds' Society, Chess Club, Draughtsclub, Church Lads' Brigade, Church Mothers' Meeting, Church of England Men's Society, Folk Dance Society, two or three friendly societies, The Free Church Mothers' Meeting, The Gardeners' Society, Grocers' Society, Farmers' Union, National Union of

Teachers, Radio Society, Woman's Institute and Workers' Educational Association".[1]

Another common form of extension work is that of arranging for public lectures in the premises of the library. For this purpose all modern library buildings are provided with spacious lecture halls, fitted with a stage, a magic lantern, a cinema apparatus and other related appliances. In addition to the local associations being invited to hold their public lectures in the library's lecture hall, the library frequently arranges for special library talks either by the members of its staff or by outside experts. One special feature of such library talks is the announcement of a select list of books on the subject-matter of the talk that could be consulted in or borrowed from the library. The subjects chosen for such library talks are usually of local or topical interest. Scientific subjects also come in for a good share. Such talks ought not to be exclusively confined to topics of a religious, philosophical or puranic nature. But care should be taken to widen the range of subjects and give a chance for every phase of current thought. Whenever possible, it would be an advantage to illustrate the talks with lantern slides and moving pictures. The unique South Indian Institution of *Kalakshepam,* with its happy blend of music and talk, presents enormous potentialities as an instrument of this form of extension work. But due care should

---

(1) McCOLVIN (Lionel R.): *Library Extension Work and Publicity*, p. 142.

be taken, in this case also, to lift the *Kalakshepam* from the narrow rut of subjects to which tradition appears to have assigned it.

In western countries where this institution is unknown, the lecture hall is used for musical concerts as often as possible. This enables the Third Law to find readers for the comparatively large quantity of printed music that is usually available in those libraries.

It is not uncommon to display in the lecture hall the resources of the library bearing on the event that is happening there. Sometimes, a regular exhibition of such materials is also arranged in an adjoining hall, through which the occupants of the lecture hall have to pass at the close of the function. The books referred to in the lecture hall are carefully spread on tables, the most attractive plates greeting the passers by. Smart attendants of the library patiently stand by the side of the exhibits waiting for the man whose glance would fall on them. The moment such a man is spotted out, the face of the attendant immediately brightens up and with an inviting smile she offers the book for his home use. Perhaps the man being a non-member feels puzzled; but, before his shyness is got over, the experienced attendant volunteers, "Never mind, if you are not a member, you can have privilege issue to-day, if you so desire". As these words are being uttered a few red and green slips are inserted in the book before it is offered to the wondering man with the encouraging words

STORY HOUR, CHILDREN'S LIBRARY, BARODA.

"Take it with you—Will you mind remembering to return this as soon as you finish it or this day fortnight, whichever is earlier?" When this wondering man reaches home and turns the pages of the book with subdued excitement, the red and green slips greet him with legends like "You are paying for the maintenance of this library; why don't you use it?" "To become a member it needs no more formality than signing a card." And so on. The audacious psychology of this form of extension work seldom seems to result in the man deliberately appropriating the book permanently for his private use.

Similar to the library talks for adults, libraries arrange also for story hours, lantern talks, dramatisations and other attractive forms of extension work and similar privilege issues, to establish contact with the children of the locality. Again it is not unusual for the library to arrange occasionally for dramatic performances by amateur troops. But in all such cases the performances do not form an end in themselves but they are all made to serve as aids to the ultimate satisfaction of the exacting Third Law.

Another form that extension work takes is the celebration of local festivals and special days of the year dedicated to particular persons or ideas and participation in local fairs. Here again the demand of the Third Law is always kept in the forefront. In our own country, where such celebrations are still attracting large crowds of people, this form of extension work is full of great potentialities for the cause of the Third Law.

BOOK-SELECTION

Before taking leave of the Third Law, it may not be out of place to mention an important bearing of this Law on Book-Selection. In discussing the financial implications of the Second Law we had occasion to deal with this question from a slightly different point of view. It can be easily seen that one of the means of fulfilling the demands of the Third Law is to give full weight to the tastes and requirements of the *clientele* of the library in Book-Selection work. Some of the factors from which the tastes and requirements of the *clientele* could be inferred are:—

(1) the suggestions received directly from the readers,

(2) the suggestions recorded by the assistants at the Ready Reference Desk,

(3) the notes made from day to day by the Reference Staff on floor duty,

(4) the main vocations of the Local Public,

(5) the prospective events of national or local importance,

(6) the impressions gained in interviews with the leading members of the local community and so on.

If, in this manner, books are selected with full attention to probable demand, the difficulties of the

Third Law would be minimised to a large extent. But it should not be inferred from this that the library should slavishly follow the demands of readers and that it has no responsibility in steadily and consciously directing the reading tastes of its *clientele* along healthy channels. The Third Law would have no quarrel whatever with this aim of Book-Selection but it would remonstrate against haphazard selection which is utterly indifferent to the immediate and prospective requirements of the readers. The threat of the allotment lapsing in a few days sometimes forces a Library Authority to rely solely on the first trade list or catalogue, that chance might put in the way. This is a danger that should be avoided. Book-Selection is work that should be done from day to day taking into account the demands of readers, the progress of publication and the funds available.

CHAPTER VI

THE FOURTH LAW

We have seen in the last five chapters that the main concern of the first three Laws of Library Science is to get the books of the library used as fully and by as many persons as possible. We have also seen that, however axiomatic those laws appear to be, they have really begun to assert themselves as ruling concepts only during the last few decades. We further examined some of their implications and described the changes they are bringing about in the outlook of libraries and in the various aspects of library policy and administration.

We shall see in this chapter what further light is thrown on some of these problems by the Fourth Law of Library Science. This law makes its approach from the side of the readers as was the case with the Second Law. Perhaps it may even be said that the interest of the Fourth Law almost completely centres round the readers. Taking for granted that BOOKS ARE FOR USE, that EVERY READER SHOULD BE SERVED HIS OR HER BOOK and that EVERY BOOK SHOULD BE HELPED TO FIND ITS READER, it proceeds to fashion the library administration accordingly. In company with the Fifth Law, it concerns itself with the situation that should arise as the requirements of the first three laws come to be increasingly fulfilled. In dealing with the new problems of such a situation, it introduces the element of time and concentrates its attention entirely on the time-aspect of the problem.

SAVE THE TIME OF THE READER—that is the Fourth Law of Library Science. Perhaps this law is not so self-evident as the others. None the less, it has been responsible for many reforms in library administration and has a great potentiality for effecting many more reforms in the future. Perhaps the most convenient method of studying the consequences of this law will be to follow a reader from the moment he enters the library to the moment he leaves it, critically examining each process, which he has to go through, with an eye to the economy of time that can be effected at each stage.

OPEN ACCESS, *vs.* 'CLOSED' SYSTEM

Perhaps the first thing that a reader does, on entering the library, is to discharge the used up books. But it will be convenient to postpone the consideration of this process and take it up along with the method of charging, as the details of the two operations are, by their nature, interdependent. Hence, the main process that should be first studied in the light of the Fourth Law is the choice of books. In a 'closed' library, this has to be done entirely with the aid of the catalogue. The catalogue of a growing library is either of the card form or of the paste-down form. If it is of the latter form, even in a small library like the Madras University Library with but 70,000 books, the catalogue runs through fourteen folio-volumes. In the British Museum Library, the paste-down "general catalogue now fills over 1,000 volumes".[1] A common heading like 'Smith' takes a volume all for itself. Further the inevitable occurrence of certain general headings, such as 'Academies' and 'Periodicals' add further complications. A good deal of time is naturally wasted in hunting out for the required title in such a labyrinth of entries. Having got them, one has to write them out with great accuracy on separate slips and hand the slips over to the man behind the barrier. Then follows the harassing interval of waiting—for several minutes in small libraries and even for hours in large ones. It is not unusual for readers of the British Museum Library to apply for their books in the forenoon and call for them after lunch. Some readers with forethought would also send their slips overnight to save time on the next day.

If the library is popular, the loss of time due to the search for entries and to the waiting at the counter may recur several times before the right book is got. The recurrence may be due to many causes. After some time, the slip may be returned with the endorsement "entry incorrect". The spelling of some essential part of the entry may

(1) RAWLINGS (Gertrude Berford): *The British Museum Library*, p. 164.

be wrong. This would render the tracing of the book impracticable. The group of figures, constituting the press-mark or call number as it is called, might have been wrongly copied. Substitution of a small letter for a capital or omission of a dot or a comma might make all the difference. Or the slip may come back with the endorsement "on loan" or "engaged". Then the old process of selection and waiting will have to be gone through once again. Before the Madras University Library changed to 'open access', several cases used to occur almost every day when the process had to be repeated half a dozen times before a reader got some book. Again, when the book is actually produced, it may turn out to be spurious or, for other reasons, unsuitable to the reader. The catalogue entry might not have given a clear enough indication of the nature of the book. That means the repetition of the whole process over again. These features would "make the selection of books a heart-break and a labour tinctured with disgust".[1]

The average amount of time that a reader had thus to waste at the counter in the Madras University Library in 1928 (just before the open access system was introduced) was about half an hour. The colossal nature of this waste can be realised if we integrate over a full year the amount of time thus wasted by the community as a whole.

(1) BROWN (James Duff): *A Plea for Liberty*, reprinted in STEWART (J. D.) and others: *Open Access Libraries*, p. 218.

Let us take as a convenient unit of measure one person working for one hour. Let us call this a 'Man-hour'. Now, the average number of visitors in the library was 200 per day. Thus, 100 man-hours were wasted per day or 36,500 man-hours per annum. To realise its economic significance, we must convert this into money. A salary of Rs. 75 per mensem would correspond to half a rupee per man-hour. Even with this low equivalent, the wastage for which the 'closed system' of the Madras University Library was responsible in 1928 amounted to nearly Rs. 18,250 per annum. In discussing the profit and loss account of the open access system, one should give due weight to this aspect of the matter. The Fourth Law would insist that, in deciding large questions of policy, such as open access *vs.* 'closed' system, the spirit of the modern method of cost-accounting should be adopted and long, broad and full views should be taken, dealing with the community and the library as a whole. An alarmist attitude should not be developed by isolating the probable or actual loss of a few volumes in a year or by taking any other partial view of the matter.

In modern communities, such as those of America and England for whom time is money and money is time, the slogan of the Fourth Law—SAVE THE TIME OF THE READER—seems to have produced a profound impression. Further, the recent tendencies in the evolution of business methods and the rapid diffusion of the 'cost-accounting' consciousness not only among the leaders but even among the masses have led those communities to conclude that the balance of advantage is decidedly in favour of the open access system. In this system, the wastage due to waiting at the counter is eliminated fully and the wastage due to wading through cumbrous catalogues is reduced to a minimum and may even be altogether unnecessary for many ordinary readers.

Historically, an attempt was first made to eliminate the loss of time due to books being on loan. This was done by the ingenious invention of the 'indicator system'. "A library indicator, as its name implies, is a device for indicating or registering information about books. The information usually conveyed to the public is some kind of indication of the presence or absence of books, and the methods of accomplishing this almost invariably take the form of displayed numbers, qualified in such a way as to indicate books *in* and *out*".[1] Several patterns of indicators were invented from 1870 onwards. In all cases, a large run of counter space had to be given up for accommodating these mechanical contrivances and this created new problems. But as the Fourth Law gradually asserted itself still further and insisted that the time wasted in tracing the titles in catalogues and waiting thereafter for the books to be brought by

(1) BROWN (James Duff): *Manual of Library Economy*, p. 342.

attendants should also be saved, the indicators were slowly given up and the open access system came to be regarded as the only satisfactory device to SAVE THE TIME OF THE READER. Thus, the claims of the open access system, already advocated by the Second and the Third Laws, came to be reinforced by the Fourth Law, on grounds of national economy.

SHELF-ARRANGEMENT

The interest of the Fourth Law is not exhausted however with the introduction of open access. It has an equal interest in reforming the shelf-arrangement. In an open access library, the nature of the shelf-arrangement can make or mar the mission of the Fourth Law. One old fashioned method which still seems to persist in some of our libraries is that of alphabetic arrangement by the authors. But in the majority of cases, the interest of readers goes by the subject rather than by the author. Even in literature, the authors of the biographies and the critical works are not as important as the author forming the subject of biography or criticism.

Let us now follow our reader, for whom the Fourth Law has secured admission into the stack-room and let us assume that he is interested in Wave Mechanics and that he desires to see as many books as possible on that subject. If the library is an alphabetically arranged one, he will have to browse from A to Z to spot out his books as there is a nearly equal chance for each letter of the alphabet to be the initial letter of the names of the authors of the books on that subject. For example, here are some titles on Wave Mechanics, that the library may possess:—

BIGGS (H. F.): Wave Mechanics.
BIRTWISTLE (George): The New Quantum Mechanics.
BLIGH (N. M.): The Evolution and Development of the Quantum Theory.
BORN (Max): Elementare Quanten Mechanik.
CONDON (Edward U.): Quantum Mechanics.
DE BROGLIE (Louis): La Mecanique Ondulatoire.
DE BROGLIE (Louis): Selected Papers on Wave Mechanics.
FLINT (H. T.): Wave Mechanics.
FOWLER (R. H.): The Passage of Electrons through Surface and Surface Films.
HAAS (Arthur): Wave Mechanics and the New Quantum Theory.
LANDE (A.): Die Neuere Entwicklung der Quantentheorie.
RICE (James): Introd. to Statistical Mechanics.
SCHRODINGER (E.): Coll. Papers on Wave Mechanics.
SCHRODINGER (E.): Four lectures on Wave Mechanics.
SOMMERFELD (Arnold): Lecture on Wave Mechanics.
SOMMERFELD (Arnold): Wave Mechanics.
WILSON (W.): Relativity and Wave Mechanics.

Let us look at the length of shelves his eyes should travel. Assuming that twelve volumes will, on an average, go into a foot, his eyes will have to run through the backs of a little over a mile of books, even in a library of 70,000 volumes. Just imagine the time that will be involved in this process. On the other hand, suppose that the books of the library are arranged in a minutely classified manner, on a subject basis. Then, Wave-Mechanics will be one of the ultimate classes and his eyes will have to run only through the backs of a foot or two of books. In other words, he could see them all almost at a glance. This has led the Fourth Law to press the claims of the classified mode of arrangement. We have seen that the Second and Third Laws also prefer such an arrangement. Each law approaches the problem of shelf-arrangement from a different angle; but, fortunately, their conclusions are all concurrent.

The Fourth Law would throw some further light on the arrangement. In the first place, it would recommend that the classes accommodated in adjacent shelves should have the greatest possible affinity. A reader that is primarily interested in philosophy is sure to have some interest in religion and psychology. Hence, to SAVE THE TIME OF THAT CLASS OF READERS, it would be advisable to put religion on one side of philosophy and psychology on its other side. In a similar manner, the Fourth Law must be constantly borne in mind in fixing the relative position of the other classes as well.

Apart from relative position, the absolute position of the classes also will have to be determined in conformity to the Fourth Law. The class of books that is most in demand should be put on the nearest shelves of the stack-room and the class that is least popular should, ordinarily, be put at the farthest end. It is known for example that for every geological book issued, more than a hundred books are issued in literature in the Madras University Library. The accompanying histogram showing the relative popularity of different classes of subjects in the Madras University Library may throw some light on the importance of this aspect of shelf-arrangement. It can be seen that about a third of the issues of that Library is from the literature class. Then, in order to save the time of the greatest number of readers, that library should accommodate its literature class close to the

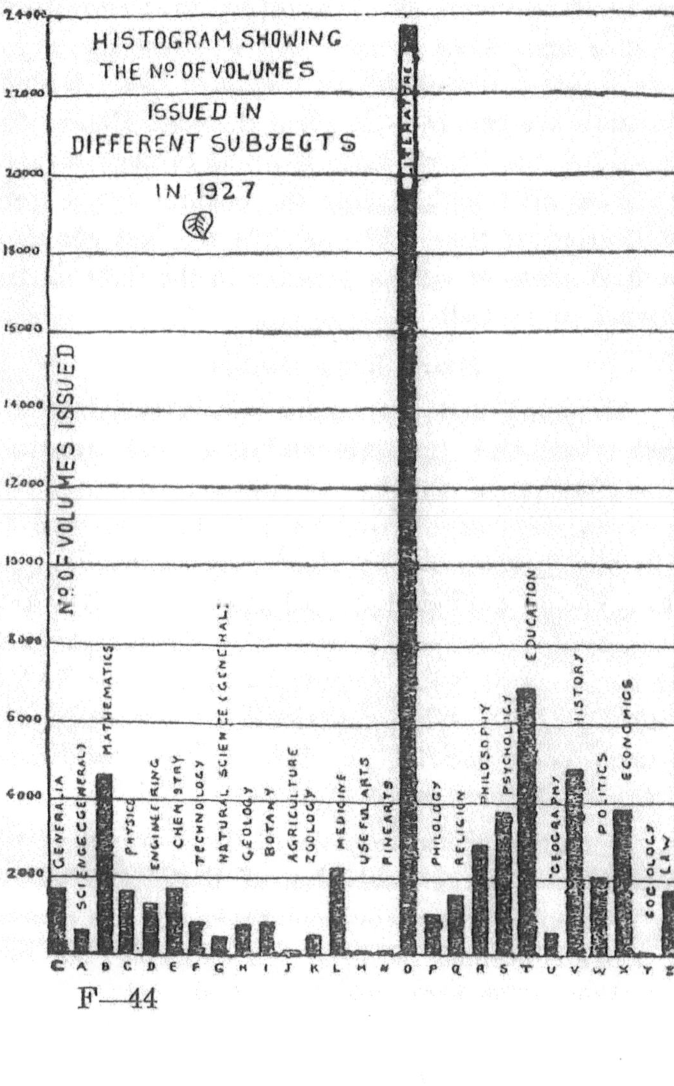

F—44

of book-racks should be furnished at each end with a "signal" guide on which the classes accommodated in the row are indicated in a manner calculated to catch the eye of the reader. In the Madras University Library they are inserted in rectangular wooden frames 18" × 6" projecting from the side of the end rack of the row as shown in the accompanying picture. Some libraries, that keep open after sunset, use illuminated signal guides.

In addition to this, every shelf-plank should also be provided with the necessary number of shelf-labels. The number of such shelf-labels is likely to be very great. In the Madras University Library, the number of shelf-planks in use, at present, is about 3,500. They are furnished with as many as 6,000 shelf-labels. The proper maintenance of such a large number of labels is a problem in itself. The serious nature of the problem will be brought out fully when we view it in the light of the Fifth Law. It is enough to say here that so many are necessary to SAVE THE TIME OF THE READER effectively. At the same time, however, it must be said that shelf labelling should not be overdone. Too many of them may cause confusion to the reader. Most of the shelves may take two labels, while a few may take one and a few others three. There should not be need for more than three per plank. The Madras University Library generally uses spoiled catalogue cards for the purpose. They are cut into labels 5" × 5|8". Each card gives four such labels. The name of the ultimate class of books just above the label is written on it in bold detached library hand of half inch size. The number of the class is also prefixed whenever there is space.

Thus, we shall imagine our reader first consulting the plan at the entrance of the stack-room. Then, with the aid of the signal guides greeting him at the end of each gangway, he will easily enter that particular gangway which contains the subject in which he is interested. As he passes along the gangway, he will run his eyes through the shelf-labels until he comes to the shelf containing the ultimate class in which his books are likely to be. Then he will examine the collection in that ultimate class and make his selection. If, on the other hand, he has already made up his mind about the particular book he wants, there must be some further help to enable him to pick out that particular book without loss of time. In such a case, the most expeditious method of his getting the book will be to find out, beforehand, the exact call number of the book from the catalogue cabinet. Assuming that he will do this, it can be easily seen that there should be further guides showing the call number of each book. They should consist of tags or labels affixed to the backs of books.

These tags should be applied and the call number written on them, when the book is being catalogued. It is very difficult to get a tag that will firmly stick to the back of the book for an appreciable time. Even if it does, it gets dirty in course of time and the letters become indistinct. It has been found to be ultimately more economical to buy specially made tags, than for each library to prepare its own tags in its own crude way. Dennison's white circular tags, number A-144, which are coated with thin gum, have been found to be most serviceable. They cost about one rupee per thousand. They are available at Libraco Ltd., 62, Cannon St., London, E. C. 4. The durability of these tags can be increased by applying paper varnish to them after they are fixed. Even then, they should be replaced periodically and systematically. There is nothing more offensive to the eye than a dirty half-torn tag disfiguring the back of a book. It further produces an impression of slovenliness which is inimical to the bright business-like look that a library should present to the reader. In the Madras University Library which issues about one hundred and fifty thousand books per annum, it has been found necessary to set apart an attendant for about ten hours in the week for renewing the tags. So much of an attendant's time has to be spent, in order to SAVE THE TIME OF THE READER at this stage. While it may look like a great expense when considered from the isolated library-point-of-view, it can be seen to be really economical from the larger community-point-of-view.

Before leaving this question, it may be well to say that the attractiveness of the shelf can be considerably increased by fixing the tags in such a way that they are all in a line when the books stand erect on the shelves. Apart from the look of slovenliness, it will be tiring for the reader's eyes if the tags appear at all heights indiscriminately. Experience has shown that the most suitable standard position for the tag is one inch from the bottom of the book.

The labour involved in the frequent repasting of the tags can be avoided by having the call number printed directly on the back of the book. For this, ordinary binders' gold lettering method should be adopted. It may be advantageous to train a library attendant to do the lettering in the library premises. If it is not practicable, the books may be sent to the binder to be numbered.

Details like these may appear to be trivial to those who have had no inside experience of a library. With the limited experience of handling a few stray books in his private study, the layman cannot easily imagine what proportions these apparently small matters assume in a growing library dealing with thousands of volumes and thousands of readers. Hence, in a country like ours with hardly any modern library tradition, the handicaps of the librarian are likely to be greatly increased by a lack of appreciation of the magnitude of the problem on the part of others. But the librarian has to devote his thought to such problems and solve them so as to SAVE THE TIME OF THE READER.

Catalogue

Another factor that may lead the reader to waste his time in getting his materials is due to the inevitable composite nature of most of the books. All books are not monographs. Very often an excellent account of a specified topic may occur in a chapter or even in a few pages of a book whose main interest may be some other topic or topics. A careful student would desire to know all the resources of the library on his subject of study, whether it be a monograph or a portion of a bigger book. If a catalogue is made up only of a single entry for each book and makes no attempt whatever to give analytic cross-references, the only course open to the reader is to examine every book to see if it gives any information on the subject of his study.

Suppose, for example, that the reader is interested in critical literature dealing with Matthew Arnold. There may be about half a dozen books in the library dealing exclusively with this subject and they can be found together on the shelves. But, a patient search by the reader will disclose to him that the library possesses also many other materials on the subject. Here are some items that he may find to be useful:—

ARNOLD (M.): Poems, pp. 4-16.
PALGRAVE (F. T.), Landscape in Poetry, pp. 257-278.
SWINBURNE, (A. C.), Essays and Studies, pp. 123-183.
HUTTON (R. H.), Literary Essays, pp. 310-360.
QUILLER-COUCH (A.): Studies in Literature, pp. 231-245.
KER (W. P.), The Art of Poetry, pp. 139-160.

DRINKWATER (J.), Victorian Poetry, pp. 86-90; 96-100; 121-123.
GRIERSON (H. J. C.), Background of English Literature, pp. 68-114.
GRIERSON (H. J. C.), Lyrical Poetry from Blake to Hardy, pp. 90-121.
SQUIRE (S. J.), Essays on Poetry, pp. 88-97.
MONROE (H.), Poets and Their Art, pp. 175-178.
ELLIOTT, (G. H.), The Cycle of Modern Poetry, pp. 58-63.
PAUL (H. W.), Matthew Arnold, pp. 16-50; 99-105.
ENGLISH ASSOCIATION, Essays and Studies, Vol. III, pp. 71-91.
TRAILL (H. D.), The New Fiction, pp. 76-103.
HUTTON (R. H.), Modern Guides to English Thought, pp. 105-149.
HUTTON (R. H.), Brief Literary Criticisms, pp. 256-281; 288-303.
STEPHEN (L.), Studies of a Biographer, Vol. II, pp. 71-114.
COLLINS (J. C.), Posthumous Essays, pp. 171-198.
HENLEY (W. E.), Views and Reviews, pp. 75-82.
BIRRELL (A.), Collected Essays and Addresses, Vol. II, pp. 170-198.
RALEIGH (W.), Some Authors, pp. 300-310.
SAINTSBURY (G.), Essays in English Literature, Vol. II, pp. 265-275.
GOSSE (E.), More Books on the Table, pp. 381-387.
WILLIAMS, (S. T.), Studies in Victorian Literature, pp. 71-160.
HARRISON (F.), Selected Essays, pp. 1-19.
WALKER (H.), Age of Tennyson, pp. 214-219.
ENGLISH ASSOCIATION, Essays and Studies, Vol. XV, pp. 7-19.
HUTTON (R. H.), Contemporary Thought and Thinkers, Vol. I, pp. 214-226.
FITCH (Joshua, *Sir*), Lives of Thomas and Matthew Arnold, pp. 241-274.

Now, to discover these references for himself the reader may have to go through most of the books in the literature shelves. The library may have some hundreds of books in literature. Even if the reader has the patience to make a search in a thorough manner, there is no doubt that he will require many hours and perhaps days to prepare the above list.

Let us take another example. A few weeks back an eminent research worker felt the need to consult all the literature that our library had on the Zeeman Effect. We had only four books exclusively devoted to the subject and hence they were the only books that were found on the shelf having the shelf-label "Zeeman Effect". But, our catalogue contained the following seventeen references.

HAAS (A.), Introd. to Theoretical Physics, Vol. II, pp. 125-132.
KONEN (H.), Licht und Materie, pp. 360-388.
WATTS (W. M.), Study of Spectrum Analysis, pp. 167-173.
BALY (E. C. C.), Spectroscopy, pp. 529-558.
CAMPBELL (N. R.), Series Spectra, pp. 73-78.
JOHNSON (R. C.), Spectra, pp. 27-30.
KAYSER (H.), Handbuch der Spectroscopie, B. 2, pp. 611-672.
BACK (N.), Handbuch der Experimental Physik, B. 22, pp. 1-189.
VAN VLECK (J. H.), Quantum Principles, pp. 230-257.
HUND (F.), Linienspectren, pp. 78-111; 201-207.
CAMPBELL (N. R.), Modern Electrical Theory, pp. 83-102.
ABRAHAM (M.), Theorie der Elektrizitat, B. 2, pp. 71-79.
STONER (E. C.), Magnetism and Atomic Structure, pp. 212-244.
SOMMERFELD (A.), Atomic Structure and Spectral Lines, pp. 294-303 and 384-405.
BIRTWISTLE (C.), Quantum Theory, pp. 112-118.
BALY (E. C. C.), Spectroscopy, Vol. III, pp. 308-416.
ANDRADE (E. N. da C.), Structure of the Atom, pp. 501-581.

When he was shown these seventeen red cards he was immensely delighted and he said that we had saved much of his time by the preparation of these cross-reference cards.

This brings us to the economic aspect of the cross-referencing work. Such analytic cross-reference cards can be prepared only if the library has an adequate technical staff with high academic qualifications and thorough professional training. It has been found from four years' experience that a full-timed staff of five is necessary to deal with the annual accessions of a library, adding 6,000 volumes a year and that a volume requires six cards on an average. Roughly speaking this amounts to an average cost of about ten annas per volume.

To decide whether it is wise to spend this amount and to maintain such a staff, the Fourth Law would urge the library authorities to view it from a different angle—from the national angle so to speak. If it is not done, what is the wastage that would be involved in our talented high paid research worker spending some hours of his time in the search? Further if the work is not done once for all and in a thorough manner by the library staff, in the days and years to come the time of many such persons interested in Zeeman Effect will have to be wasted in going through the same process of search. This would mean repeated wastage not only of the nation's money but also of its best brains. Research should not be allowed to degenerate into a search of this type.

All the countries of the world are really competitors in matters of research; and the workers in any branch of research in our country should not be subjected to avoidable handicaps. Their precious time should be saved as much as possible by the libraries undertaking to do thorough cross-referencing work.

Similarly, consider the national wastage that would be involved in professor after professor and student after student—and that from year to year—pulling out book after book from the large literature collection of the library to make out an exhaustive list of its resources on Matthew Arnold. Is it an economical way of utilising the brain power and time of erudite professors and students? The Fourth Law would ask, "Is it not more economical from the national point of view, to introduce a division of labour here, by setting apart a few persons to prepare such exhaustive lists in all possible subjects?" Such work once done will be of use for ever.

BIBLIOGRAPHY

While examining this aspect of the Fourth Law, it may be well to raise the issue, "Is the cross-referencing to be confined to regular books or is it to be extended to periodicals also?" There is no doubt that the contents of periodicals should be indexed in a classified manner to SAVE THE TIME OF THE READER.

The number of periodicals in the field runs to thousands, (60,000 is one of the estimates). Even the Madras University Library gets about a thousand of them. The Yale University Library gets as many as 11,500. The articles on any topic get widely scattered in many of them. The time involved in listing them together is bound to be very large. It is not proper to divert the time of busy researchers to the task of listing them. On the other hand, it would be more economical, from the point of view of the community as a whole, to get it done by a special staff and make it available to all researchers. The Fourth Law would in fact go to the extent of lifting it, not only from the sphere of individual workers, but also from that of individual libraries and even of individual nations and would assign it to international organisations.

Let us take for example a recent subject like 'Raman Effect'. Since Sir C. V. Raman announced his discovery of a new radiation in his historic inaugural address before the South Indian Science Association at Bangalore on the 16th March, 1928, many physicists all over the world have turned their attention to this new phenomenon—its elucidation and its applications—and the periodicals in Physics are being flooded with the results of the work done on and with the aid of the Raman Effect. Both to avoid unnecessary duplication of work and to cut out new lines, it is desirable that all the results are rendered easily available to all the workers in the field. The publication of a bibliography of Raman Effect as Part IV of the IV Volume and in pp. 256-283 of the V volume of the *Indian Journal of Physics,* listing about 550 titles, has resulted in a substantial economy of time. In deference to the Fourth Law, many such special bibliographies are being published. Here are a few examples:—

International Catalogue of Scientific Literature.

Revue Semestrielle des publications mathematiques.

Science Abstracts.

Chemical Abstracts together with the cumulative indexes.

Bibliography of American Natural History.

Bibliographia Genetica.

The Annual Bibliography of English Language and Literature.

Orientalische Bibliographie.

Religionsgeschichtliche Bibliographie.

Bibliographie methodique du pragmatisme americain.

Psychological Abstracts.

Bibliographical Bulletin of International Affairs.

Bibliographie der Sozialwissenschaften.

Index to Legal Periodicals.

A detailed account of such bibliographies published so as to SAVE THE TIME OF THE READER will be found in Chapters III to XI of the book entitled '*Bibliography, practical, enumerative, historical*' by Henry Bartlett Van Hoesen.

The influence of the Fourth Law has even gone to the extent of bringing about the publication of bibliographies of bibliographies, such as the following:—

DARROW (K. K.): Classified list of published Bibliographies in Physics.

WEST (C. J.) and BEROLZHEIMER (D. D.): Bibliography of Bibliographies in Chemistry.

MATHEWS (E. B.): Catalogue of published Bibliographies in Geology.

PEDDIE (Robert Alexander): List of Bibliographical Works published since 1893.

One should not leave this section without referring to the great help that the Fourth Law can derive from the *Reference Catalogue*, the annual volumes of the *English Catalogue* and the *Subject Catalogue* of the British Museum Library and the short bibliographies appended to the articles in the *Encyclopædia Britannica*. Many of the problems of the readers can be solved expeditiously with the aid of these volumes. Hardly a day passes in a library without recourse to them. The Madras University Library has been systematically preparing cross-reference cards for all important bibliographical lists found at the ends of chapters or at the ends of books. This is a simple piece of work which every library can undertake to do. These cross-reference cards which have now accumulated to a large number are rendering invaluable service in SAVING THE TIME OF THE READER in the Madras University Library.

The chief contribution of the Fourth Law to Book-selection is that a fair and representative selection of bibliographical publications should be acquired. The *English Catalogue* or a corresponding annual is absolutely necessary in any library. What further bibliographical materials should be bought will depend on the nature of the library, the interests of its readers and its financial resources. A Scientific or University Library should carefully watch the announcements of cumulative indexes of the periodicals current in it and acquire them as a matter of course. It should also buy all possible bibliographies of individual authors in literature and as many subject bibliographies as possible. A public library should go in either for Poole's *Index* or for the British Library Association's *Index to Periodicals.* It may with advantage, subscribe also for the bibliographies published from time to time by the National Book Council.

REFERENCE WORK

We have seen in the last two sections the various types of bibliographical tools which are either constructed in the library or are constructed elsewhere and are bought by the library. Whether we consider an elaborate well-prepared catalogue with a profusion of cross-references or the numerous other bibliographical aids that are likely to be available in the library, it may not be an easy matter for an average reader to derive the fullest advantages of these time-saving devices. In the first place, some personal initiation will be essential to SAVE THE TIME OF THE READER in getting himself acquainted with their correct use. Even after the initiation, most readers will stand in need of the bibliographical service of the Reference Staff. With their constant practice, the Reference Staff are sure to acquire not only greater precision but also a much higher speed than the readers in handling the bibliographical apparatus. Again in spite of the initiation, the reader cannot become as familiar as the staff with the order in which the books are arranged. The librarian's intimate acquaintance with classification and cataloguing gives him an immense advantage over the reader in arriving quickly at the desired book or information. He knows the order in which the books fall. He knows the ins and outs of his catalogue. He can wield all kinds of indexes and catalogues with greater ease and speed. Hence the Fourth Law also would join hands with the first three Laws in pressing the need for an adequate Reference Staff in all libraries. The money spent on such a staff comes back to the nation in ever-increasing measure in the saving of the precious time of its best brains. That this is an economically sound proposition can be inferred from the fact that commercial and business libraries, maintained by business houses ungrudgingly pay for an adequate Reference Staff. They know the economic value of time. But academic libraries seem to be lacking in their power to perceive the value of time and are hence halting in appreciating the need for such a staff.

From the point of view of the Fourth Law, the work of the Reference Staff falls into two divisions: (1) Ready Reference Work, and (2) Reference Work proper. For purposes of Ready Reference Work, libraries that have faith in the Fourth Law maintain *information desks* and place them in a prominent position so as to attract the attention of the reader early in his transactions. The problems that frequently fall within the sphere of the persons in charge of the information desk are—

(*i*) the direction of the readers to the different parts of the library and to the appropriate members of the Reference Staff, if prolonged and intensive help is necessary;

(*ii*) instruction to new comers in the use of the library, particularly in the use of the catalogue and the other bibliographical tools available in the library and in the general outline of classification and shelf-arrangement; and

(*iii*) the supply of answers to simple queries, involving a minimum amount of search and the use of the few ready reference books such as year-books, directories and calendars usually kept at the information desk.

A good deal of the service rendered by the information desk may have to be over telephone wires. A retentive and associative memory coupled with capacity to do several things at once without flurry and the ability to turn from one subject to another with quickness and ease are essential if the service of the person at the information desk is to SAVE THE TIME OF THE READER substantially. Slow, dull-witted, immobile and absent-minded persons cannot be of any service to the Fourth Law.

Let us now turn to Reference Work proper. Let us follow the reader in the stack-room. If the library is ideally organised, he will soon find himself in charge of one who is a specialist in the bibliography of the subject in which he is interested. Such a reference-librarian will greet him with a smile and begin to talk to him in the language of his subject. Being put at ease by these circumstances, the reader will state his problems and his requirements as definitely as he can. The reference-librarian will unreservedly place at his disposal his varied bibliographical experience, built up by years of contact with several specialists seeking his help and by the constant handling of the tools and the resources of the library from various points of view. This will SAVE THE TIME OF THE READER considerably and enable him to get at his materials far more expeditiously than otherwise.

The reader may be a young inexperienced student who is unable to find out the relative value of the different books that bear the same class number. Then, the reference-librarian will SAVE HIS TIME by readily picking out the volumes whose standard is within his reach. The reader may take an amateur's interest in a subject. Then the reference-librarian will ascertain his previous equipment and work out for him a graded reading course, so that he can get the necessary acquaintance with the subject without any loss of time due to the unaided choice of incomprehensible books in an inconvenient order. The reader may be a busy administrator or specialist. In this case, the reference-librarian will pick out and assemble in advance all the materials that may be relevant to the topic pursued by him so that he can refer to them without wasting his precious time in knocking about in the different parts of the library to collect his materials.

Not long ago, a Sanskrit scholar came from an up-country town in search of some materials on certain aspects of Indian Philosophy. The Sanskrit books usually have perplexing titles, with hardly any indication as to the nature of the contents. Hence, he knew that there was no short cut to ascertain their value for his purpose except to open out each book and look it through. But he knew nothing either of the classified arrangement of the books or of the analytic nature of the subject catalogue. Nor did he know of the existence of the Reference Staff. On the other hand he had persuaded himself that, since his books would be in the Devanagari Script and his subject was an abstruse branch of ancient philosophy, he should not expect any assistance from anybody. Hence, he came prepared to spend some days to get his work done. On the first day, in spite of repeated offers, he declined all help and began to carry a few books at a time to his work-table. After about an hour or two, when he was beginning to show signs of exhaustion, he was again approached in a tactful manner and he consented to be shown round the stack-room. That gave a splendid opportunity to the reference-librarian to explain the various arrangements that the library had made to SAVE THE TIME OF THE READER. He was eventually taken to the Indian Philosophy region. After a talk for about an hour, he went out for lunch. Without going into further details it may be stated at once that at about 4-30 P.M., he sought permission to use the office telephone to request the station-master to get his berth reserved that very night. Nor is it necessary to reproduce here his many words of surprise and thanks for the manner in which the library staff had SAVED HIS TIME.

CHARGING AND DISCHARGING METHODS

Let us now move on with the reader. We shall assume that he has finished all the reading he intended to do within the library itself and that he is ready to go home. Let us assume that he desires to take a few books home. The process of making the necessary entries before permitting him to borrow the books for home reading is spoken of as the 'charging work'. The reverse process of receiving the books back when he returns them and releasing him from all further responsibility about those books is known as 'discharging'. Before the advent of the Fourth Law, the method of charging and discharging was very cumbrous and wasteful. Even to-day, such antiquated methods still prevail in many of our libraries. It will be shown when we consider the Fifth Law that those methods will absolutely break down if the library functions up to the ideal of the first three laws. Here we shall confine ourselves only to the time aspect of the process.

The method that is prevalent in most of our libraries may be described as that of the *Day-book and Ledger*. In this method the reader fills up his name and the author, title and call number of the book in a printed form. The counter clerk copies these details in the Day-book and posts these daily records in a personal ledger to avoid searching through the Day-book to find a given entry. A few pages of this ledger are assigned to each reader. The call number of the book drawn and the date of issue are noted in the columns ruled for the purpose. On the return of the volume the date of return is set down in another column. If a book is returned after the due date the amount of fine due and the date and the number of the receipt of collection are entered in additional columns. Certain libraries get all these details posted also in another ledger in which each book gets a page. Apart from the impossibility of keeping up the alphabetic or call number order in such ledgers, the process of making the entries both while charging and discharging makes the reader wait long at the counter. It is made still worse in rush hours since only one person could use this record book at a time. When this system was in vogue in the Madras University Library till three years ago, the average time wasted by a reader as a result of this old fashioned method of charging and discharging was about fifteen minutes.

But the recognition of the Fouth Law has led the library profession to overhaul the charging system completely. To effect this overhauling the purposes of the present day charging system had to be critically analysed. The charging system should answer the purposes of three definite records, *viz.*, a time record, a book record and a readers' record. In other words it should give ready answer to queries of the following type:—

(1) What and how many books are lent on any date.

(2) Who has each volume on loan on any date.

(3) What books are due on any date.

The most economical charging system that has been devised to answer all these purposes and at the same time fulfil the requirements of the Fourth Law may be described as the 'Two-card' system. In this system each book is given a book-card which is inserted in a book-pocket pasted on the inside of the front cover of the book, and each reader is provided with as many borrowers' tickets as the number of volumes which he is entitled to remove from the library at one time.

Now let us follow our reader. He will bring up to the counter the books he desires to take home. He will present these books with an equal number of his tickets to the counter clerk at the exit gate. This clerk will immediately stamp the due date on the date labels of the books, release the book-cards from their respective pockets in the books and couple each of them with one of the reader's tickets. As soon as this is done the reader will be at liberty to go home with his books. The time taken by this process of charging will be far less than the time taken to describe it. In fact it should be possible to charge at least a dozen books in a minute. Perhaps it is only in the charging method that the ideal of the Fourth Law has been actually reached.

Different devices are employed to couple the book-card and the corresponding reader's ticket. One popular method is to make the reader's ticket in the form of a stiff pocket and insert the book-card in it. Whatever be the means of coupling them, these coupled cards are arranged in a tray by the call number behind a date guide showing the due date.

When the book is brought back to the library the counter clerk at the entrance gate finds out the due date and the call number from the date label and with their aid he picks out from the charged tray the book-card coupled with the reader's ticket. The book-card is inserted into the book pocket and the reader's ticket is handed over to the reader. This process also takes as little time as the charging process. There are many variations of this method which it would be out of place to dilate upon in this book. It is hoped to have in this series a separate volume on counter work, which will appropriately deal in detail with as many systems as possible.

THE TIME OF THE STAFF

We have seen that one of the methods employed to SAVE THE TIME OF THE READER is to provide an adequate number of hands for reference work. Hence it follows that the greater the number of such hands and the longer the period for which they can be spared for actual reference work, the fuller will be the extent to which the purposes of the Fourth Law would be fulfilled. It follows as a corollary from this that the Fourth Law implies also that the time of the staff spent in routine work should be minimised as much as possible. This appeal of the Fourth Law has been engaging the attention of libraries for a long time and has produced splendid results. While a full account of the evolution of the methods of library routine will be given in a special volume on library routine, it may be stated in a word that the effect of the Fourth Law has been to revolutionise the method of keeping library records. The old bound books have been completely given up and loose cards have taken their place. It may even be claimed that the card system which appears to be now fast entering into all kinds of business houses and offices is a most noteworthy contribution of Library Science to modern administrative methods in general. It must be admitted that, in its turn, Library Science owes the invention of the card system to a sincere desire on the part of librarians to satisfy the Fourth Law in all possible ways.

We may perhaps illustrate the extent to which the card system can SAVE THE TIME OF THE STAFF by considering one set of library records, namely, those that deal with book selection, book ordering, book accessioning, book cataloguing and withdrawal. Perhaps the chart in the next page showing the inter-relation or the linking up of the records relating to these processes will simplify the discussion of this question. The first row indicates the sources for book-selection. The nature of the records mentioned in the second and the third rows is obvious. The fourth and the fifth rows show the different channels through which books may come into the library. A popular alternative name for 'accession cabinet' is stock-register. The withdrawal cabinet contains the list of books lost, worn out by use, or otherwise ceasing to be part of the library. The registers in each of any two consecutive rows are linked with each other by certain common entries, *e.g.*, the order number is posted in the vouchers, and the voucher number, in the order registers.

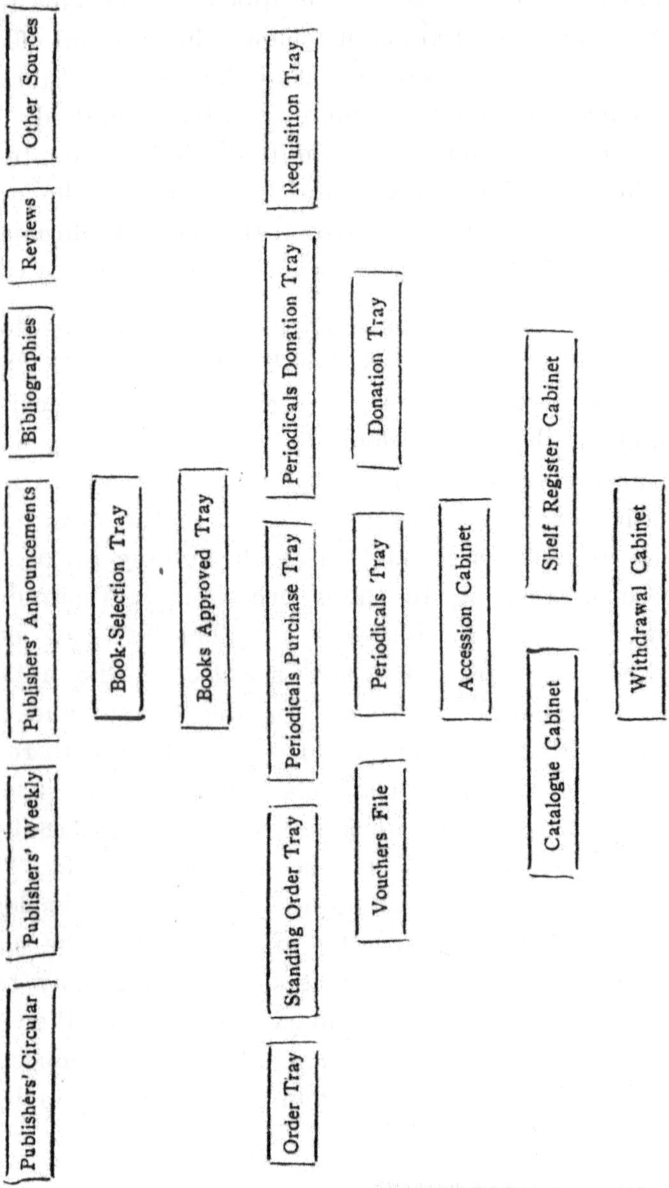
Publishers' Circular
Publishers' Weekly
Publishers' Announcements
Bibliographies
Reviews
Other Sources
Book-Selection Tray
Books Approved Tray
Order Tray
Standing Order Tray
Periodicals Purchase Tray
Periodicals Donation Tray
Requisition Tray
Vouchers File
Periodicals Tray
Donation Tray
Accession Cabinet
Catalogue Cabinet
Shelf Register Cabinet
Withdrawal Cabinet

In the pre-card days the titles of the books for consideration would be written either on sheets of paper or in note-books. Books not approved would be struck off. If too many items were struck off, it might become necessary to re-write the remaining items. Then, in the course of checking this list with the existing stock of the library, several items may have again to be struck off and notes about edition or year of publication, etc., of the existing books may have to be made against some of the items. At this stage again if the pages become too congested the surviving items might have to be re-written once again. Then the 'order' list would be prepared. It is very unlikely that all the books of an 'order' would be supplied on the same day. As the books come they would have to be listed. This might be the fourth occasion of writing out the entries. This fourth list would really constitute the Stock-book or the Accession Register as it is usually called. Then the catalogue cards and the shelf-register cards would be written and lastly it might be necessary to keep a separate register for the books withdrawn from the library. Thus, excluding the writing out of the catalogue and the shelf-register, the details of every book would have to be written about five times. In the card system, on the other hand, it is enough if the details are written once instead of five times. This gives a measure of the extent to which the card system SAVES THE TIME OF THE STAFF.

Ac. No.	Cl. No.	Wl. No.	
Don. No.			
Auth.			
Title.			
Size.	Colln.	Edn.	Yr.
Pubr.		Pub-price.	
Series, etc.			
Review.			
M.U.L.			

Vendor			Cost. Indian. Foreign.						
	Date.	Initials.							
Seln.			Order No.						
Apprd.			Voucher No.						
Order.				Cur. Yr.			Total.		
Recd.									
Paid.			Sub. No.						
Accnd.									
Cut.			Lang No.						
Clasd.									
Cat.			Cost.	Rs.	A.	P.	Rs.	A.	P.
Shld.			Sub.						
Bound.									
Wl.			Total.						

In the card system one and the same card serves the purposes of five different record books. A form of the card which is of the standard size 5" × 3" is shown in the previous page.

It would be realised as we describe the use of this card that, in addition to saving time, it affords many other conveniences.

A separate card is used for each item selected. All the details in the first page of the card except accession number, call number and withdrawal number are entered as soon as the selection is made. The entries about review may perhaps have to be written at a later stage when the review becomes actually available. The source from which the details about the book are taken is indicated near the left-hand bottom corner of the first page. The person making these entries puts his initials and date in the first row on the second side of the card. All such cards are roughly arranged in a classified manner to facilitate the work of those who have to approve the indent finally. The approving authority has just to sort it into three groups:—"selected", "rejected", and "deferred consideration". Then the cards of the first group are transferred to the "approved" tray and the cards of the other groups, into corresponding trays. Then, the person responsible for the ordering work checks each card with the stock of the library and after the cards relating to books already in the library are eliminated, the surviving cards are transferred to the "order" tray with the notes in the cards themselves.

If the library purchases the books through an agent the "order" is typed straightaway from these cards. If, on the other hand, the library purchases the books directly from the publishers the cards in the "order" tray are first sorted according to the publishers and separate orders are typed for each publisher. In any case the "order" number and date of order are entered in appropriate places in the second page of the card. The vendor is usually instructed to mention the "order" number and date in the bill accompanying the supply, and the cards themselves are kept in the "order" tray behind the date guides showing the date of order.

On the arrival of the books the cards relating to them are readily lifted from the "order" tray and inserted in the title page of the corresponding books. The accessioning clerk carefully scrutinizes the books by comparing them with the entries in the cards with regard to author, title, size, collation, edition, date of publication, publisher, and series if any, and also checks the amount claimed in the bill with the published price noted on the card. If the supply is correct, the bill is passed for payment and the voucher number and the date of payment are noted in appropriate places in the card. The accession number is put in the book, on the card and in the bill also.

Then the books and the cards are passed on to the classifier and the cataloguer, who prepare the necessary catalogue cards and shelf-register cards and post the call-numbers in the cards. Then, the shelf-register cards and the accession cards are tallied by the accessioning clerk, after which the shelf-register cards are filed in the shelf-register cabinets and the original cards are transferred to the accession cabinets, and form part of the accession register.

Lastly, when the book has to be withdrawn from the library, the corresponding card is transferred from the accession cabinet to the withdrawal cabinet and given a withdrawal number. Thus, we have seen, one and the same card is made to migrate by successive stages from the "book selection" tray to the "withdrawal" tray and thus SAVE THE TIME OF THE STAFF and also add considerably to their convenience. Roughly speaking, for every minute required in the card system, five minutes would have to be spent in the old system. Further, the initials against the different items in the second column would make it possible to trace to the right persons the responsibility for any mistakes detected at any subsequent time—however late it may be. Experience has shown that this has a wholesome chastening effect on the staff. The progressive tabular statements indicated in the backside of the card enable the staff to furnish, without any loss of time, replies to the queries that are not infrequently put by the managing authorities. The confusion, dislocation of work and the excitement caused by queries of this type are well-known. In spite of the time wasted, satisfactory and accurate replies are seldom obtainable. But it has been found that this type of card has made work of such a nature not only accurate but also quite easy and expeditious.

In a similar manner, the routine work of libraries is being simplified in many other ways, in order to SAVE THE TIME OF THE STAFF and thereby to SAVE THE TIME OF THE READER.

CENTRAL CATALOGUING

Another direction in which an attempt is being made to SAVE THE TIME OF THE STAFF is that of central cataloguing. From the larger national point of view, much time is wasted as a result of every library continuing "to catalogue its own books, regardless of the fact that the same books undergo similar treatment in some hundreds of libraries throughout the country". Even as early as the last quarter of the nineteenth century, the American Library Association began to devote its thought to this problem and experimented on a small scale, in the production and distribution of printed cards, in order to SAVE THE TIME OF THE STAFF of individual libraries. But, a large-scale organisation for central cataloguing was started only in 1901. The circular on the *Distribution of Catalogue Cards*[1] issued by the Library of Congress on October 28, 1901, marks an epoch in the achievements of the Fourth Law of Library Science. The difficulties experienced in the earlier years of this bold experiment are fully described

(1) *Report of the Librarian of Congress*, 1901, pp. 68-73.

by the Chief of the Card Division[2] in his *Reminiscences and Observations on the Card Distribution Work of the Library of Congress.*

But, the American libraries were not slow in recognising the value of central cataloguing to the cause of the Fourth Law. In the year 1929-30, the number of subscribers to the printed cards was as high as 5,011. Even foreign countries like China and Russia have begun to purchase these cards for their libraries. This wide market has naturally resulted in reducing the cost of these cards. The approximate cost of the cards required for a volume is estimated as four annas, whereas, as it has been already stated, the cost of preparing the cards in the library itself is as high as 10 annas per book in a Madras Library. The number of books for which congress cards are now available is 1,135,265. Till now, these cards contained only the Congress call number. Arrangements have now been made to print on them the Dewey number also. The success of this American experiment is leading many other countries to start similar organisations to SAVE THE TIME OF THE STAFF of their libraries. "The Russian and German governmental libraries already have card printing and distributing agencies. The Czechoslovakians and the Spaniards have started similar activities." There are indications that the countries of South America are also contemplating the inauguration

(2) *Essays offered to Herbert Putnam . . . on his thirtieth anniversary as Librarian of Congress*, pp. 195-206.

of central cataloguing, through a governmental agency. The Public Libraries Committee of England and Wales have strongly commended the proposal for establishing a Central Cataloguing Agency in the British Museum. They urge in its support that "a very large amount of work, time and skill would be saved" and that, as a result of the Library of Congress Scheme, "Time and money formerly spent by individual libraries on cataloguing the same books have been directed to more useful purposes".

The Fourth Law would urge the library world to reconcile the differences in the cataloguing codes of different countries so as to make the way clear for international co-operative cataloguing.

LIBRARY LOCATION

So far we have been dealing with the problem of saving the time of the reader after he enters the library. But, the Fourth Law is interested also in the time taken by the reader to reach the library. In other words, a library should be so located as to SAVE THE TIME OF THE READER. In a college, the library should be centrally located so as to be easily accessible to the students of all the classes. The research departments of a University should, as far as possible, be housed in the library buildings. The research laboratories, in which the scientific departments have to be housed, should be built in the same compound as the library.

But the location of a city-library cannot be made to satisfy the Fourth Law in such an easy way. It would be impossible to find, in a big city, any site which would be equally accessible from all parts of the city. The larger cities of the West are reconciling this geographical difficulty with the demand of the Fourth Law by establishing branch libraries and delivery stations in all their divisions. We had occasion to give some examples of this practice, when we were discussing the subject of library location in the light of the First Law.[1] The ideal should be to provide a sufficient number of branch libraries, so that every citizen may find a branch within ten-minutes' walk from his residence.

Rural readers suffer even more from the difficulties caused by distance in the operation of the Fourth Law. A branch library cannot be built near every farm home as it can be built near homes in the cities. The only means available to SAVE THE TIME OF THE RURAL READER is to put the library on wheels and take it to him from time to time. A good selection of books, chosen by a trained librarian, should be put in a motor van equipped as a travelling library and sent out for periodical exchange in small village libraries, delivery stations and isolated farm homes. Where villages or homes are inaccessible to motors, special arrangements should be made for the conveyance of books by hand from and to the nearest highway.

"Do you mean to say that the District Board can afford to take books out into the country in

(1) *Vide* p. 10.

this manner? Ridiculous! Let country people come to the town library and get their books as we do," some of the city-dwellers may say. But time is as precious to the rural reader as to the town reader and the Fourth Law is not meant merely for the town libraries. The Fourth Law would argue "There is nothing more ridiculous or more expensive in the institution of the travelling library system by a District Board than in the maintenance of the postal delivery system by the government. Is not a letter taken many miles into the country? Whereas the mail has to be taken to every rural home every day, the books may have to be taken to each village, perhaps only once in a month!" In recent years, these arguments of the Fourth Law have carried conviction to most western countries and Rural Travelling Libraries on a District basis are being rapidly established. They aim at adequate library service within easy reach of every one. They are operated from the district headquarters library through deposit stations and branches. The accompanying diagram illustrates the ideal way in which the Fourth Law is observed by one of the County Libraries of the State of New York. It delivers books within a mile from each home.

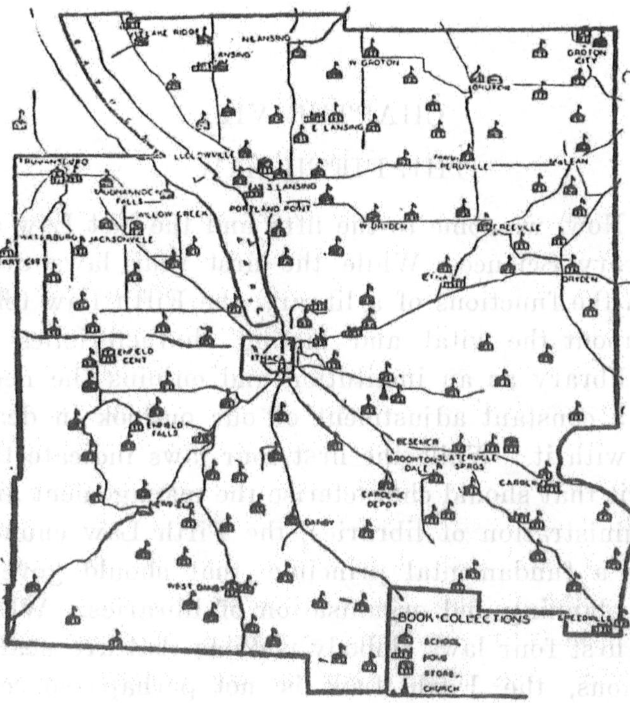

TOMPKINS COUNTY, NEW YORK STATE

Area—476 square miles.

Number of branch-stations visited by the book-van of the County Library—160.

One station for every three square miles.

CHAPTER VII

THE FIFTH LAW

Now, we come to the fifth and the last Law of Library Science. While the first four laws deal with the functions of a library, the Fifth Law tells us about the vital and lasting characteristics of the library as an institution and enjoins the need for a constant adjustment of our outlook in dealing with it. While the first four laws indicate the spirit that should characterise the management and administration of libraries, the Fifth Law enunciates a fundamental principle that should govern the planning and organisation of libraries. While the first four laws embody maxims that are nearly obvious, the Fifth Law is not perhaps so self-evident.

The Fifth Law is: A LIBRARY IS A GROWING ORGANISM. It is an accepted biological fact that a growing organism alone will survive. An organism which ceases to grow will petrify and perish. The Fifth Law invites our attention to the fact that the library, as an institution, has all the attributes of a growing organism. A growing organism takes in new matter, casts off old matter, changes in size and takes new shapes and forms. Apart from sudden and apparently discontinuous changes involved in metamorphosis, it is also subject to a slow continuous change which leads to what is known as 'variation', in biological parlance, and to the evolution of new forms. This change is so slow but so effective that the protagonists of evolution assert that it is the shapeless undifferentiated protozoa of the *Palaeozoic* age that has transformed itself, by successive stages of variation, into the most differentiated specimen of creation—the human being. The one thing that has been persisting through all those changes of form has been the vital principle of life. So it is with the library.

GROWTH IN SIZE

We shall first trace the consequences of the simple growth in size. For this purpose, it may be convenient to examine the main parts of the organism that are capable of growing. They are the books, the readers and the staff. It is well to repeat here that a modern library is a trinity of these factors. It must be clearly realised that a collection of books without readers has no more right to be called a library than a group of readers without books and that the mere juxtaposition of books and readers without the service of a staff, that know to effect contact between the right reader and the right book, at the right time and in the right manner, cannot constitute a library either. The modesty with which library authorities underestimate the rate of growth of each of these factors is unimaginable. We shall have occasion to give instances of this modesty as we go into details. But a far less pardonable thing is to set about organising a library as if it would be stationary, as if neither the books, nor the readers, nor the staff would grow in number. There could be nothing more reprehensible than a faulty organisation obstructing the free development of a library, or indeed of any institution, to its full stature. The frequent recurrence of this fatal mistake in library matters is due to the failure to realise a fundamental fact, *viz.*, an organisation which may be suitable for a small library may completely fail when the library grows big. Technologists know from painful experience that a successful laboratory method may not always turn out to be a successful manufacturing method. Physicists too are now beginning to realise that what may hold good in situations of an infinitesimal order may cease to do so in similar situations of a finite order. The library organisation should not short-sightedly allow itself to be unduly influenced by the present size but should plan its lay out in such a way as to make it easy to keep pace with the necessary growth of the library. Let us now take up each of the three elements of the trinity and trace the consequence of its growth on the different aspects of library organisation.

BOOKS

Let us first take the books. The number of books in a live library must and does grow. We shall assume that there is hardly any probability for the recurrence of the familiar anecdote of the

Kansas legislator who objected to an appropriation for more books for the University library with the eloquent words, "Mr. Speaker, I object to spending this money. Why, they've got forty thousand books there at Lawrence now, and I don't believe any one of them professors has read 'em all yet!"[1] We shall also assume the impracticability of the Quincy plan, which is to equalise the rate of weeding out and the rate of accessioning, after the size of the collection reaches an arbitrary norm. While finance is no doubt the ultimate deciding factor, it cannot be denied that some light is thrown on the average rate of growth of the book-collections of libraries by the following tables giving the annual rate of book-production in some of the important countries of the world.

Table I giving the number of books published in some of the foreign countries in 1927 is extracted from p. 281 of Vol. CXV of the *Publishers' Weekly*. I am indebted to the Educational Secretary to the Government of India for Table II giving the number of books published in some of the Indian Provinces in 1927.

TABLE I.

International Book Production Statistics for 1927.

Name of the Country.	No. of books published.
1. Russia	.. 36,680
2. Germany	.. 31,026

(1) BISHOP (William Warner): *Backs of Books*, p. 5.

Name of the country.		No. of books published.
3.	Japan	19,967
4.	Great Britain	13,810
5.	France	11,922
6.	United States	10,153
7.	Poland	6,888
8.	Italy	6,533
9.	Holland	6,103
10.	Denmark	3,293
11.	Sweden	2,652
12.	Spain	2,374
13.	Switzerland	1,909
14.	Norway	1,238

TABLE II.

Book Production Statistics of India for 1927.

Name of the Province.		No. of books published.
1.	Madras	4,042
2.	Bengal	3,425
3.	United Provinces	3,298
4.	Punjab	2,537
5.	Bombay	2,211
6.	Bihar and Orissa	1,500
7.	Delhi	414
8.	Central Provinces	217
9.	Burma	122
10.	Assam	54

To view the subject from another angle, here is a table giving the annual rate of accession in a few libraries:—

Name of the Library.		No. of Vols. added in a year.
1.	Library of Congress ..	202,111
2.	Boston Public Library ..	94,339
3.	Cambridge University Library.	90,916
4.	Birmingham Public Library.	28,566
5.	New York State Library ..	23,313
6.	Imperial Library, Calcutta ..	7,832
7.	Madras University Library ..	5,628
8.	Aberdeen Public Library ..	3,726

STACK-ROOM AND FITTINGS

We shall first trace the effect of the growth of stock on Library Architecture. The part of the library building that is primarily concerned with this is the stack-room. Its size, its relative position, the book-rack forming the unit out of which the stack is built, the parts of the book-rack, the shelf-planks, label-holders and all such things relating to the housing of the books will have to be examined in the light of the inevitable growth in stock.

Taking the size first, it is seldom that the Fifth Law does not outwit the library authorities. To take an example, the managing committee of a certain library estimated as follows in the year 1911: "In order to accommodate the books which the library already possesses together with those that the committee expects to purchase during the next year, a room 40' × 40' × 18' would be required. To accommodate books to be added . . . during the next twenty-five years (on the assumption that the annual allotment will continue the same) another room of the same size will be necessary". But by about 1922, the committee was led to modify its estimate as follows:—"The two rooms each measuring 40' × 40' × 18' provided for the storage of books may be raised to three as future additions are likely to be much more than was originally anticipated". Later experience has shown that the stock, which was 7,000 in 1911, grew to as much as 70,000 in 1930. The stack-room had to be actually designed to consist of four tiers each 144' × 34' × 9', with provision for doubling the space as and when required.

The amount of forethought that the Fifth Law has induced in American Universities is illustrated by the following description of the planning of the Yale University Library. "The problem of the general library was to provide adequately for present needs and for future needs so far as they could be foreseen. The programme therefore asked for suitable accommodation for three million volumes on the day of opening, and ultimately for four million volumes".

Apart from emphasising the need for a generous provision for the future, the Fifth Law has been slowly eliminating the old alcove and gallery forms of construction for the storage of books. The stack form is steadily gaining ground and a further development in stack architecture is the stack tower. Another solution which has been proposed to meet the increase in stock is the building of repositories of the warehouse type for the close packing of the book-racks for the economical storage of books infrequently used. Each rack is provided with wheels, so that it can be pulled out from its neighbours, when a book on its shelves is required for use. No doubt this way of meeting the Fifth Law would be prejudicial to the interests of the Third Law. It is a case of compromise here. It is only books which are entirely out of date and are not likely to be of any but antiquarian interest that would be consigned to such closely packed racks.

As the size of the stack-room must grow with the stock of books, it is necessary that the architectural features and the lay out should admit of an easy extension of the stack-room. Horizontal expansion may not always be possible. Hence, it is desirable to make the foundations of the stack-room strong enough to take extra tiers.

The unit racks of which the stack-room is built should all be equal in every way, so that the additions can be made by any number of units at a time. In particular, the shelf-planks should all be of identical dimensions, so that they can be interchanged in any manner. They should also be adjustable. While steel-shelves can be made universally adjustable, even wooden shelves can be made adjustable to an inch with the help of Tonk's fittings. The need for interchangeability and adjustability can be understood if we put together the Fifth Law and the fact that the books are to be arranged in a classified manner on a subject basis. As further additions are made, the books will have to be shifted from shelf to shelf, to keep their relative order intact. As books will be of all sizes, full freedom of adjustment of shelves will be necessary, to avoid waste of space.

Another consequence of shifting the books as the library grows will be the need for frequently changing the shelf-labels. We have already seen the need for a very large number of shelf-labels. In fact, a shelf-label will have to be assigned to every group of twenty books on an average. The frequency of shifting them as a result of the Fifth Law is bound to be very great. Hence, much thought has been devoted to the invention of a suitable form of label-holder. Primitive methods of shelf-labelling, such as sticking the labels to the edge of the shelf with gum or writing out the name of the class on the edge with a piece of chalk, will prove unmanageable in a growing library. A common form of label-holder consists of a piece of transparent xylonite bent at right angles and fixed to the underside of the shelf with a pair of drawing pins. The labour involved in pulling out and fixing the pins turns out to be prohibitive. Another form of label-holder is made of sheet metal, with the upper and lower edges flanged so as to form grooves to receive the labels. They are fitted to the shelves by projections at top and bottom, and are capable of being moved forward and backward as required. But the simplest and the cheapest method is to cut a groove of a suitable cross-section in the edge of the shelf itself. The shelf planks of the book-racks designed by me for the Madras University are one inch thick. A slightly wedge-shaped groove cut in its front edge takes a shelf-label 5|8" wide. The label can be moved from end to end and can be inserted or removed without disturbing the shelf and its contents. This design has proved to be quite satisfactory. There are no sharp edges in this device and there is nothing involving waste of time.

PERIODICALS ROOM

Another part of the library building which needs careful designing in the light of the Fifth Law is the periodicals room. Its size and its furniture will have to be examined in the light of the inevitable growth in the number of periodicals current in a growing library. The rate of increase is indicated by the following figures:—[1]

Name of Library	In Year	No. of Periodicals	In Year	No. of Periodicals	Amount of Increase.
Madras	1908	160	1931	913	571%
Ames	1900	200	1925	1,414	707%
California	1913	7,000	1925	11,179	160%
Illinois	1900	414	1924	9,943	2401%
Iowa	1900	213	1925	1,176	552%
Michigan	1900	775	1925	3,361	434%
Minnesota	1906	321	1925	1,715	534%
Oregon	1909	158	1925	778	492%
Yale	1920	8,890	1925	11,548	130%

(1) The figures for American Libraries are taken from WORKS (George Allan): *College and University Library Problems*, p. 124-*a*.

Another factor to be remembered in this connection is that the number of scientific periodicals published in the world is estimated to exceed 25,000, while it would exceed 60,000 if non-scientific periodicals are taken in the count.

To satisfy the first four Laws in general, and the Third Law and the Fourth Law in particular, it is necessary that the current numbers of all the periodicals taken by the library should be displayed in a classified order in a special periodicals room. The periodicals room should be of a sufficiently large size and should be so located and designed as to admit of extension. Further, to economise in table space, at least four rows of periodicals should be accommodated on each table. The periodicals should be put in good leather binders and made to stand vertically with the front cover facing the reader. The rows should be one behind the other in ascending steps, so that the periodicals in all the rows are clearly visible.

CATALOGUE ROOM

Another part of the library building which should be generously provided for in consequence of the growth in stock is the catalogue room or the room in which the catalogue cabinets are kept. A standard unit cabinet, which occupies a floor area of 23" × 28", can hold 48,000 catalogue cards We have seen that each book may have to be given six catalogue cards on an average, if the Second, Third and Fourth Laws are to be satisfied. Thus, a unit cabinet is required for every eight thousand volumes. One can also infer from this the rate at which the number of catalogue cabinets will increase in a growing library. This consequence of the Fifth Law should be borne in mind in designing the catalogue room. Not only should that room be made sufficiently big to begin with, but provision should also be made for its extension. The Fourth Law would, on its part, urge that it should be located just near the entrance to the stack-room.

CATALOGUE

We shall next consider the effect of the Fifth Law on the physical form of the catalogue. If A LIBRARY IS A GROWING ORGANISM, it follows that the library catalogue will also be a growing one. In fact, the rate of growth of the catalogue may be said to be six times the rate of growth of the number of books, as a book requires six entries on an average. Hence, the first effort of the Fifth Law in the matter of the catalogue was to fight against the printed catalogue. Taking a library which adds 6,000 volumes a year and assuming that a page of the printed catalogue can take 20 entries, a volume of 300 pages would be necessary to print a catalogue even on the basis of one entry for a book. But, if, in accordance with the requirements of the other Laws, the catalogue should be of the classified form with an alphabetic index and a profusion of cross-references, the volume would swell to 1,800 pages. The time taken to see a catalogue of that size through the press would keep it always behind date at least by a year. That is to say, the latest books, which are of the greatest interest, would not find a place in it. Further, there is the question of cost, and that of cumulating the annual volumes from time to time. On the other hand, a library catalogue never sells even when the price is nominal. Persons familiar only with libraries which are either stationary or at best grow inordinately slowly do not easily appreciate the waste and confusion involved in printing the catalogue of a growing library. Accustomed to the periodical supply of printed lists by libraries of slow growth, such persons fret and fume if printed catalogues are not supplied. If one attempts to convince them by argument, they refuse to listen and express their bitterness by saying that it is all the tyranny of experts. It may be more truly called the tyranny of large numbers or the tyranny of the Fifth Law. And the experts only try to find a way out of that tyranny.

But a more inexcusable attitude was that of the principal of a college, who said that the college did not mind the cost, since it realised the whole amount by forcing each student to buy a copy. What a narrow view! Was money to be wasted simply because it came from the pocket of the student? If money can be extracted from the students, can it not be utilised to enrich the library collection, instead of being wasted on an unwanted, out-of-date, poorly made list, passing under the dignified title of *Library Catalogue?* It is notorious how considerations of economy begin to loom large when the question of staff or the allotment for books is brought up. But all sense of economy seems to vanish away when the annual or biennial printing of the catalogue is undertaken.

Assuming that the catalogue can not be printed and that it should be only a manuscript one, let us examine what form the Fifth Law would recommend for it. It was the bound book form that was in use for a long time. But, in a growing library, the need for interpolating entries to keep up their correct sequence soon led to the adoption of the "paste-down form". In this form, the entries are written, typed or printed on narrow strips of paper, which are pasted down on the pages of a bound book, leaving ample interspace for future interpolations. If any region gets congested, the strips in that region are lifted up and redistributed. Apart from such paste-down catalogues soon becoming an eye-sore, the time and labour involved in lifting and pasting are prohibitive.

The next stage of evolution to which the Fifth Law brought the catalogue was the loose-leaf form. Here, each leaf is made to take about half a dozen entries and the relative order of the leaves can be easily maintained. Several forms of loose-leaf binders have been invented during the last twenty or thirty years. The Kalamazoo binder is of a strong and convenient form although it is a little too costly. The loose-leaf idea, thus originated by the force of the Fifth Law of Library Science, has now spread everywhere. Most of the business houses are now bidding good-bye to their bound books and are introducing loose-leaf ledgers in their place. Atlases, encyclopædias, directories and such other publications, parts of which frequently become out of date, are nowadays issued in loose-leaf form, so that they may be maintained perpetually up-to-date, with the least cost and the least waste.

But, even in the loose-leaf catalogue, the insertion of more than one entry in a leaf led to a break in the sequence, which became increasingly inconvenient as the library grew more and more. To avoid this, the size of the leaf was reduced and only one entry was put on a leaf. It was next felt that it was inconvenient to handle such small thin leaves.

This brought into the field the card form of the catalogue. After a good deal of experimentation, 5″ × 3″ has now been accepted as the most convenient size. Each card gets one and only one entry. Hence, the right sequence is always maintained. Cards of .01 inch thickness are found to be suitable. As the cards should stand wear and tear, tough cards of close texture should be selected. Library suppliers like the Libraco, 62, Cannon St., London, specialise in the production of such cards. Their "35 cards, medium thickness, round punched," which cost about Rs. 8-8-0 per 1,000 including freight and customs duties are found to be quite serviceable. As in the case of the loose-leaf ledger, the card system is another epoch making contribution of the library profession to the business world in general. It has introduced great convenience, freedom, neatness and up-to-dateness in the maintenance of all kinds of records.

SHELF-REGISTER

In the same manner the shelf-register, which shows the books in the order in which they occur on the shelf and is indispensable for checking the stock of the library, has also passed through similar stages of evolution and has finally assumed the card form, as a result of the Fifth Law.

CLASSIFICATION SCHEME

Another important matter that needs to be examined in the light of the Fifth Law is the classification of books. In the first place, as A LIBRARY IS A GROWING ORGANISM and as knowledge itself is growing, it is necessary that the "classification must be comprehensive, embracing all past and present knowledge and allowing places for any possible additions to knowledge". Indeed this has been set down by Mr. Sayers as the first canon of classification. To quote Sayers again, "A classification must be elastic, expansible, and hospitable in the highest degree. That is to say, it must be so constructed that any new subject may be inserted into it without dislocating its sequence". Cases like that of *Wave Mechanics, Matrices, Raman Effect, Internal Combustion Engine, Radium, Behaviourism, Dalton Plan* and the entire subject of *Sociology* have had to be accommodated within living memory. It can not be said that all the printed schemes in force have come quite unscathed out of this trial.

In addition to the scheme of classes being comprehensive and hospitable, the notation attached to them should be perfectly flexible. The greatest service done to Librarianship by Melvil Dewey is the demonstration of the immense potentiality of the decimal notation in meeting the difficulties due to growth. It is regrettable that the influential scheme of the Library of Congress should have failed to utilise the services of such a flexible type of notation and have adopted the primitive method of leaving gaps in the ordinary serial use of numbers. The Fifth Law will soon outgrow the gaps, however farseeing and generous they might be. It is only the decimal notation that will remain unbaffled by that law. Indeed the brilliant success of the decimal notation in overcoming the trials of the Fifth Law of Library Science is leading to its adoption in other spheres as well. Analytically minded authors like Jesperson and Whittaker, are beginning to number the paragraphs and chapters of their writings in a strictly decimal way. Some authors even claim that the use of the decimal notation adds substantially to clarity of thought.

It is by no means easy to secure hospitality of classes and flexibility of notation to the full satisfaction of the Fifth Law. Un-thought-of difficulties are likely to crop up as the library grows. One should not light-heartedly venture to construct schemes of classification. The old plan of dividing a library into about a dozen or two main classes and numbering the books in each class consecutively as received will soon prove inadequate and lead to confusion as the library grows. It is only ignorance of the Fifth Law that makes many of our libraries adopt such a plan. The best course is to follow a recognised printed scheme of classification. There are four such standard schemes used in English speaking countries. They are *Brown's Subject Classification*, *Cutter's Expansive Classification*, *Dewey's Decimal Classification* and *The Library of Congress Classification*. Of these, *Dewey's Decimal Classification* is the most popular. It is used in about 14,000 libraries. *The Library of Congress Classification* is also being largely used in America. The supply of printed catalogue cards by the Library of Congress has made this scheme very popular. Cutter's scheme and Brown's scheme are not used in many libraries as there is no agency to bring them up-to-date from time to time. E. C. Richardson's *Classification, Theoretical and Practical* contains an essay on the bibliographical history of systems of classification. There are no less than 161 systems mentioned by him. But, as has been already said, it is only two of these that have stood the test of time.

I have constructed a new scheme known as the *Colon Classification*. It is adopted in the Madras University Library and in a few other Indian libraries which are beginning to classify their books. The notation of the scheme is a mixed one and has taken full advantage of the flexibility of the decimal use of digits. It has also many mnemonic features. The conscious use of multiple characteristics as basis of classification, without leading to cross classification, has made its classes greatly elastic. The next volume of this series will give an account of this classification.

Before proceeding further, it may be advantageous to mention here a practical detail which should be borne in mind along with the Fifth Law. The call number which individualises the book, has to be written in practice in a dozen places, *viz.*, the back of the title page of the book, the date label pasted in the book, the back of the book, the book card, the shelf-register, the accession register, and each one of the catalogue-cards corresponding to the book—and we have already stated that the average number of catalogue-cards is six per book. This should make it plain that it is no ordinary matter to change the classification of a library. The labour, the time and the cost involved will be prohibitive.

This practical difficulty should dissuade libraries from adopting a scheme in part. It is not uncommon for libraries, that have not realised the full implications of the Fifth Law, to mutilate the chosen scheme—say, to three figures of Dewey or four figures of Dewey as they desire. But as the library grows the need for fuller details would arise and it would be no easy matter to change or extend the call numbers of all the books. An equally dangerous course is to modify the chosen scheme here and there; but one should not venture such modifications without seeing far into the future and examining whether the modifications proposed will not, at some time or other, come into conflict with the mnemonic features of the notation, or with the methods of division into classes. It is not enough if the modifications appear to be feasible with the existing classification. A mutilated scheme, that may appear to work well under certain conditions of size, will seldom work successfully as the library grows. In Engineering, it is a well-known fact that the construction of small models is often quite an easy matter, whereas to develop them on a large scale presents serious technical problems which can often be solved only by some new method of attack. So it is with classification. As A LIBRARY IS A GROWING ORGANISM, there is a great need for prudent planning on account of the difficulty of changing the scheme later. The wisest course is to adopt a tried scheme as it is, without modifying it here and there.

READERS AND ISSUE OF BOOKS

We shall next consider the increase in the number of readers in the light of the following factors:—

(*a*) the size of the reading room;

(*b*) the issue method; and

(*c*) certain safeguards.

READING ROOM

Taking the size of the reading room first, it is seldom that the Fifth Law does not outwit the library authorities. To take an example, the Managing Committee of a certain library stated, in 1911, that it would be satisfied with a reading room 60' × 24'. But, by 1926, it had to ask for rooms measuring, on the whole, 220' × 35'. If the present rate of increase of its readers persists, it may not be long before it will have to ask for additional accommodation for readers. The generous way in which the Yale University has met the demands of the Fifth Law in this matter can be seen from the following account:—"The reading rooms included a general room seating 260 readers, and shelving 15,000 reference books; a reserved book room, seating 220 readers, and shelving 25,000 volumes of duplicates for class use, with provision in the basement for as many more volumes, a periodical room, seating 120, with wall shelving for 2,000 different current serials; a special room for undergraduates, seating 165, and shelving 30,000 of the best books in English on all subjects. A 'commuters' study' in the basement shelved 1,000 of the most important reference books, and provided 90 seats".[1] Thus, this library has made provision for nearly 1,000 readers.

---

(1) *Proceedings of the Fiftieth Anniversary Conference of the Library Association*, 1927, p. 76.

ISSUE METHOD

Increase of readers leads to increase of issue. Here are some figures showing the rate of increase of issue in certain University Libraries:—

Name of Library.		In year.	No. of Vols. issued (in round figures).	In year.	No. of Vols. issued (in round figures).	Amount of increase.
Madras	..	1914	5,000	1930	113,000	2,260%
California	..	1910	184,000	1925	896,000	487%
Cincinnati	..	1905	21,000	1925	134,000	690%
Columbia	..	1905	232,000	1924	1,206,000	520%
Michigan	..	1910	204,000	1925	477,000	234%
Minnesota	..	1910	105,000	1925	441,000	422%

The following table, relating to some British Municipal Libraries, not only shows the magnitude of the issue work as it is now, but also throws some light on the scope for a still greater issue. As the Second Law would not be satisfied until the percentage of borrowers to population reaches 90, it follows that there is much room for increase in issue in almost all the towns mentioned in the table:—

Town.		Population.	Borrowers.	Percentage of Borrowers to Population.	Total issues.
Wigan	..	91,200	8,002	8·7	258,908
Twickenham	..	34,790	4,404	12·6	142,838
York	..	84,039	12,116	14·4	380,576
Walthamstow	..	129,395	19,043	14·7	632,517
Cheltenham	..	50,630	8,030	15·86	279,105
Willesden	..	177,973	29,192	16·4	908,980
Swinton and Pendlebury	..	34,750	5,814	16·7	217,205
Southend-on-Sea	..	128,500	22,628	17·0	770,414

Town.		Population.	Borrowers.	Percentage of Borrowers to Population.	Total issues.
Chorley	..	30,581	5,663	18·5	162,024
Kirkaldy	..	45,000	9,916	20·0	229,257
Stockport	..	123,315	26,704	21·7	545,020
Northampton	..	90,895	19,984	22·0	552,790
Royal Lamington Spa	..	29,450	7,107	24·1	216,249
Darwen	..	38,200	11,733	30·0	323,241
Montrose	..	10,979	6,624	60·3	131,770

This great increase in issue has to be borne in mind in planning the issue methods. When the issue amounts to hundreds per day, the old fashioned method of making an attendant pick out the books asked for and dole them across the counter would require the full-timed service of about twenty attendants. As the issue grows further, the staff of attendants would stand in need of proportionate strengthening. Such an indefinite increase of men, for doing the mechanical work of issuing, is considered uneconomical and the library authorities are being driven to recognise that the 'open access' system is the only method of meeting the Fifth Law.

Further the ledger method of issue simply breaks down. The average number of volumes issued is usually double the number of readers visiting the library. The number of operations involved in the issue of a volume by the ledger method has been indicated in the last chapter. It can be seen from these data that the process of making the entries in the ledger method of issue would involve the employment of several counter clerks, and even, with them, it would be hardly

AN EVENING IN THE MADRAS UNIVERSITY LIBRARY.

practicable to cope with the situation in rush hours. Evening hours, just before the library is to close, are usually rush hours. The accompanying plate shows a portion of the reading room of a library in such hours. Most of the readers would be leaving the library in the last few minutes of the day and the ledger method of issue would become simply impossible. On the other hand, the crowd can be handled most expeditiously by the 'reader's ticket-book card' method mentioned in the last chapter.

Further, this method automatically solves the problem of identifying the borrowers. This problem becomes serious, as the number of borrowers increases. It becomes impossible to depend on one's memory for faces. Big colleges and popular public libraries find it increasingly difficult to handle this problem. The introduction of the reader's ticket transfers the responsibility from the counter-staff to the readers themselves. Each reader is made responsible for the books drawn on his tickets and it is his business to keep the tickets in his personal custody and prevent their use by others.

Further, the issue of as many tickets as the number of volumes which the reader is entitled to and the locking up in the library of one ticket against every book in his possession automatically secures that he does not remove from the library at any one time more volumes than he is entitled to. It is hardly practicable to secure this in the ledger method as the number of readers increases.

Again, as the reader's tickets coupled with corresponding book-cards are arranged behind the date guide in accordance with the call number on the book-cards, the different statistics of the daily issue are obtained with the least loss of time and labour. On the other hand, in the ledger method, in which the books will be entered only in the order of issue, the collection of these statistics will involve much labour and inconvenience and may become impracticable as the daily issue grows in bulk.

EVEN FLOORS

The issue aspect of the Fifth Law has some bearing on library design also. Increase in issue implies also increase in the number of volumes to be replaced. In the earlier stages, the few volumes to be replaced can be conveniently carried by hand. But, as the issue increases, it may not be convenient to do so. It will become necessary to carry them on a book-trolley. It means that the room of the library should be devoid of raised thresholds and that the floor should be throughout even and in one level, so as to admit of the wheeling of the book-trolley to any part of the floor. If there be more than one floor, they should be connected by a lift large enough to carry the book-trolley.

SAFEGUARDS

As the number of readers increases, the problem of preventing unauthorised removal of books from the library becomes acute in open access libraries. It is not practicable to watch every reader unless certain safeguards are introduced. The safeguards should really secure that all the readers can leave the library only one at a time through a particular door, at which a vigilant clerk is posted. The safeguards consist of the following arrangements:—

Entrance to the library must be by one and only one gate and exit also must be by one and only one gate. The gates should be normally in the locked position. They should open only if the counter-clerk releases the catch. The moment the reader leaves it, it should automatically lock itself. The gate way should be big enough to allow one and only one reader to pass through it at a time. All other doorways and windows should be fitted with *jali-work* shutters or expanded metal shutters, whose meshes are too small for a book to be passed through. Further, no reader should be allowed to replace the books on the shelves.

The great need for such safeguards may not be realised when the number of readers and the issue are small. But it will become serious as the library grows, particularly as the issue grows. Perhaps, the greatest disservice to the open access system is done by the imprudent enthusiasts who introduce the system without the necessary safeguards. As the library grows, loss exceeds a reasonable limit and the system is hastily condemned. Such mistakes should be avoided from the very beginning, *i.e.*, even when the library is small—as the LIBRARY IS A GROWING ORGANISM, which grows constantly and by imperceptible degrees.

STAFF

We now turn to the third factor—the staff. Even those, who realise the truth of the Fifth Law in regard to the books and the readers, fail to recognise the need for the growth in the third factor. The safeguarded open access system and the modern issue method eliminate the need for growth in the counter staff and considerably minimise the need for growth in the number of attendants. But, the book section, the periodicals section, the cataloguing section, the binding section and the reference section have to grow as the library grows. Of these five sections, the growth of the first three depend only on the rate of growth of the first factor—books. But, the growth of the last two sections depends not only on the growth of the stock but also on the growth of the number of readers. The Fifth Law would urge library authorities to remember that the efficiency of a library cannot be maintained at the proper level, unless provision is made for the necessary growth in all these five sections of the library staff.

Granting that the library authority provides for the growth of the staff to the needed extent, the growth of the staff brings, in its train, certain new problems of organisation. With a large staff, more machinery of supervision and more records become necessary. With a staff of one efficient person, we get maximum results. With a staff of two equally efficient persons we may perhaps get twice the work done. But, with a staff of ten, we cannot get ten times the work; the ratio is bound to be much less. It is the task of the organiser, the man at the head, to keep this ratio as high as possible. A recognised method of doing this is to seize the opportunity for specialisation which size undoubtedly brings with it. Such specialisation should be carried one step further, every time the staff are increased.

As soon as a library increases the staff from one to two, the counter work and reference work should be separated from all other items of work and assigned to one of them. At the next stage, it may be desirable to form three sections—the administrative section, the technical section (classification and cataloguing) and the counter section. At the next stage, a reference section may be formed. If the staff are increased still further, the administrative section may be split up into order section, accession section, periodicals section, binding section, accounts section, correspondence section and so on, as opportunity presents itself. Similarly, the technical section may be bifurcated into classification section and cataloguing section. It may further be a great advantage if the members of the reference section specialize in different subjects, as the section grows in strength.

When the library staff are divided into many sections, it is necessary to determine carefully the section to which each member of the staff is best fitted, physically, academically, and temperamentally. While periodical inter-sectional transfers may be desirable from the point of view of the staff, such transfers should primarily be subject to the principle that the library should get the best service which each person is capable of.

STAFF-COUNCIL

In a library with a large staff, it may be useful to form a staff-council. The council may be made up of the librarian, the heads of sections and one representative of each section. The staff-council may advise the librarian—

(1) in the systematization of the work of the sections with due regard to efficiency and economy of energy and time;

(2) in solving problems involving inter-sectional relationship;

(3) in developing the book resources of the library in a harmonious manner;

(4) in devising methods for improving the service to the public; and

(5) in organising extension work of all kinds.

Incidentally such a council will develop good comradeship and *esprit de corps* among the members of the staff and train the junior members in organisation and original thinking. It will also develop in them a sense of responsibility and ownership. While the librarian may preside over the meetings of the council and of the general body, it may be useful to make the heads of sections themselves preside over the meetings of the respective sections. This will give increased opportunities for them to develop powers of leadership. If at all, the librarian may be present at the meeting and take part in discussion without the power of vote.

THE SPIRIT OF THE HIVE

As a library has to work on all days and for long hours, the organisation of the reference section and the counter section requires the greatest skill and care, so that there may be absolute continuity in the work and that the change of shift could be effected smoothly and quickly with the least dislocation of work. Indeed the readers should not be able to perceive that a change in personnel had come. The details of this organisation and the machinery that has to be set up to secure proper control and co-ordination will be discussed in later volumes. But there is one factor that may be mentioned here. That is the spirit of the staff. The members of the staff should be on the most cordial terms among themselves. They should be willing to co-operate with one another in every possible way. There should not be the least trace of jealousy or envy. The propensity to claim credit exclusively to oneself should be completely got over. Self should be suppressed to such a degree that every member is prepared to pass off all work as anonymous. Maeterlinck's picture of the work in the bee-hive contains the most vivid and accurate description of the spirit that should come over a library staff, as it inevitably grows in accordance with the Fifth Law, if it is to function with maximum efficiency.

"She . . . , like the foundresses, abruptly departs and abandons her model. Her place is taken at once by an impatient worker, who continues the task that a third will finish, while others close by are attacking the rest of the surface and the opposite side of the wall; each one obeying the general law of interrupted and successive labour, as though it were an inherent principle of the hive that the pride of toil should be distributed and every achievement be anonymous and common to all, that it might thereby become more fraternal".[1]

The spirit of the hive should prevail among the library staff if the inconveniences due to the Fifth Law are to be avoided.

EVOLUTION

So far, we have dealt only with the consequences of growth in size. We shall now turn to the other attribute of a growing organism, *viz.*, variation and evolution of new forms.

In the earliest days, a library is said to have been denoted by a word which meant a place for

---

(1) MAETERLINCK (Maurice): *The Life of the Bee*; Tr. by Alfred Sutro, Chapter III, Section 54.

hiding books in. Later on they seem to have been literal prisons for books. That prison life of the books appears to have been much more rigorous than that of even some of the C class prisoners of to-day. I believe it is not every C class prisoner that is kept chained all the hours of the day; but the libraries of the medieval days kept their books perpetually in chains. It was only in the seventeenth and the eighteenth centuries, that the inhuman aspect of this way of preserving books appears to have been realised. Even then the freedom that was first given to the books was only comparable to the freedom given to A class prisoners. That is to say, they were given freedom of movement only within the four walls of the library, even as an A class prisoner is perhaps permitted to take his constitutional walks within the boundary of the prison walls. Then came the period of grudgingly lending them out. In that period the libraries appear to have devoted their main attention to the stock-taking process, to the number of books lost, to the number of books damaged—never mind even if it was due to the wear and tear of legitimate use—to the fixing up of the responsibility for such loss or damages, and to such other factors almost to the exclusion of the statistics of issue, the statistics of membership, the percentage of the community that was still keeping out from libraries and the means of bringing them under the influence of the libraries. But the slow change that began to appear at the turn of the present century attained a huge amplitude as a result of the Great

War and the highly differentiated and complicated character of the organisation of the library of to-day makes it as far different from the ancient Chinese "place to hide books in" as the human group is from the protozoa group or the Atlantic Liner of 60,000 tons is from Columbus's 'Santa Maria'.

What further stages of evolution are in store for this GROWING ORGANISM—the library—we can only wait and see. Who knows that a day may not come—at least Wells[1] has pictured a world in which dissemination of knowledge will be effected by direct thought transfer, in the Dakshinamurti[2] fashion, without the invocation of the spoken or the printed word—that a day may not come when the dissemination of knowledge, which is the vital function of libraries, will be realised by libraries even by means other than those of the printed book?

VARIETY OF FORMS

Without indulging in such speculations, we may have a look at the variety of forms into which the library organism has differentiated itself in our present day. We have the Municipal or City library, the Rural or District library, the academic libraries such as the School library, the College library and the University library, the Business library, the Commercial library, the Seafarers'

(1) WELLS (H. G.): *Men Like Gods.*

(2) According to a traditional verse, Siva, as Dakshinamurti, is said to sit under a banyan-tree in the midst of his disciples and to resolve all their doubts by the eloquence of his very silence.

library, the Children's library, the Intermediate library—a species that is just beginning to appear —the library for the blind and many other special libraries. Each one of these species has problems and peculiarities of its own, in addition to certain common features. It will take us beyond the scope of this book to deal with each of them in a detailed manner. There are special treatises that deal with each such species.

THE VITAL PRINCIPLE

But the vital principle of the library—which has struggled through all the stages of its evolution, is common to all its different forms and will persist to be its distinguishing feature for all time to come —is that it is an instrument of universal education, and assembles together and freely distributes all the tools of education and disseminates knowledge with their aid. This vital principle—'the spirit of the library'—persisting through all its forms is like the inner man; and to it are applicable the words[1] of the Lord:—

As a person casts off worn-out garments and puts on others that are new, so does the embodied soul cast off worn-out forms and enter into others that are new.

Weapons do not cleave him; fire does not burn him; water does not make him wet; nor does the wind make him dry.

---

(1) *Bhagavad Gita*, II, 22-24.

He cannot be cloven; he cannot be burnt; he cannot be wetted; he cannot be dried; he is eternal, all-pervading, steadfast and immovable; he is the same for ever.

वासांसि जीर्णानि यथा विहाय
नवानि गृह्णाति नरोऽपराणि ।
तथा शरीराणि विहाय जीर्णा-
न्यन्यानि संयाति नवानि देही ॥

नैनं छिन्दन्ति शस्त्राणि नैनं दहति पावकः ।
न चैनं क्लेदयन्त्यापो न शोषयति मारुतः ॥

अच्छेद्योऽयमदाह्योऽयमक्लेद्योऽशोष्य एव च ।
नित्यः सर्वगतः स्थाणुरचलोऽयं सनातनः ॥

APPENDIX

SPECIFICATION FOR A TEAKWOOD BOOK-RACK

The standard unit-rack that I have designed for the Madras University Library has two faces. Each face has two bays, so that the unit rack is a four-bayed rack—two bays on each side. While the height may be 7 ft. in adult libraries, it should not exceed 5 ft. in children's libraries.

The detailed dimensions of and specification for an adult library unit are as follows:—

(*a*) External dimensions 6' 6" × 1' 6" × 7'.

(*b*) Three uprights, each 2" × 1' 6" × 7'.

(*c*) Seven shelf-planks, each 3' × 8½" × 1"

Two of the shelf-planks are to be fixed ones —one near the top and the other near the bottom. The other five are to be movable ones supported by Tonk's fittings, so that they can be adjusted to an inch. It may be an advantage to provide two spare shelves for each unit.

(*d*) The book rack is to have sanitary bottom, *i.e.*, the lowest shelf is to be fixed at a height of 6 ins. from the floor to facilitate cleaning the floor beneath the rack and easy vigilance. The topmost shelf is to be fixed 6 ins. below the top of the uprights.

(*e*) To prevent the books on the shelves in one face getting mixed up with the books on the corresponding shelves in the other face, an expanded metal partition is to separate the two faces. It is to accommodate this frame that the planks are made only 8½ inches broad, thus leaving a gap of 1 inch in the centre of the rack. The expanded metal partition is to begin only from a height of 6 inches from the lowest fixed shelf and go right up to the lower side of the uppermost fixed shelf. The advantage in beginning it only from a height of 6 inches from the lowermost shelf is that giant folios, which are more than a foot broad, can be made to lie flat, on the bottommost fixed shelves, extending from one face to the other. If the expanded metal is of steel and not of brass, it should be coated with an anti-corrosive paint.

(*f*) The front edge of each shelf is to have a wedge-shaped groove cut in it, to hold the shelf-cards. If the groove is carefully cut, the shelf-cards can be easily slided from end to end, as the books are necessarily moved in course of time.

(*g*) The three uprights are bound together by the four pairs of fixed shelves. It would be an advantage to reinforce this by means of two steel tie-rods binding them together, one at a height of 2½ ft. from the bottom and the other at a depth of 2½ ft. from the top. To accommodate these rods it may be necessary to make the expanded metal partition in three parts, the rods running between the frames of the parts.

(*h*) It may be convenient to fix spring blind-holders to each bay to hold maps. At least two maps can be accommodated in front of each bay. The maps are to be normally in the rolled-up position. Whenever necessary, they are to be pulled out for reference and then released.

(*i*) The teakwood used should be well-seasoned and the contractor should make good any crack that it may develop within a year of supply.

(*j*) The length of all the shelf-planks should be quite accurate, so that they can be interchanged without any restriction.

This unit rack requires about 10 c.ft. of teak-wood. It has 84 running ft. of shelf-space. It can accommodate, on an average, 1,000 volumes. When full of books, it will weigh about 1 ton. Its estimated cost is Rs. 175 if steel Tonk's fittings are used and Rs. 230 if brass Tonk's fittings are used.

INDEX

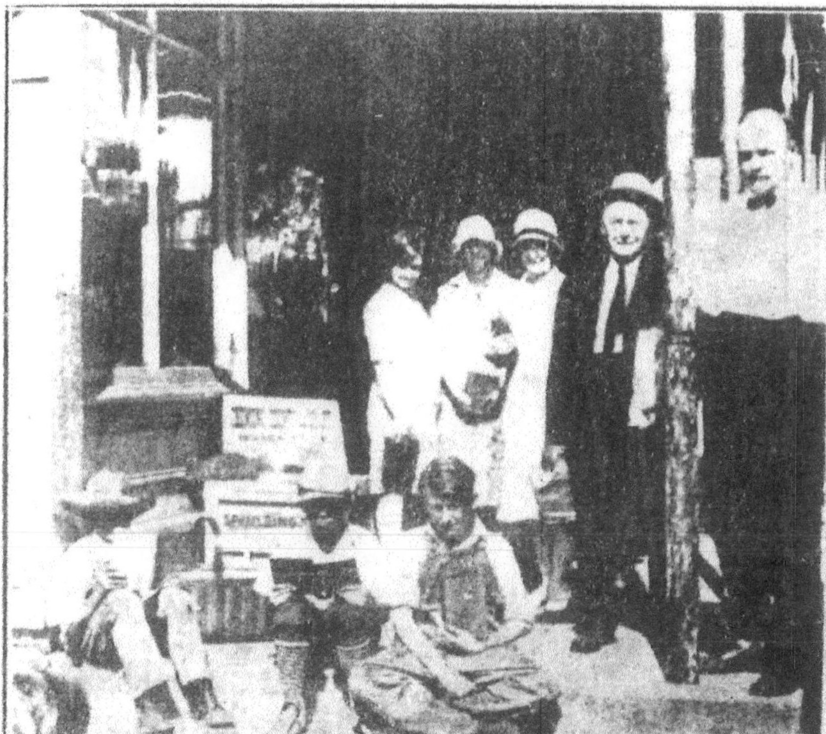

STORE USED AS LOCAL CENTRE.

18